D1255388

THE AGE OF INDISCRETION

THE AGE OF INDISCRETION

Clyde Brion Davis

J. B. LIPPINCOTT COMPANY
Philadelphia *New York*

PRINTED IN THE UNITED STATES
AT THE COUNTRY LIFE PRESS, GARDEN CITY, N.Y.

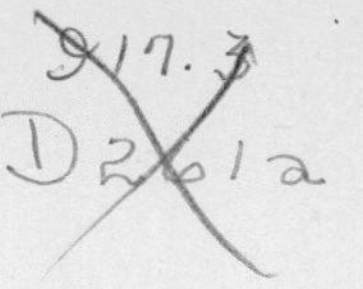

To G. S.

CONTENTS

THE AGE OF INDISCRETION

I

WOODEN NICKELS

We can assert with some confidence that our own period is one of decline; that the standards of culture are lower than they were fifty years ago; and that the evidences of this decline are visible in every department of human activity.—T. S. Eliot in *Notes Towards the Definition of Culture*

I CANNOT HOLD that the above is unmitigated nonsense for the reason that I personally know of no absolute in the realm of nonsense and I am not sure even whether there is a definite par for the course.

However—" 'Tis not so deep as a well, nor so wide as a church door; but 'tis enough, 'twill serve."

The renowned Dr. Eliot is far from alone in his fuzzy conceit. Besides a spate of nostalgic fiction and autobiography glorifying the good old days of Queen Victoria and Edward VII and William McKinley, there has risen from behind the crystalline barricade of belles lettres a blue fog of sighs for the old days, the better days, the blessed, golden, gaudy days of the turn of the century. I remember those days better, I think, than most of the yearners and especially better than Dr. Eliot who, in 1900, was a boy of twelve attending Smith Academy, a private school in Missouri, and probably very unhappy. At this same time there were, of course, many thousands of other young boys in Missouri, some of whom grew up into such diverse characters as Harry S. Truman, Reinhold Niebuhr and

Thomas Hart Benton, and others who merely grew up. In the latter classification was one six-year-old, slightly bewildered but still very interested in the world about him, who developed a pretty good memory for knickknacks, if nothing else.

Yes, I can remember those good old days of the Twentieth Century's first decade very well indeed, and I say anyone who would trade 1950 for 1900 would trade a brand-new Cadillac for a second-hand velocipede, and not even a rubber-tired velocipede at that. I say that affairs in general, including culture, have improved in the last fifty years, not as much as they should have improved considering the opportunity, but still immeasurably.

If T. S. Eliot were alone in his position it could be laughed off as a quaint aberration of genius, but he is not alone. He has become the unofficial leader of a cult of reactionary esthetes which is making its influence felt in important quarters, particularly in the field of education.

It is the fashion for intellectuals to poke sneers at modern man. They are always sure of publicity if they can think of a sufficiently extravagant exaggeration.

Thus Dr. José Ortega y Gasset is widely quoted when he says man is the only congenitally unhappy creature in the animal kingdom. I shall grant that the people of Dr. Ortega's native Spain have some reason for unhappiness in their government, but I shall also say he is better versed in philosophy than in zoology if he believes wild mammals from chipmunks to polar bears lead lives of unworried bliss. Wild animals as well as Spaniards have their terrors and empty bellies, jealousies, physical pains and apprehensions of the unknown.

But true or not, just what was the purpose of this remarkable statement?

And Chancellor Robert M. Hutchins, of the University of Chicago, at that curious Goethe festival held in the remote Rocky Mountain village of Aspen, Colorado, attended also by Drs. Albert Schweitzer and Ortega, said, "All the work mankind has put forth through countless ages to ease the path of generations yet unborn, all this work has ended up in what? In Coney Island."

Even if Dr. Hutchins meant that only as a wise-crack, it still is unworthy of a man of his reputation and responsibilities. Coney Island is *not* representative of American culture. But it does provide a little fresh air, recreation and earthy fun for hundreds of thousands who have not enjoyed Dr. Hutchins' opportunity for cultural advancement, and I, who have had experience with both Coney Island and those quaint peasant festivals of Europe which excite the patronizing praise of Eliot and his boys, feel that one is no more vulgar than the other.

Consciously or unconsciously Dr. Hutchins here was chiming in with the Eliot clique of esthetes who are chipping away so industriously at the institutions of democracy, particularly at public education, and this indeed is strange coming from the Chancellor of the University of Chicago.

In this same address at Aspen, Hutchins saw us confronted by two alternate fates—being blown to bits or being bored to death. Perhaps these dangers do exist, but my conception of a cultured person is one with sufficient intellectual resources never to be threatened with boredom in this fascinating, exciting world, without recourse to bridge or other time-killers.

Even Dr. Irwin Edman, Columbia's sprightly professor of philosophy, seemed to see something of this danger in *The Saturday Review of Literature,* of Sept. 10, 1949 when he wrote, "It is conceivable that we may achieve a world free from war and from want and that in that world life might not be worth living. . . . Something has gone from our lives in the way of the love of excellence. . . ."

Then, however, Professor Edman went on to say, "Widespread education is making us more widely sensitive to excellence, more eager to have excellence itself more pervasive. Art, music, and ideas have larger audiences and more discussions than existed only twenty-five years ago. . . . Not everyone can be an original artist or thinker. But many can be educated to disinterested and undistracted criteria of judgment in these matters. . . . What is security for but to give human beings their chance to achieve their full stature of humanity?"

What, I might add also, is education for otherwise? Or life itself?

And what is this thing they call culture?

Well, I am quite willing to accept one of Dr. Eliot's definitions that "culture may even be described simply as that which makes life worth living."

I should be willing to accept his definition even if he had narrowed it by half—which would be more in line with his subsequent arguments—because this definition surely would include such varied items as biochemistry, the internal combustion engine, plenty of ice in summer, a central heating plant capable of keeping one's abode at approximately 70 degrees fahrenheit in winter, percolated coffee, mass production, the forty-hour week, the electro-magnetic principle, aspirin, the photoelectric cell, no taxes for support of an hereditary nobility, the electric phonograph, sufficient production of foodstuffs for large exports to the hungry old cultures of Europe after taking care of the homefolks, and a whole catalogue of similar comforts, luxuries and gadgets peculiar to life in that curiously haphazard wilderness of the United States of which the state of Missouri happens to be close to the geographical center.

While I endorse these items as making life "worth living," I never should have the temerity to class many of them as "culture" except in the very broadest sense. The definition is Dr. Eliot's, not mine, and I am merely taking it as a gift.

I decline, however, to accept his dogmatic statements about the decline of culture in the last fifty years because, despite his acknowledged scholarship, his reasoning often is as narrowly inconsequential as a quodlibetarian gravely arguing about the angels on the point of a needle. It obviously has been quite a while since he looked at the scoreboard.

Dr. Eliot's intellectual and mystic snobbishness puts him in the unfortunate position of a sitting duck. You could knock him over with a stick. I am spared, however, the necessity of unsportsmanlike action by the fact the Missouri-born and reared Dr. Eliot does not concern himself with culture in the United States, patently holding that there *is* no culture in the United States.

As converts frequently become the most pious of Catholics, so do naturalized Englishmen often become the most English of chauvinist Englishmen, and excessively superior. And if one is so constituted that one must feel superior for mental and physical health, it usually is possible to find *some* protuberance upon which to hang the superiority.

I could, for instance, feel superior to cats and Englishmen because I do not eat entrails and they do. And if someone tried to wean me from my folly by pointing out that cats can climb trees better than I could even in my more agile days, I could still cling to my superiority by declaring haughtily that no one ever had to call the fire department to get me out of a tree once I was up.

However, in this respect at least, I am too realistic to believe dietary aberrations are very important. I eat and drink some things that most cats and Englishmen scorn, and I realize that the general run of cats are much more beautiful and graceful than I, diet or no diet.

Well, well. In his dissertation on culture, Dr. Eliot condescends to mention the land of his birth once in connection with Edgar Allan Poe, whom he calls "An American of Irish extraction." It is neither here nor there that Poe was of English extraction rather than Irish, but the Nobel Prize winner surely is going out of his way to mention "extraction" at all in Poe's case, inasmuch as it was the poet's great-grandfather who emigrated to America by way of Ireland.

The admittedly brilliant brain of this native of a great corn and hog state (Dr. Eliot doubtless refers to corn as "maize" now) has been so thoroughly steeped in the lore, language and superstitions of the ancients that he can accept as advanced thought quaint ideas and theories which were discarded and forgotten by thinkers before the reign of George III (an English king of German extraction who had some trouble with his American colonies) and never seriously revived until they were dragged out of the rag bag and polished up by an Austrian mystic (of God knows what extraction) named Adolf Hitler.

I shall not take the space to discuss Eliot's "élites" nor his plea for the preservation of provincialism (keeping the damn peasants in their place); maintenance of a controlled friction between groups of families "persisting from generation to generation" in a "healthily stratified society" (to keep their silly little minds off the exploiting elites); his bland assumption that the relation between culture and religion is perpetually irrevocable because it once was irrevocable in regions where the Church dominated all human activity and thought; his arrogant opposition to equal educational opportunities for all, nor any of the rest of his reactionary poppycock.

Instead, I shall try to show that Thomas Stearns Eliot is an incompetent witness, that he is psychologically incapable of judging whether culture has retrogressed in the last fifty years or advanced or remained static, because his memory cannot be trusted.

We all live, more or less, in a graveyard of our dead memories. Those memories which are happy are embalmed like the body of Lenin and glorified and honored periodically with garlands of hyperbole. But the unhappy memories, the humiliating memories, the shameful memories, we try to bury deeply in unmarked graves where we hope they may be forgotten.

All too often, however, the soil of the unconscious is too thin for a proper burial and there seems to be an impervious stratum of granite close to the surface which defies our spade. So we do the next best thing. We construct a sort of mausoleum over the unhappy memory as best we can with the only building material at hand, which rarely is substantial enough to give a sense of security.

As we approach middle age the souls of most of us are so full of these flimsy shacks, each hiding its own sad secret, that they look like plywood shantytowns. The more imaginative (those talented in kidding themselves) decorate the plywood mausoleums with paintings of gay scenes, much as the circus luggage wagons used to be painted to make country people believe they contained all manner of fascinating creatures instead of drab canvas and blue boards, and these talented people look not upon the truth hidden behind the plywood mausoleums but upon the scarlet and gold of the decorations and speak of the joys and glamor of the good old days. But even as they speak they live in terror of a high wind coming up some night and blowing that gaudy plywood shanty-town helter-skelter, revealing to all the world what was hidden.

As this is written the United States of America is without question the most important nation in the whole wide world, speaking from a practical, down-to-earth point of view. The American eagle is doubling in brass for God's ravens, dropping manna to the destitute of many lands, perhaps without an air of noblesse oblige, or without the sweet song of the lark, but still dropping the manna.

And the United States *does* have a culture. Really. Despite our heterogeneous population, despite the most restrictive definition oolong-sipping esthetes can devise, there is actually a pretty vital indigenous culture in America as well as cultures brought here from Europe, the Near East, the Far East, Africa and the Islands of the Southern Seas. And because the United States is also demonstrably the *least* provincial of all major powers (including the United Kingdom) the various cultures native to such taproots of culture as France and England and Wales and Scotland and Ireland and Prussia and Bavaria and Poland and the Levant and the Orient and the Balkans and the Congo tend in part to be absorbed by the sometimes amorphous, sometimes crude, sometimes astonishing, but at all times living and bubbling native culture.

I am out of patience with the wailing prophets of doom who weep because life cannot be one perpetual honeymoon with Santa Claus bearing gifts down the chimney at least once a week. I do not believe the world is necessarily rattling to hell on a handcar any more today than it was in 1850 or 1750 or 1550 or 950.

I am a little tired too of these painted mausoleums, the nostalgia books which have been riding through the best-seller lists for the last ten years or so, the fiction and so-called non-fiction which spread a cake-frosting of glamor over the good old days, the better days of a half-century or more ago. Some of them have been good books and some of them bad, but I am not concerned at the moment with their literary quality. What does concern me is that they have had a cumulative effect on the popular audience, giving an impression that the days of long ago were more interesting, more romantic and happier than today and that impression by and large simply is false.

I could not begin to name all of the books in this category, but among them are *Life with Father, Chicken Every Sunday, Country Lawyer, Big Family, Cheaper by the Dozen, Excuse My Dust, One Foot in Heaven, Mama's Bank Account, Mother Wore Tights, Genius in the Family, My Old Kentucky Home,* etc., etc.

Despite these romances, despite the dissertations of philosophers and the mooning of poets, I know from personal experience that the United States is a better place in which to live, a better place for adults and a better place for children than it was at the beginning of the Twentieth Century. And I propose to show that this is so.

I am pleased rather than otherwise that mechanical miracles have brought war to the civilian population because life can be just as sweet to a twenty-year-old conscript as to a fire-eating grandmother or to a bellicose though prostatic statesman, and international difficulties may not be so impossible of compromise when it is fully realized that the alternative puts newspaper editors, academically virile ministers of the Gospel and articulate grandmothers immediately into the front lines. There's that chance.

Well, fifty years ago the population of the United States was 75,994,575. Of this number only 24,056,562 lived in communities of more than ten thousand population. Our population at that time was preponderantly rural with 51,938,013 living on farms, ranches and in towns of less than ten thousand.

Chillicothe, Missouri, with a population of 6,905 in 1900, was a fairly typical small town near the geographical center of the nation, where life in its fundamental aspects must have been quite like that of the great majority of Americans.

It was in Chillicothe, Missouri, that I first became aware of things not directly concerned with my own bodily comfort, and that would have been in 1898 or 1899. I lived in Chillicothe until the fall of 1908 when I was fourteen years old, and the humiliations, disappointments, frustrations, injustices and shameful acts which fell to my lot up to that time are far enough behind me now to be viewed safely without bitterness or cringing, and, for that matter, without a sentimental desire to make the picture pretty.

For that reason I believe I can view the turn of the century without distortion. In some respects it was a dreadful period. In other respects it was quite funny.

We have grown wiser in many ways. Our manners have improved. We have jettisoned a number of our communal asininities and, while we may have acquired some new ones, the balance is favorable. We have grown astonishingly in our appreciation of the arts—all of the arts. Our provincialism and chauvinism have been reduced remarkably by education, increased travel, and a better understanding of the world beyond our shores. These are extremely good things for all concerned, despite T. S. Eliot's curious arguments.

Partly because of enlightened social legislation, partly because of a growing consideration for our fellow-man's welfare, and even more because of unbelievable inventions and discoveries, the great mass of Americans lead much healthier lives than they did fifty years ago.

And I am completely convinced that there is more happiness per capita today than in 1900.

II

THE GOOD OLD DAYS

In the last flutter of the Nineteenth Century, which, by merit of half a hundred round trips from Aphelion to Perihelion, has now become the "good old days," there were people who spoke dreamily of the good old days.

In Chillicothe, Missouri, if these people were venerable enough, they meant the good old days before the war—and not the Spanish-American War just finished so gloriously, but the *other* war, the war between the Blue and the Gray.

The old folk in 1900 mourned for the glamorous old days before the Hannibal and St. Joe Railroad was pounded across the state, frightening the deer and bear and wild turkeys clear out of the country, when people were good neighbors and you could borrow a bucket of fire without being expected to return it with interest, when the skies were bluer and the winters colder and the girls were prettier and the young men hardier.

"Yes," they said in 1900, "things were different back in 1850. In those days a man was proud of himself and glad for a chance to work for a living—none of this cry-babying for a ten-hour day the way some of these anarchists and Socialists are doing now in the cities—and any woman worthy of the name had from ten to fourteen children instead of thinking five or six made a family."

On every hand in 1900 the observing and thoughtful could see signs of decadence. For instance, wasn't a farmer revealing something of his character when he bought a sulky plow? Wasn't he showing an inclination to sit down at his work? Wasn't that something for the bank to consider when the farmer asked for credit?

There was reason to be disturbed over a growing flightiness among young people. Oh, it wasn't imagination. Not only were the boys restless and talking about going to the city, but so were their sisters. Even the most carefully reared girls were trials to their parents with their flip expressions such as, "Did you ever get left?" and "Go way back and sit down," as well as slang that often approached perilously close to profanity.

The *Ladies' Home Journal* published a story in point, a story about a gently reared girl—and a minister's daughter at that—whose parents sought to give her every advantage and sent her to Vassar College. After four years the girl received her bachelor of arts degree, came home and swaggered—that was the word, *swaggered*—into the parlor, sailed her rolled-up diploma across the library table, spread her arms and proclaimed in a loud voice—*"Educated, by gosh!"*

It all made one wonder.

The bicycle craze wasn't helping things. While a young man's steadiness might not be suspect necessarily just because he rode a bicycle, it still didn't hurt to watch him. There were a lot of stories about bicycle riders, and one of the most popular concerned an Indian seeing his first cyclist. The Indian said, "Ugh! Paleface heap lazy. Sits down to run."

That Indian wasn't so slow. Perhaps he was looking deeper into the bicycle craze than most white people. The Indian sensed riding a bicycle was violent exercise from an unnatural position, just as doctors were sounding warnings that such concerted exertion from a humped-over position brought on a dangerous malady called "bicycle heart."

Bicycling was bad enough, goodness knows, for the young men, but the fad had also spread to the young women, and the manufacturers were encouraging it by marketing "wheels" with no cross-bar for the gentler sex, making it unnecessary for the girls to wear bloomers or divided skirts——unless, of course, they really *wanted* to make spectacles of themselves.

Intelligent older men—the ministers, the editors and other molders of public opinion—were truly worried about young women and bicycles, but it was a subject which had to be dealt with delicately. They couldn't blurt right out that there were certain physiological facts which made bicycle riding perilous not only to a girl's health, but to her very character—to say nothing of her ordained future as a mother.

Fathers passed on the warnings to mothers and mothers presumably passed on the warnings to daughters who in 1900 paid just as much attention to common-sense advice as they did in 1850 and as they do in 1950. They went right on riding bicycles, and that may account very well for the shape their children are in today. Yes, and their grandchildren too.

Despite the yearnings of gaffers and gammers for the good old days, at the turn of the century there had been little change in Chillicothe, Missouri, in fifty years. It was much the same sleepy town which was occupied in 1861 by Colonel Ulysses S. Grant after a skirmish at Graham's Mill and capture of the square brick powder magazine near the Livingston County fair grounds. The buildings around the Square were much the same, the ivy-covered Town Hall was the same; more than a decade must pass before the trees of Elm Park would be cut down to make way for the new stone Court House. Children had been born, people had died, a few families had moved away, a few families had moved in, but the population remained fairly constant—something less than seven thousand.

Chillicothe was and is county seat of Livingston County, in central Missouri, north of the Missouri River. It is about ninety miles from Kansas City and two hundred and ten miles from St. Louis. Incorporated as a city in 1869, it was an attractive small town in 1900 and still is—although the Chamber of Commerce claims thirteen thousand population and school and water estimates indicate about ten thousand.

Except for the river bottoms, which are flooded at least once a year, Chillicothe is surrounded by some of the finest gently rolling land in America. It is of marked glacial origin, and is especially good for grain and pasture. The native timber was varied—oak, hickory, black walnut, soft maple, but with white elm predominating.

The name Chillicothe is Shawnee, meaning "Our Big Town," and, according to legend, was adopted from an Indian village which stood in the vicinity. It seems probable that Chillicothe, Missouri, and Chillicothe, Ohio, were named independently because the Shawnees inhabited both regions and "Our Big Town" is a fairly obvious name, especially for an Indian.

Daniel Boone is said to have spent the winter of 1799-1800 near the river forks west of town and to have been the first white man to build a shack in the vicinity, and if the Missouri State Historical Society hasn't found any proof of this yet it isn't my fault. Forty-odd years ago Sliver Elvin and I caught a giant snapping turtle near the forks and carved into his tough old lid, "D. Boone, A. Elvin, C. Davis, 1799." As snapping turtles are supposed to live for hundreds of years, this fellow may still be carrying his historical gem. We also carved into the trunk of a hardy sycamore, "D. Boone killed bar here Dec. 1799," and I hope this relic has been found and preserved.

The settlement of Chillicothe was started early in the Nineteenth Century on relatively high ground, almost surrounded by the north fork of the Grand River to the north and west, the main river to the south and Medicine Creek to the east. These pioneers were pretty optimistic and believed the Grand to be navigable, but it wasn't until 1840 that anything of greater dignity than a skiff or flatboat attempted this capricious stream from the Big Muddy to Chillicothe. Then the steamer *Bedford* came up with a cargo of goods and went firmly aground on a bar at the forks. A few other steamboats made the trip at high-water periods later, but Chillicothe finally resigned itself to being an inland town. There was plenty of water but it wasn't concentrated in the right places. The swampy country south of the river was spangled with ponds and oxbow lakes such as Roach Lake, Half Moon Lake and Bear Lake, but in recent years the river has recaptured Bear Lake.

Like so many midwestern communities, Chillicothe was built, Mexican style, around a square or plaza, and there are stories of Mexican traders coming in with their high-wheeled carts to trade fine silverwork for firearms and other manufactured goods.

The original settlers seem to have been largely immigrants from Kentucky and Virginia with a sprinkling of French adventurers. Later a good many arrived from Illinois and Indiana, but they came mostly after the Civil War.

In 1900 Chillicothe's industry consisted of the Chicago, Milwaukee & St. Paul Railroad shops and roundhouse, later moved to Laredo when the division was extended; Milbank's flour mill; the Chillicothe Foundry & Novelty Works; the Jenkins Hay Rake Co.; Jackson's Axe Handle factory; Brownfield and Bird candy factory; the Crow Cigar factory; the Chillicothe Box Manufacturing Co. (in which my father was about to acquire controlling equity); Slifer's Steam Laundry; the Chillicothe Gas and Electric Co., and the Chillicothe Water Co.

The streets were lighted by carbon arc lights suspended at alternate intersections downtown and in the better residential districts. A very few homes and business houses were illuminated by Edison's incandescent bulbs. Some were lighted with the piped-in artificial gas manufactured by retorting naphtha. A few others used acetylene gas or gasoline, but a majority of homes got along with kerosene, or, as they were called, "coal oil" lamps.

A prominent feature of Chillicothe in 1900 was the water company's red iron standpipe in the southwestern end of town. I don't know how tall this water tower was. They had to take it down years ago when it became shaky in high winds. But I do know it seemed higher than the Tower of Babel pictured in our big Bible.

One Halloween night some unnamed boys stole an unpopular

citizen's rubber-tired buggy and hauled it, laboriously and dangerously, piece by piece, to the top of the water tower and put it together again canted on the big fish weather vane. The fire department and the police department and the water company all looked up at the rubber-tired buggy, which seemed very strange and remote and small, and they wanted no part of it, so the rubber-tired buggy clung to the weather vane for a long time until at last a March gale lifted it one night and it came down by itself. The owner threatened to sue the water company so the water company threatened to sue the owner because his buggy had bent their weather vane. I think the whole thing ended in a compromise.

In 1900 Chillicothe was proud of its educational system. I am inclined to believe it was below average for comparable towns of the period, but it may be unfair to judge by what I learned in the schools; I probably had an especially high resistance to education.

The Central School, which was the high school in 1900, was a big three-story brick structure with mansard roof, two fancy towers and high arched windows. It cost $35,000 to build in 1876. They changed the doors to open outward and put fire escapes on the architectural monstrosity in the spring of 1908 following the Collingwood, Ohio, school fire, and they held fire drills several times a week then for all except a fat boy named Clarence. Clarence was required to stay disconsolately in his seat—never quite sure whether it was just another drill or whether he soon would be sizzling in the flames—because the school authorities had no confidence that the flimsy fire escape would support Clarence's bulk. I have wondered what psychological effect this sort of discrimination would have on a boy.

Three of the four ward schools carried pupils through the sixth grade and fed them into the Central School for the seventh and eighth grades. The fourth was the William Lloyd Garrison School for Negroes and its curriculum extended, supposedly, through the ninth grade. Negroes, of course, were not eligible for high school education in those days and that region, and if anyone in town, white or black, considered the system discriminatory, I'm sure I never heard of it. On the contrary, I remember more than a little grumbling about wasting the taxpayers' money for any Negro education. "Take and learn a nigger how to read and write and you just make him biggety and ruin him for being a good nigger."

I entered the second ward Eugene Field School in September, 1900, and the "plant," as educators like to call school equipment, consisted of a three-room brick building set in a small cindery yard. Each room averaged about sixty pupils. Each room was heated by a round-bellied soft coal stove. Each room owned a red composition water bucket and tin dipper which was passed around periodically in the hot days of fall and spring—a democratic gesture designed for equitable distribution of all communicable maladies. But there really was no democracy.

The pupils of the Field School were divided sharply between "Highviewites," who lived east of the Milwaukee tracks, and the comparatively rich children of railroad engineers and conductors and merchants and traveling salesmen and professional and business men who lived west of the tracks.

It was easy to distinguish Highview people from us quality folk. Even our speech was different. They said "Hain't" instead of a genteel "ain't." They said "winder" for "windah." They said "them kind" instead of "those kind." Their ancestors probably came from Indiana or Illinois. Our proud neighbors were mostly from the beauty and chivalry of old Virginia with a generation's stopover in Kentucky.

A lot of the Highview children were depigmentized towheads, no doubt prey to all deficiency diseases, as well as malaria, ringworm, itch and head lice. We pretty generally escaped the last three by scrupulously avoiding contact with the little pariahs except for an occasional fight. There was no playing together at recess because there never were any recesses, and I have no idea whether this was a device aimed at avoiding class war or whether the school board merely regarded recesses as a loss of time.

Teachers arranged to place Highview children as far as possible from the stove, not only because they reputedly were sewed up for the winter in their underwear but because numbers of them wore asafetida bags around their necks to ward off sickness.

The most curious difference in clothing between us of the elite and the Highview children was in footgear. In the winter we wore shoes that were bought for us individually. They wore no shoes even in winter months except in very cold or slushy weather. Then Highview boys and girls alike wore women's shoes—high button shoes usually—that turned up at the toes like the strange old-time slippers of court jesters or Persian potentates. It was very funny indeed to see a tough Highview boy hobbling along through the slush in a pair of suede-top high-heeled female shoes, and you could yell at him, "Hey, Snotty, where you get the shoes?" provided, of course, that you had your gang with you and he didn't have his gang with him.

Several times I heard neighbor women complain bitterly about the necessity of sending their gentle little girls and boys to classrooms infested by Highview children, and mourn that the Garrison School was too far from Highview to warrant turning the Negroes out and sending the Highview offspring there.

But the Highview problem diminished progressively with time. Each year more of them dropped from school and scarcely any finished the sixth grade. Some of them were expelled, usually for not studying their lessons—"I hain't learned it 'cause I hain't got no book and Paw, he says does the school want me to have a book let the school buy it." More simply dropped out quietly to get jobs at eleven or twelve or to run away and become tramps.

Yes, we had a "stratified society," and perhaps twelve or fourteen per cent, representing the Negroes, was born irrevocably into the very lowest stratum and lived in shanties in the southeast of town. Next were the Highview people, and their status was not irrevocable—provided God had a miracle left up his sleeve. Third were the people of "The Levee," a delapidated slum joining the Negro district north of the Wabash and Hannibal & St. Joe tracks. No one seemed to know why this district was called the Levee unless it was because it was suggestive of a river city's levee region. The Levee was and is a greater trouble spot for the police than Highview, but greater stigma was attached to residence in Highview than on the Levee. The distinction, of course, was marked by railroad tracks. Highview was across the tracks. The Levee wasn't. The Levee had no definite boundary. There was greater clannishness among the youngsters of Highview, greater antipathy toward aliens. I thought nothing of traversing the Levee each evening with my newspaper sack. No one but a Highview boy would have dared serve that region across the Milwaukee Railroad.

Then came us.

Of course there was a small section on the West Side which considered itself the super-elite, but that was plain snobbishness. They obviously couldn't be any better than we. After all, what did the Declaration of Independence say? After all, weren't all men (meaning members of the elite, of course) born equal?

Some of the West Side boys came to school wearing stiff linen collars as a badge of rank to distinguish themselves from boys who wore celluloid collars. That was a very silly affectation. Linen collars scratched one's neck and actually weren't as neat as a celluloid collar a lot of the time because most of those West Siders would try to get through the school week on two collars while we could wash our nice, shiny celluloid collars every morning before putting them on.

Also, who had the Governor? Was it the snooty West Side? It was not. The birthplace and home of Governor Alexander M. Dockerey was the cottage just west of our home on East Calhoun Street. The Governor's father, the Reverend Willis E. Dockerey, lived there all the time and sat in a chair outside the house whenever the weather permitted and sometimes when the weather did not permit, if they happened to forget him. He was a very old man and I suppose he may have wanted the sun, but I assumed at the time that they kept him outdoors because he didn't smell nice in the house. He would sit out there in his chair killing flies and mumbling about the good old ante-bellum days before Culture had retrogressed, when a servant knew he'd be flogged if he didn't hop when his master called.

Governor Dockerey himself wasn't there often, being busy running the state in Jefferson City, but sometimes a shout would go up, "There's the Governor!" and sure enough there would be Governor Dockerey without his silk hat or frock coat and with his fawn-colored vest unbuttoned and the tab of his stiff-bosomed shirt unbuttoned and hanging outside his trousers, a burly but slightly stoop-shouldered man looking very thoughtful as he sauntered to the privy. Then, if you waited with the crowd, you'd see him again when he emerged from the privy, looking very thoughtful as he went back to the house.

The West Side didn't have anything like that.

Unfortunately, we didn't have it indefinitely either. Long before he went out of office in 1905, the Governor severed ties with Chillicothe. Old Reverend Dockerey died and the Governor sold the ancestral cottage to a German immigrant who was prospering in the junk business, and the German tore down the old Dockerey place and built a fine big white house complete with indoor plumbing.

In 1900 Chillicothe had several other distinctions besides Governor Dockerey.

It was the seat of the State Industrial Home for Girls, which was a very fine thing because housewives of good Christian reputation could get reformed girls paroled to them, thus obtaining household help very cheaply indeed.

It was the birthplace of Sloan's liniment, good for man or beast, which was orginally concocted by the Sloan brothers in their livery stable.

It was the home town of a celebrated Confederate general who was killed at the battle of Pea Ridge but rather neglected by historians, and his name was William Y. Slack.

It was the home of the beautifully matched chestnut-roans, Joe and Dan, who gained national fame on July 4, 1899, as the fastest fire team in the world.

Ordinarily Joe and Dan stood directly under their highly polished automatic harness which dropped on their backs at the clang of the fire gong. Joe and Dan did the rest.

In the firehouse hung a large framed photograph taken on the day Joe and Dan set the record and the inscription on the frame read, "On July 4, 1899, they made a run of 591 feet, laid 100 feet of hose and had water on the fire in 36 seconds." Inasmuch as nothing is said about human assistance in laying the hose and turning on the water, it must be granted that that is a wonderful record for a couple of horses.

Joe and Dan were very close friends of mine. Sometimes I was even allowed to brush their glossy coats. I learned how to run by chasing them to fires. We could really go, Joe and Dan and I.

Chillicothe also was distinguished by being the final resting place of Nelson Kneas, and if a lot of people from outside never heard of Nelson Kneas they would hear of him soon enough if they visited the home of a loyal Chillicothean, and no doubt be taken out to Edgewood Cemetery to see his grave.

Nelson Kneas (sometimes spelled Kneass) wrote the music to Thomas Dunn English's poem "Ben Bolt." At least he wrote the third version of the muisc, the score made immensely popular forty years or so later by use in Du Maurier's *Trilby*. Kneas is said to have admitted that he adapted his composition from "an old German tune." Inasmuch as he was employed at the time as a singer in a Pittsburgh beer garden, he probably was familiar with many old German tunes.

In any event, Nelson Kneas came to Chillicothe with a group of minstrels and was critically ill with pneumonia when he arrived. He died in the old Browning House, which stood on the southeast corner of the Square until it burned shortly before the Civil War, and he was buried in a favored spot in Edgewood Cemetery, a spot over which the willows sighed and the mocking-birds sang and where the springtime violets bloomed larger and more lushly purple than anywhere else.

"Sweet Alice, Ben Bolt violets" were cherished and put into

small special vases. I remember my sister was not quite orthodox in this regard and she would put mignonette in the "Sweet Alice, Ben Bolt" vase, but of course not with the violets. Mignonette also had some meaning to her.

While Nelson Kneas' association with Chillicothe was brief and unhappy, Chillicothe still reveres his memory. The newest and finest movie theater in town is named the Ben Bolt.

In 1900 Chillicothe had thirteen saloons and thirteen churches. All were pretty well attended.

Today Chillicothe has seventeen churches and no open saloons where anything stronger than beer is sold. People have to buy their hard liquor in bottles if they want to obey the law. I don't know whether that system is better or worse from a point of morals. But it is cheaper.

Despite the increase in churches and in church membership I wouldn't be too sure that the people are more prayerful now than in 1900. But I also am not sure that spirituality necessarily is a corollary of prayer. I should think it would depend on the kind of prayer. So many prayers, public and private, are practically requisitions for material advancement of one sort or another.

I remember when I was a young child that I had the Holy Trinity somewhat confused despite the care of my religious upbringing. It seemed to me that the Trinity consisted of Father, Son and Santa Claus, and I prayed to them collectively and individually. While I realize this is an abstruse matter which had better be left to those trained in ecclesiastical doctrine and dialectics, I still can't refrain from saying that I see little spirituality in praying for a bicycle, a boom in the button-hook business or success in battle.

Perhaps a decrease in the requisition type of prayer could mean a decrease in spirituality, but I think it also could mean that the people are doing better and that they are less distraught, and that they might even be more thankful to their anthropomorphic and omnipotent Almighty.

I suspect from reading a number of the popular novels of fifty years or so ago, novels which were freighted with a sort of religiosity, that there was a tendency to confuse spirituality with sentimentality.

At the turn of the Century the moneyed "aristocracy" in America was making a vulgar display of its wealth by erecting baronial castles and competing with one another in the Oriental splendor of their entertainments. Of course they were only trying to imitate the royalty and nobility of Europe, but I am not disconsolate over the fact that royalty, nobility and the American rich have been forced to shorten sail because of economic vicissitudes. Some people used to refer to these extravagant displays of wealth as the "finer things in life," and some now mourn the passing of the days of "gracious living," when many families could afford to be vulgar in a really grandiose manner.

Vulgarity brings up another ubiquitous little item of 1900, and that was the spittoon, called "cuspidor" in more elegant circles. Almost every parlor or "sitting room" had a china cuspidor, often hand-painted with posies, on the floor by father's chair and another handy for guests. Virtually every office and waiting room had at least a couple—flaring-mouthed copper urns, squat utilitarian porcelain vessels, homely pots of soldered sheet metal or, in the pastoral regions, plain boxes of sawdust. The sidewalks were spangled with wet, brown stars as were the wooden-floored halls of office buildings. The pristine beauty of a new-fallen snow was quickly defiled by tobacco juice, with efficient help from equus caballus, and despairing managers of theaters and other gathering places were forced to nail up such signs as, "Gents will not spit on the floor; others must not."

Well, I suppose if one were in the cut plug business the decline in tobacco chewing could seem to be a decline in culture.

The dragging skirts affected by women of the period did only a fair job in sweeping up the tobacco quids and horse droppings, but the women were pretty valiant about their Herculean task, considering the fact that there were no dry-cleaners in those days. Yes, they were brave and they were dogged, but it was still a relief to them when streets ceased to be a morass of mud in wet weather and two inches deep with dust in dry weather, and the horse began to retire in favor of motor vehicles and a young man no longer felt his masculinity was suspect if he didn't chew tobacco, and dry-cleaning was developed, and there no longer was any real necessity to wear dragging skirts and petticoats, and a woman could wear a dress that hung no lower than her shoetops without occasioning leers from strange men and consternation on the part of her family and friends.

Yes, the lot of gentle woman was wonderful in the good old days. Go into any cemetery of that period and look at the number of girls who were buried between the ages of sixteen and thirty. Go into a library and look over the files of women's magazines of from 1895 to 1905. Read the articles of advice. Read the advertisements. Read the fiction directed at the tender minds of the well-protected fair sex.

There may be some significance in the fact that among the retrogressionists who long to go back to the good old days you don't find many middle-aged women.

III

THE ALIEN ADULT

ONE OF THE developments toward civilization in the last half century is an improvement in relationship and understanding between adults and boys of the Cro-Magnon stage. I do not hold, by any means, that peace has come to the warring factions. But some important steps have been taken in the right direction.

I know there are a few fundamental errors in the concept of such organizations as the Boy Scouts, the Y.M.C.A., and most church groups, and that frequently the personalities of adult supervisors are unfortunate. I do not expect to see all these items corrected, because the situation is delicate and complex, and homo sapiens, by and large, is a clumsy creature of emotions. Except by accident, you can't repair a watch with a corn cob.

By a good deal of uninhibited retrospection, allowing one incident to bring up another, I have built up a picture in my own mind of what life was like for a boy between the ages of nine and fourteen in the years 1904-1908 at Chillicothe, Missouri, and I think that picture is about as truthful as it is possible for an unbiased human brain to make it. I believe the locale was fairly representative of America as a whole. And, while my own situation was perhaps in some ways extreme, I still believe it could be regarded as representative of other boys of that period from middle-class, white, God-fearing families.

My father, like most Victorian heads of families, was the domineering male who permitted my mother no word in either business or family affairs and closed his ears to her petitions, complaints, admonitions and faint-voiced naggings. My father was an unrealistic product of the mid-Nineteenth Century.

He was born in 1849 on the west shore of Lake Canandaigua in New York State and by the time he was ten was riding tow horse on my grandfather's Erie Canal boat. Thrown in with what was probably as tough a company of young boys as this country ever saw, I don't believe, from his later attitude, that he ever quite accepted them, or they him. "Scum of the earth," he used to say of those boys. "Nothing in the world too low or filthy for them to do."

I believe his association with those Erie Canal boys influenced his whole life. Certainly it affected his attitude toward my brother and me, whom he was determined to rear as Christian gentlemen.

According to family legend, my father's first Davis ancestor in America came from Wales in the Seventeenth Century. I have no idea of his social status. He may possibly have been an indentured servant, but I doubt that he was a convict because the legend holds he was a public official in Connecticut for many years. But in America the Welsh blood became mixed with English, Scotch and heaven knows what else. So far as I know there were no criminals, men of great wealth, geniuses, paupers or actually insane people in the strain, although there were screwballs aplenty and those who approached religious fanaticism perilously close. The only men of prominence with even remote family connections that I know of were Stephen A. Douglas and General John Brown Gordon of the Confederate Army.

It is possible that these connections influenced the attitude of my father's father toward the Civil War. He believed the conflict should be avoided, even if the government must issue bonds and buy all slaves. He was a militant copperhead, which was a far from popular position around Canandaigua, New York, or on the Erie Canal, and, according to my father's stories, Jeremiah Davis whipped everyone who challenged his views from Canal Street,

Buffalo, to Rome. That took in quite a bit of very tough territory, and, granting Jeremiah Davis extraordinary physical strength, pugnacity and agility, and remembering what a fetish my father made of veracity and how many times he flogged me for the slightest deviation from the exact truth, I still would be willing to discount that *everyone* at least five per cent.

My father did not boast of my grandfather's prowess. Rather, he was proud that he, the son of a reckless, hard-drinking, profane canaller, had become an ardent prohibitionist in silk-lapelled frock coat who said his prayers at least four times a day and never uttered an oath except when he talked in his sleep—which was practically every night.

My father apparently got his religion from his grandfather, David Davis, who fought in the War of 1812, read the Bible forty-seven times, kept his eye constantly on heaven and thundered warnings as a prophet of doom. He invented happy aphorisms such as, "There's nothing in this world worth the smile of a toad."

Apparently my father got his hatred of liquor from his mother, who was born Eliza Martin in Tonawanda, New York (an Erie Canal port) and who must have had quite a time with her husband, to whom she bore eight children.

When I was born my father was nearly forty-five and was fifty by the time I have a clear recollection of his appearance. At that time he was a heavy man just under six feet with dark curly beard and hawk nose and ruddy, weathered complexion.

He was about the best horseman I ever knew. Even at seventy he rode like a cavalryman, and as a young man was renowned as a breaker and trainer of wild horses. He spoke a horse's language and he had that rare quality of voice which can soothe a "spooked" team under most difficult situations.

I have been told by old Nebraskans that hopeless "outlaws" were brought hundreds of miles to him and that he almost never failed to ride them and make friends with them and to cajole them into law-abiding servitude. He loved all animals, and he made pets of horses, cows, pigs, sheep, goats, game cocks, rabbits, crows, song birds, white rats, cats, dogs, foxes, pigeons and squirrels so that they followed him around like the pictures of St. Francis.

Once I saw him threaten to kill a man for beating a horse, and the next day he beat me twice as severely for half the reason.

When I was a young child my father was very kind to me. He loved to tell stories and in me he found a very appreciative audience. For years almost every evening I sat on his lap while he related his boyhood adventures on the "old scow" sailing Lake Canandaigua, or on the Erie Canal or with the strange people who inhabited the green hills of Ontario County, and he frequently would draw maps of the region so I could understand just how this or that event took place. He told of his going to Nebraska at sixteen, of being pursued by a band of howling painted Indians and of outriding them; of driving the stage coach into Julesburg, Colorado—all manner of personal experiences, plus an unending serial fantasy about Pat and Mike Malloy who came over from old Ireland and became owners of a wonderful railroad.

Until I was about nine years old and it became necessary for him to pay half fare for me on trains, he took me with him on scores of business trips over the country and, without realizing it, turned me into a confirmed tramp. I can't understand why he bothered himself with me so often. I remember definitely being told time and again that I could not accompany him and begging until he gave in. But he was utterly impervious to my pleadings in other regards.

It's possible that he feared my mother's hand was not strong enough to keep me from "associating with tough boys" during his absence (which was quite true) or that I might addle my brain by reading storybooks and *The Youth's Companion.* Or I suppose he may have thought I might learn something of what he considered proper business tactics by watching his dealings with the heads of various firms which had use for wooden boxes and crates.

I believe his greatest weakness as a businessman was an overwhelming optimism, a faith that he could afford to take great chances because God was on his side, giving him every break over those sinful men who used profanity, tobacco and alcohol. He had a perfect understanding with God. When the cards were not stacked in his favor but actually seemed to be stacked against him, my father realized that God was merely testing his mettle and he knew that God was chuckling to Himself and saying, "That man Davis is a wonder. You don't see him whining or grumbling over a disappointment. Look at him smile. I've got to do something real good for him and right soon."

In that regard I have another definition of a pessimist: A pessimist is the son of an optimist.

I believe my father may have been a better than average salesman. He exuded vitality and confidence. And, while his education was extremely sketchy and he read almost nothing but the newspapers, he was a glib speaker with an arsenal of oratorical clichés which he could adapt to almost any purpose. But it took very little to swing him from box shooks to William Jennings Bryan ("Only one greater and purer man ever lived on the face of this earth and *He* never trod American soil.") or to the "Liquor Question." ("There are two sides to every question on earth except one, and that one is the liquor question. There was never a single case in history where anyone was helped one iota by a drink of intoxicating beverage, but rum, whisky and beer have been responsible for most of the misery, crime, poverty and divorce in the world and I think it's safe to say that for every drop of intoxicating beverage consumed by men in America, two tears have been shed by women and children.")

I suppose one might say that liquor ruined my father—but not in the usual way. Living in an era of expansion, he took advantage of opportunities to become comfortably well-to-do, but his zeal for battle against John Barleycorn led him to neglect his business in favor of publishing miserable little weeklies in the interest of the Anti-Saloon League and W.C.T.U.

When national prohibition finally came he was happy in the thought that he had played his part in bringing the reform and he never lived to see the "noble experiment" discredited and junked.

He was just as bitter about gambling, tobacco, Sunday baseball and other breaches of the Sabbath. But he did not consider betting on horse races gambling—not for him. "I have the utmost contempt," he would say, "for men who bet on horses when they don't know a gaskin from a croup. But for a student of horseflesh, placing money on a race is not gambling in any respect. It's simply a matter of using your knowledge and judgment to direct a business investment." Never in his life was he wrong in his judgment of a race. If his horse didn't finish in the money it was because of the stupidity of the jockey, an accident or crookedness or some other obvious reason. His selection was still the best horse.

During the years when he took me on so many business trips he and I were very close, and I naturally regarded him as the fountain of all wisdom. Sometimes my mother objected to his taking me out of school, but he declared that I learned more from travel and association with him in a week than I could in a month at school, and I quite agreed with him. It's just possible that I still agree. In any event I saw a good deal of accommodation trains, country boardinghouses, second-rate city hotels, all manner of manufacturing plants, wholesale establishments and warehouses.

The break came when railroad conductors began to ask my age. Then I was left at home. And then I began to see how much fun I had been missing through obedience to my father's orders.

Naturally, I think, I was a gregarious extrovert, but my father's determination to keep me isolated from "toughness" drove me underground for a while to a land of fantasy.

For the life of me I can't imagine how he thought I should occupy myself. True, I had certain household chores such as churning, helping my sister with the dishes, keeping the kitchen wood box full and weeding the yard and garden, but these things took little time. I could play with Maurine and Mary Sweeney, who lived across Woodward Street to the east, but we had nothing in common and our play usually broke up in a row.

Because my sister Una, ten years my senior, had taken the trouble to teach me, I could read when I was five years old—a year before I started school. So I read. In a hot upstairs storeroom were stacked a ton or more of old magazines which had come in exchange for *The Missouri Stock Journal,* which my father published until he acquired the box factory. There were years and years of *The Youth's Companion, The Scientific American, Cosmopolitan, Leslie's, McClure's, Harper's, Century, Ladies' Home Journal* and others, and I devoured practically the whole store, acquiring in the process a most curious perspective on my world.

My first deliberate disobedience centered on that stock of old magazines. I was completely a slave to the vice of reading before my father discovered me "addling my brain, ruining my health and burning out my eyes" in the storeroom. He commanded me to cease my evil practices under penalty of the lash, but he did not realize I already was too far gone for redemption. At every opportunity I would sneak into the storeroom to read and re-read the *Ladies' Home Journal's* serialization of Ernest Thompson Seton's *Two Little Savages;* or *Track's End,* or *The Bold American* in *The Youth's Companion.* At least twice I was apprehended and thrashed, but that only made me more crafty.

My mother, on the other hand, tacitly encouraged my reading by not opposing it when he was away from home. She liked to read fiction herself and we had perhaps a couple of hundred novels in the house ranging from Laura Jean Libbey and Bertha M. Clay through an assortment of temperance propaganda works such as *The Temperance Doctor, His Wife's Wedding Ring, Ten Nights in a Barroom, Minnie Hermon or the Curse of Rum* and *The Hard Master* to *Les Miserables* and *Vanity Fair.* She also had a paper-bound set of Dickens which had been a premium for something or other that she kept in a box upstairs, and she did a good deal of trading and borrowing from various neighbors, especially from Mrs. Hornback who owned a rather good library.

My father used to criticize my mother as a horrible example of what happened to people who "sat around with their noses in books filling their brains with stuff and nonsense."

I was about eleven and pretty well alienated by my father's arbitrary strictness when I took ill-advised issue with him. I said, "Well, you hadn't ought to talk. Maybe you wouldn't have spent all the money on that silly pump if you'd read a few more books." The words "silly pump" were direct quotes from my mother but that didn't help any when we retired to the kitchen for a painful session with Dr. Hickory.

The incident referred to was an invention of my father's, an automatic pump designed to keep a proper water level in the factory's steam boiler. I don't know the principle of the thing, but I do remember my brother Glen, who had studied some physics, protesting vehemently that it couldn't possibly work.

"Why, Pop," Glen said, "if that would work you'd have perpetual motion."

"All right," my father said, "then we'll have perpetual motion."

As I recall, it cost him something better than a thousand dollars to discover he *didn't* have perpetual motion, and my mother thought the money could have been spent better in buying some new furniture (and perhaps a few nineteen-cent standard books) from Sears, Roebuck and having the house redecorated.

Items like these tumbled my father from his early pedestal of infallibility. If he could be wrong once or twice he could be wrong whenever his opinion conflicted with my wishes—which seemed to be most of the time. My unquestioning childish devotion changed to a rebellious surliness. He in turn was disappointed in me and shocked and apprehensive. He attempted to "lick it out of me" and that only made matters worse. Where once I believed him always right, I came to think of him as always wrong. And my filial attitude was far from unique.

Most of my boy associates seemed to think of their fathers as Number One enemies, as cruel but stupid despots. Circumventing paternal tyranny was one of the first purposes of life, a game exciting and filled with danger but definitely worth while. Even more daring and more filled with delicious fun was playing tricks that humiliated momentarily or deflated pompous adults, particularly a father.

I think it may have been typically Nineteenth Century, this attitude of patronizing dignity that fathers held for their young sons. I believe it came as something of a shock to the average boy when he realized there was a good deal of pompous sham to Papa and, consciously or unconsciously, the boy resented it. The broad comedy of *Peck's Bad Boy* and the "Katzenjammer Kids" in puncturing adult dignity appealed to children who were confronted with similar Nineteenth Century situations.

In other words, the children were native realists and they were moved instinctively to bring posing adults down to earth.

My father was a staunch advocate of woman suffrage, believing that women in politics not only would put crooked machine politicians to flight, but institute prohibition of tobacco as well as of intoxicating liquor. Yet I doubt if he ever asked my mother's opinion before issuing a family interdiction. She, poor woman, had read too many books to be taken seriously.

I don't suppose my father ever heard of Arthur Schopenhauer. Generally speaking, I imagine my father would have called the German a "contemptible, whining pessimist." But I'm sure my father would have gone right along with Schopenhauer on thinking for oneself. He would have agreed that "the safest way of having no thoughts of one's own is to take up a book every moment one has nothing else to do. It is this practice which explains why erudition makes most men more stupid and silly than they are by nature. . . . Reading is nothing more than a substitute for thoughts of one's own. It means putting the mind into leading-strings. The multitude of books serves only to show how many false paths there are, and how widely astray a man may wander if he follows any of them."

On the matter of reading, I remember my mother once attempted to make a minority report, but was quickly withered. She then informed me privately that my father was prejudiced against reading fiction, and that it was quite all right for me to read storybooks if I didn't let my father catch me at it.

That seemed to me to be the perfect omnibus solution.

On my own initiative I had discovered that the Catholic boys were not at all imps from hell as he pictured them, but swell kids. So it would be quite all right for me to run with them if I didn't let my father catch me at it.

On my own initiative I had discovered that baseball was a wonderful and utterly fascinating sport and not a device of the devil aimed directly at desecrating the Lord's Day. I could play baseball if I never let my father catch me at it. I had money from my paper route and I could buy a finger mitt and a dollar-and-a-quarter Spalding ball if I kept them carefully hidden where my father never would see them.

So I came to what seemed a logical conclusion: What my father called bad was probably pretty good; what my father said was good was probably pretty dull.

My father was bitterly opposed to tobacco. At eleven I began to smoke cigars—when I could win one at the shooting gallery on my paper route. My father believed liquor to be the greatest evil in the world. When I got my first pair of long pants at fifteen, which in the eyes of Kansas City bartenders of that day turned a boy into a man, I went directly to a saloon and bought myself a couple of shots of straight bourbon.

When I started to the Eugene Field School I made my first real friendship (one which, incidentally, endures to this day) with a blond, imaginative boy named Chester Grace, and for several years we were inseparable. While my father did not wholly approve of this association, he still did not disapprove vigorously. Chester was indeed suspect of that dread thing, "toughness," but after all his father was a good Democrat, a total abstainer from alcohol and tobacco, and presumably as great a Christian Protestant as possible for a member of the South Methodist Church. Also, Ode Grace was a breeder of horses, which gave him something in common with my father.

I never knew why the two men were not good friends, but it is possible that Ode Grace, a graduate of the University of Missouri and possessed of a dry sense of humor, may have taken my father's frock coat, boiled shirt and ortatorical manner less than seriously.

Chester and I became conscious of adults living in another and antagonistic world, of something happening to a human being when he or she reached maturity which caused him or her to shed rationality and all sense of values.

We resented adults' taking unfair advantage of their superior physical strength and position. We accepted them as natural enemies, but we realized they could be fought only by subtle and crafty means.

We youngsters, without knowing it, were living in the fag end of an age of reform. Reformers of every complexion were being virtually canonized in America and the great ideal was to keep the new generation from growing up into human beings and to turn us into glittering saints. That ideal was quite opposed to our instincts and we naturally rebelled.

The age of reform came to its dying climax with enactment of the Eighteenth Amendment and resulted in the discrediting and in the virtual extinction of the genus reformer.

It would seem scarcely necessary to make categorical statements now that relations between adults and children have improved. Parents, by and large, ceased long ago the hopeless attempt to turn young flesh and blood into living but hallowed ectoplasm. School teachers, by and large, are more competent and more realistic in approaching their jobs. Consequently the little darlings are more open in their deviltry because there is less reason to be furtive.

For a while, particularly in the Nineteen-twenties, reaction to old standards surely went too far and especially in the case of parents who dove overboard in adopting the cult of Behaviorism. Lack of any discipline can be as bad as, or worse than, too much discipline. Now, for some years, there has been a leveling-off toward a common-sense basis and I think this is reflected in the improved attitude of boys and girls, generally speaking, toward parents, teachers and adults at large. They are still living in different worlds, it is true, but the important fact is the wide recognition that this is natural and inevitable.

We adults do not believe we are so wise today, and consequently we are wiser. Because boys and girls are regarded as boys and girls and given opportunity to *be* boys and girls, they are healthier, brighter, more candid and happier than were the children of forty or fifty years ago.

IV

REVOLT OF THE YOUNG BULLS

Adults of forty-five or fifty years ago had either forgotten what it was like to live in the Cro-Magnon cave man stage of human metamorphosis or wished they could forget and were resolved that their own offspring should be better than they themselves were as boys. The common attitude of a Victorian American father was determination that his sons should be little gentlemen—even if cringing little gentlemen.

This paternal attitude had the logical effect of driving sons underground and banding them together in warfare against the common foe, the community's adult population.

It was guerrilla warfare against a vastly stronger enemy, and, consequently, was characterized by brief sorties, sabotage, ambuscades and particularly by insidious annoyances designed to humiliate the foe and make him lose face. It was a hit-and-run fight against authority, but a great deal of fun—except on those rare occasions when you got caught and licked.

In my own case there was first an alliance with Chester Grace, an oath of eternal brotherhood signed with blood pricked from our fingers and buried in a can under our front porch, where it may still rest. But presently I found myself in an anomalous situation and practically living a double life. While my first pal Chester was vigorous and athletic, he just didn't care much for baseball as a game. I loved it. And, while it may have been a matter of personalities, he also didn't seem to care much for gang activities with the boys of my neighborhood who were mostly pupils in the Catholic parochial school, the same "tough" boys my father had expressly forbidden me to associate with. I did not find them tough. I found them wonderful, especially one ingenious lad named Allan Elvin.

I wanted to take Allan—commonly called Sliver—into our fraternity and, while Chester was not enthusiastic, I do not recall that he offered serious objections to Sliver's initiation.

Once the door was opened for Sliver, however, other boys began to slip in until there were enough of the elect for a baseball team and a football team. Then, while it was nominally one gang, there really were three circles—Chester and me, Sliver and me, and Sliver and the gang and me—and we developed into something approximating a European political party and quite subversive.

Being, as I say, in the cave man period of our development, we were naturally fascist. In fact Chester and I selected what we believed to be an Indian insigne—the swastika—probably at least ten years before Adolf Hitler ever saw that sign.

It was quite fortunate that I did not learn the art of tattooing until several years later or I surely would have pricked our swastika under the skins of our inner circle at least. From about 1932 on, owning a swastika tattoo would have been embarrassing. As it was, Chester and I, and the gang and I, daubed that swastika sign in the dead of night all over town, including the water tower. That was to let the silly and complacent adults know an enemy lived in their midst and to give them fair warning. That was to carry consternation into the hearts of the enemy. For we were the young bulls, exiled (even if voluntarily) from the herd.

There were no formal meetings of the Swastika gang; that would have been pretentious and adult and silly. We simply got together in small groups by giving a secret sign, plotted night forays, recounted adventures of the last few days, and howled with laughter at successes and commiserated with jibes at those who were clumsy enough or unlucky enough to fail.

One common approach was wide-eyed innocence with great reverence for the dignity of the elder, inducing him to lower his guard and to pontificate.

There was poor Mr. Barry, a browbeating bully who knew the answers to every question on earth. One morning Sliver Elvin and I were going fishing and Mr. Barry yelled at us, perhaps from kindness in his heart, perhaps because he never lost an opportunity to display his knowledge. "Look here, you kids, keep away from Half Moon Lake. Rattlesnakes there."

"Gee, Mr. Barry, thank you. Did you see rattlesnakes there?"

"Did I see 'em? By God, I got bit by one."

Of course we knew Mr. Barry had been bitten by a rattlesnake but we knew also that it had occurred before we were born.

We whistled and shook our heads in sympathy. "Gosh—where'd he bite you, Mr. Barry?"

"Right on the shank, by God. Took and bit me right through my pants. Know that swampy spot just east of Half Moon? Well, right in there."

"Whew! Did you kill him?"

"You bet I killed him. Took and shot 'im. Had nine rattles and a button."

"But didn't it hurt awful?"

"Hurt? Hurt's no name for it. Worse than being shot. By God, worse than anything else on earth, I reckon. Doctor said I'd died sure enough wasn't I so strong and had a flask of corn on me."

"It leave a scar, Mr. Barry?"

"Course it left a scar. Big scar. Why wouldn't it leave a scar when not many men ever'd live through it?"

"Mr. Barry, can we see the scar?"

"Huh! Think I'm going to undress out here on the street so you fool kids can see a snake bite?"

"Please, Mr. Barry. If it's down there on your shank all you got to do is pull up your pant leg. Aw, come on, Mr. Barry. We never did see a snake bite."

"Well, by God. No."

"Aw, Mr. Barry. What's it look like, Mr. Barry? Is it green or any color? Maybe it's red, huh?"

"Well, for heaven's sake, if you're so set on seeing a snake bite—"

Mr. Barry sat down on the curbing, rolled up his trousers leg, unclasped the safety pin that held his sock to his long underwear, pulled up the underwear and proudly displayed the scar on his bulging calf. It looked like an oversized vaccination scar and slightly depressed.

We expressed admiration and horror.

"Hmm," Mr. Barry breathed modestly, "ain't nothing now."

"Gosh, I'd say it was plenty."

"Well, by God, if you think it's something now you should ought to looked at it once. Gob of proud flesh right about here." Mr. Barry touched the upper part of the scar with a gnarled forefinger.

"Can I touch it, Mr. Barry?" I asked. "I never did touch a snake bite."

"Hmmm."

I touched it. "Gee, it's kind of funny and slick, ain't it, Mr. Barry?"

"Hmm."

Sliver touched it. "Sure is slick," he said. "Dirt wouldn't stick to it like to the rest of the leg."

Mr. Barry bristled.

"Oh," said Sliver, "I didn't mean the rest of your leg is dirty *now*. I just meant that the scar is too slippery for dirt to stick to any time."

"Well, now you seen a snake bite scar and I hope you're satisfied." Mr. Barry pulled down his underwear and pinned his sock to it.

We sighed. "Gee, we're sure much obliged, Mr. Barry. I reckon there ain't many kids ever saw a rattlesnake scar. Thank you *ever* so much."

Mr. Barry, obviously pleased with himself, stood up and growled,

"Well, just see you don't never get one yourself. You kids never'd in the world live through it."

So we went sedately around the corner and lay down in the grass and laughed and cried and repeated bits of the conversation and laughed all over again and finally pulled ourselves together and went fishing at Half Moon Lake where there probably had been no rattlesnakes for ten years.

The next day we took Mox Rupp and Sliver's younger brother Johnny and hunted down Mr. Barry and cajoled and flattered and coaxed until he finally sat down and unpinned his sock and displayed the scar for them to marvel at. And the following day we rounded up three more of the gang and found Mr. Barry and despite our ostensible awe and great respect, he began to grumble. "What you think I am?" he demanded. "You think I'm a God-damn side show? Maybe I should ought to charge admission." Nevertheless he unpinned his sock and displayed the scar.

On the fourth day we had practically the whole baseball team on hand and Mr. Barry at last grew suspicious that something was happening, perhaps something almost as painful as the snake bite itself. Johnny Elvin giggled and it was like touching off a train of powder. Mr. Barry was surrounded by chortling urchins like a range cow surrounded by yapping coyotes. "Aw come on, Mr. Barry. Show us your snake bite, Mr. Barry?"

"Why, you little bastards. You trying to make fun of me or something? Why I'll flail you within—" He made a grab at Sliver who ducked easily out of his way.

We spread and yapped—"Where'd the snake bite you, Mr. Barry? Hey, show us the scar, will you, Mr. Barry? Did it hurt awful, Mr. Barry?" Then one boy blipped his lips in what he thought was an imitation of a rattlesnake and shrilled, "Watch out, there, here comes a rattler!" and Mr. Barry made an ineffectual dive at him and must have known in his sorrowing soul that he was done for, that he had been lured into the clutches of jungle pigmies from whom he could not hope for mercy.

For a while when boys yelled at him, "Where'd the snake bite you?" he would run at them, sometimes with a buggy whip in his hand, but he was heavy and slow and his tormentors were agile as rabbits and he had no chance. Then he sought to frighten them with threats of reform school, glowers and curses, and he knew he was licked, but he, like so many victims of war, not only didn't know what the war was about but didn't realize the psychological forces at work. He indubitably considered his own situation unique. Without a doubt he felt that Chillicothe was infested with a vicious breed of boys who weren't whipped enough at home and therefore would grow into criminals.

There were several in Mr. Barry's unfortunate category. Then there was the just-a-boy-at-heart, patronizing kind of adult of which Mr. Whittaker, the mail carrier, was a good representative. Mr. Whittaker "understood" children. He was blithe and hale and if he came upon a group "playing catch" in the street he'd whistle shrilly and call out, "Shoot it, Skinny!" And, if the boy, out of politeness, threw him the ball, Mr. Whittaker would burn it back quickly to some unsuspecting lad and jibe, "Butterfingers!" if the ball was muffed. With the sacred leather mail sack of Uncle Sam over one shoulder, he would engage in mock sparring bouts with boys of twelve, slapping their cheeks and guffawing at them. He wanted to be a super-boy, but he just didn't qualify.

We boys of the mystic swastika began to ignore Mr. Whittaker except for shooting him in the posterior now and then with a slingshot from a safe hiding place where there was a quick exit to the rear. I had long, strong, ten cent rubbers on my slingshot and could knock a yellowhammer off the top of a telegraph pole with it. Mr. Whittaker used to react beautifully to my pebbles, and while he would dash around madly, seeking his tormentors, we always had two or three bushwackers hidden in different quarters, so he was sure to pick up an additional pebble or two if he tarried in the hunt for his original assailant. We called this enterprise "Laying for Whittaker," and it was one of the most successful objectives of the War of the Young Bulls. At last Mr. Whittaker was transferred to the West Side (possibly at his own request) and we got Earl Blue, a quiet, pleasant man who minded his own business and had no trouble.

Chief of Police Dorney was an exciting objective, although his posterior offered a much wider target than Mr. Whittaker's and we had to strain our imaginations as to what the chief might do with his billy club and revolver.

Naturally, and particularly, the war extended into school. From the Catholic boys I heard much of a hard-boiled Sister Veronica who beat the palms of their hands with a ruler until they were purple and swollen, and it seemed to me that their retaliatory measures were innocuous and uninspired.

For some reason the "tough" Catholic boys seemed to have no fighting spirit in school. They seemed to pass up countless opportunities to make Sister Veronica's life miserable. It was difficult even to persuade them to play hookey.

We Protestant public school pupils, on the other hand, carried on the good fight grade after grade against teacher after teacher, giving no quarter and certainly receiving no quarter. While there was a chance that a teacher cared little whether we learned anything or not, it seemed probable that he or she might regard it as a personal triumph if we showed any progress. We didn't dare risk that. Far better to take our floggings and maintain an air of contemptuous, inattentive stupidity. And we lived under the curious obsession that we were pretty manly little martyrs, shedding our blood, or at least suffering welts and blisters, in the good fight against oppression.

I have given only a few examples of the scores of adults who won special attention from the young bulls. But there was the woman who threatened to call the police because we roller-skated on her cement sidewalk, and one night Sliver Elvin and I noiselessly got her garden hose, pushed the nozzle through the latticework of her back porch, aimed at the center of the closed door. Then, while Sliver waited with hand on the faucet, I knocked loudly on the back door and ran. At the sound of the door opening, Sliver turned on the water full force and we knew we got a bull's-eye from the piercing screams that followed. There was the man who threatened to send Chester and me to reform school simply because we put a couple of roosters together and let them follow their natural, God-given instincts. His front door bell was rung one dark night and he answered it to be caught in enfilading fire from shrubbery to the right and left of his house, a sneak attack with eggs, some of them the product of his own hens, which had been nurtured for weeks until they rattled ominously when shaken.

There were many, many others, and if any victim ever suspected me I had an unbreakable alibi.

When my father was home I was required to be in bed by eight-thirty. When he was away the deadline could be stretched, if I wished, until nearly nine o'clock by reading and saying, "All right, just as soon as I finish this chapter." My mother permitted me to read when my father was away.

Once in my room and with the door closed, it was simple to slip out the window to the back porch roof, shinny down and away. The return was only slightly more difficult. Both Chester and Sliver also were able to make exits by their bedroom windows after their younger brothers were asleep.

After Chester moved away my night life seemed to accelerate because Sliver was a romantic, and prowling the silent town, hiding in bushes at the approach of adult footsteps, feeding in fruit trees, fishing in the moonlight with owls and whippoorwills mourning in the black trees, and fireflies flashing in the thickets seemed the most exciting thing in the world to him.

Right there we entered into a most dangerous phase which, had our environment been a crowded city or even a rural slum, would almost inevitably have led us into crime.

We had a normal craving for adventure and a sense of independence. We were extremely anti-social as far as adults were concerned. But there happened to be relatively wholesome outlets which do not exist, for instance, in Harlem, the South Side of Chicago or the Mission District of San Francisco.

In that stage we needed not mothering love as some psychoanalysts would have it, but adult male understanding and direction into healthful, interesting daytime projects. We needed fewer restrictions rather than more. A good portion of our restrictions were impossible and they served only to drive us into night life at a cost of sleep.

The attitude toward young boys today may not be universally perfect. But the progress made in that department in the last fifty years is practically revolutionary.

If, in this account of the bulls of a half century ago, I seem to neglect the activities and adventures of the young heifers, that is because, by and large, the young heifers didn't have any activities and adventures. That is, to the best of my knowledge, they didn't.

Girls were just around and they jolly well kept their place. They wheeled their doll babies in doll buggies. They played jacks. Sometimes they rolled hoops. They stuck out their tongues at you and if you pulled their hair they screeched. If you were weak enough to be lured into playing a while with a girl it was always the same thing. "Let's play house. You be the papa." Then there'd be a tea party with doll's dishes, and God help you if some of the gang caught you at it.

A few girls were tomboys, and adults predicted no good end for them. Maurine Sweeney was a tomboy and she would even come over and work out on my trapeze. But she was very careful to put an elastic around the bottom of her dress to hold it tight around her knees. Otherwise she'd have shown her ruffled panties when she skinned the cat. You had to give Maurine credit for that much, even while admitting it certainly wasn't very ladylike in the first place for a big girl of ten or eleven to be swinging on a trapeze.

Well, if the general attitude toward young boys has improved one hundred per cent in the last fifty years, the attitude toward young girls must have improved three hundred per cent.

In Chillicothe, today, girls play softball and, even though their grandmothers may be turning over in their graves, they wear shorts and jerseys while they are playing it. They play tennis. They go on hikes and camp out. They shoot traps and skeet with their *own* four-ten and twenty-gauge shotguns. They play basketball. They go swimming in the magnificent municipal pool. This last, I think, has more significance than all the rest because I would wager that when I was twelve years old there wasn't a girl my age in town who could swim a stroke. There simply was no place for them to learn.

I myself had never even seen a bathing suit, male or female, until I was about fifteen.

As I write this I can look out my window and see half a dozen high school students passing a football. There are four boys and two girls. One of the girls, a tall, supple lass, throws the football as well as any of the boys—a long, beautiful spiral with plenty of power behind it. The boys do not patronize her as their grandfathers would have patronized her grandmother. They do not toss the ball gently to her. They really throw it, and she catches it as a football should be caught.

Today there is a companionship between young males and females which did not exist and could not exist under the silly standards of forty-odd years ago.

This new relationship, I submit, is more wholesome, more healthful and infinitely more fun for the boys as well as for the girls than was the self-conscious association of the good old days which actually emphasized sex while pretending to hide it.

Now the young bulls are generally regarded as primitive human beings, not as wild animals to be hemmed in and whipped into submission. Even parents are becoming aware that too many restrictions are almost as bad as no restrictions at all because a spirited lad simply will not submit to tyranny, and once he begins to circumvent *unjust* parental laws there is nothing to prevent his circumventing *just* parental laws.

Wise parents and directors of youth activities realize now that the intelligence of pre-puberty boys used to be grievously underrated, for the young bulls are instinctive masters of dissimulation and therefore prodigiously shrewd at detecting sham and fakery in their elders.

When I hear a father proudly proclaim that he and his sons are buddies I wonder how much the boys are taking the old man for a ride. Oh, it can be done, but it's almost impossible unless papa is a case of retarded mental development and has retained his youthful physical agility along with the twelve-year-old mind.

Buddies, necessarily, must be equals and I doubt whether that is the ideal father-son relationship. It is far better, in my opinion, for the father to conduct himself in such a manner that the boy respects the parent's judgment and especially his unswerving fairness. There is definitely an insurmountable barrier between parent and child which should be recognized in the interest of happiness on both sides, and I believe a prospective parent could do much worse than take the training required of an athletic coach.

My father, believing firmly that man was made in God's image, saw no reason why a boy could not be a demi-cherubim if properly shielded from "toughness" and if the hickory was applied consistently. The parents of most of my associates held substantially the same erroneous notion and, while their intentions may have been of the highest, they were running entirely against nature. If you seal up a vessel of water and boil it, the steam is bound to escape no matter how much you scold or pray. With us, escape was made at night through opening seams and the seams were our windows.

Sliver and I had an old sheet-iron skillet and we always had bacon filched from home and bread, and many a catfish we fried and ate in our Cro-Magnon firelight after the Big Dipper made its midnight turn. And there were frogs' legs and there were eggs, which in our code of morals were as legitimate prey as the peaches God put on trees and the grapes and watermelons that grew on vines. It definitely would have been stealing to take fruit from a grocery, but there was a saving distinction between fruit in a basket and fruit on the tree or vine or in a hen's nest.

Once we lifted a chicken which, as the saying went, was roosting uncomfortably, and we fried it at our camp. But the chicken didn't taste good and we couldn't finish it. We knew that was stealing and we knew we somehow must make restitution.

I had money from my paper route and I thought seriously of going to the owners of the chicken, confessing the theft and paying for it. Sliver was opposed for the practical reason that he knew this man and woman were of uncertain temper and might have us arrested despite our reformation. I thought then of leaving an anonymous letter with twenty-five cents (a liberal price for the chicken) on their front porch, but again Sliver was opposed because his father was a traveling postal inspector and Sliver was much impressed by methods of tracing stationery and handwriting.

Our problem of conscience was solved that fall when these people had the steam woodsaw come and zing up a huge pile of stove wood. We went to work that night, carried the mountain of wood into their woodshed and stacked it up neatly. That stint, we considered, settled the chicken account. It probably mystified the ex-chicken's owners more or less also. If they ever missed their fryer they wouldn't have been likely to associate it with the leprechauns coming to carry in their wood.

Those night rovings with Sliver and other members of the Swastika gang are among the most pleasant memories of my boyhood. Sliver was imaginative and steeped in a half-believed Irish lore which enabled him to endow a familiar mist-filled valley with strange poetry and to people it with unworldly creatures. The night world was filled with a synthesis of dew-accentuated odors that followed us from town to woods to river like soft background music. Unidentified noises, the creak of a faraway pump or slamming of a door or outcry of some small wild thing were freighted with a delicious sense of peril. One of us would whisper—"Hush, what's that?"—then dart into the brush where we'd crouch and I'd cock my twenty-two over a black-powder short cartridge, hoping that at least a wolf or wildcat would stalk out into the starlight.

In town the hollow thump of some late wayfarer's footsteps on wooden sidewalks was portentous, especially if the footsteps were approaching, and we would lie flat in the dewy grass, watching and waiting breathlessly while the slow thump-thump-thump grew louder and closer—perhaps some weary specter, hopelessly seeking sanctuary, perhaps only a drunk stumbling doggedly homeward, perhaps Policeman Ross making his rounds on the lookout for such night prowlers as Sliver and me, criminals, violating the town's eight-thirty o'clock curfew law.

But one of the greatest thrills was to hide in the shadow of the Milwaukee water tank on a steaming hot night, allowing the silver trickle to splash on our bare heads once in a while, talking in whispers while waiting for the bittersweet, lonesome, exultant whistle of the eleven o'clock southbound freight as it passed through Sturges. Maybe there would be one or more of the Swastika gang with us and we were reckless adventurers, brothers of the hoboes whose monickers were cut or scrawled in the water tank standards, especially that fabulous character who carved so meticulously with a razor-sharp knife: "A–No. 1, '06—GOING NORTH."

And the town was silent and asleep except for the agent with green eyeshade in the passenger depot and the occasional drowsy clatter of his telegraph instrument and the June bugs battering their brains out against the sputtering arc lights. And the whistle would moan again, vibrant and exciting, and the headlight would blossom suddenly up the track, quivering and dancing and shining down the bright rails, and then the sizzling black hulk of the locomotive would be upon us with a quick twinkle of Mars-red stars from the fire box, and then the slowing flutter of brick-colored box cars—Milwaukee, Burlington, Nickel Plate, Pere Marquette, Grand Trunk, Missouri Pacific, Rock Island—comprising a lesson in practical geography which the books, with characteristic stupidity, ignored. We all, and particularly the sons of railroad men, knew the route of virtually every important railroad on the continent.

Perhaps there would be a delay of some minutes while a car or two was cut from the train and sidetracked. Perhaps there would be only shouts and banter between members of the crew and the station agent before the compounder snorted monstrously and took up its southwestern course. Then we would dart from the shadow of the water tank, seize "grab-irons" and swing up the rusty ladders to cling there on the sides of the cars while the romantic and perfumed night roared and bounced past us with an apocalyptic magnificence complete with shooting stars from the engine's smoke-stack. We knew the train was required to stop before crossing the flimsy river bridge, and there we could unload and slide down the embankment to swim or fish or merely to sit listening to the water gurgling around the bridge piers while we talked seriously and interminably of the things which seem profound to a boy of twelve or thirteen and which have passed beyond the understanding of a staid adult. There was a northbound freight at about one o'clock and we could cross the trestle, climb aboard, and ride back to town.

Hopping trains was the ultimate in rebellion against adult authority. Not that Sliver or I had ever been forbidden to climb on freight cars. I was forbidden to go into the water of ponds and oxbow lakes in the region because they were supposedly filled with chills and fever. I was forbidden to go into the river because, as far as my parents knew, I couldn't swim and was certain to get drowned. I was forbidden to play baseball down at the "commons" near the Milwaukee tracks (the only possible place to play baseball in that end of town) because tough boys congregated there. So it never entered their minds that I'd even think of hopping trains.

Even after that horrible day when Floyd Whitehouse, a gentle, blond boy a year younger than I, slipped and fell under the wheels, neither Sliver's parents nor mine thought it necessary to warn us of the dangers connected with such a practice. As a matter of fact such a warning *was* unnecessary. We knew the perils quite well and the perils were what made the adventure worth while. That is a very important point which many adult directors of youngster activity do not seem to understand.

At the turn of the Century and for the first eight years of the Twentieth Century, scarcely anyone thought there was any youth problem. Free schools were provided where children could learn to read, write and do arithmetic. Every decent parent required his offspring to attend some Sunday School where he was supposed to learn to lead a Christian life. Every boy and girl had household tasks to perform. And in their free time they could act like little ladies and gentlemen or suffer the hair brush, hickory switch or harness tug.

When I put my boyhood behind me and left Chillicothe in 1908 there was not a single playground in town. There was no gymnasium. There was no public library. And in that spot of virtually tropic summers there was no swimming pool or any spot where a youngster could enter the water except the really filthy ponds and the equally dirty and dangerous river where drownings occurred every season. There was no Y.M.C.A. or Boy Scouts or any similar organization.

True, in about 1901 someone connected with the Presbyterian Church started a juvenile lodge called New Century Knights and there was a rush for membership to get the red and white celluloid buttons with the mystic letters NCK on them. Because it was very Christian in purpose I was reluctantly permitted to join, although my father suspected there might be some effort to instill us with the doctrine of predestination. His fears were groundless. After we initiates had been taught the secret grip and the secret password we met in the basement of the Presbyterian Church, boys of from about six to perhaps seventeen, and were given vague talks by an uninspired lady about Sir Galahad, together with suggestions about noble but unexciting things New Century Knights could do. Then they had a picnic.

Each boy took his lunch and we went down to Bear Lake on a hay wagon and we picnicked in a swampy spot picked by the minister because of his saintly sympathy for the billions of starving mosquitoes in that region. The minister spread out the NCK on the swampy grass and fed us to his friends. It was a pretty successful picnic for the mosquitoes, but not a complete success because no one actually died. I even could see a little out of one eye the next morning.

On the way home a group of big teen-agers began to bully a fat-faced kid of eight or nine and soon had him crying. So they branded him a baby and declared him unworthy of his pants.

Despite his kicks and screams and attempts to bite, they divested the child of his badge of masculinity and swathed him diaper-fashion in a towel. Then to their loud cries of "who's got a safety pin?" the minister provided one from underneath the lapel of his black coat and they pinned up the little boy who, thoroughly exhausted and sick with humiliation, lay on his face in the hay and sobbed steadily all the way home.

The minister probably had read *Tom Brown's Schooldays* and believed that the way to sturdy Christian manhood lay only through torture. I sat in the rear of the wagon with a boy of my age named Forrest Walters and we didn't go along with the minister. Forrest and I knew quite well that it was only by the grace of God that neither he nor I was victim of the hazing. We sympathized especially with the victim of oppression because of our own vulnerability. We deplored the fate of the small boy in the towel diaper but we did our deploring quietly and unobtrusively so as to attract no attention from the big Galahads. On the way to town Forrest and I decided to default our knighthood. We decided the NCK was boring and stupid when not parlous. I think the term we used was "buggy." Apparently a majority of the other little Galahads came to the same conclusion independently because the New Century Knights began to waste away and died within a few weeks as far as Chillicothe was concerned.

The principal trouble with the NCK was lack of a real program. Doubtless a nice lady dreamed up the idea as something which *ought* to appeal to boys. I do not know whether membership was limited, as in the Ku Klux Klan, to white, Protestant Christians. Very naturally, for that time and region, Negro boys were excluded. None of my Catholic friends belonged, but I do not know whether they actually were barred or whether they merely were forbidden by parents to join an organization connected with a Protestant church. However, there may have been Jewish members. All I knew about Jews at the time was that all the biblical heroes were

Jews and that if we were good Christians we'd go to the new Jerusalem when we died.

My point is that the New Century Knights was a stupid, sentimental club that provided no outlet for the Cro-Magnon instincts of pre-puberty boys. The Swastika gang did.

Naturally, I cannot defend the unseemly career of our gang. I realize quite well that we were only one step from the gangs of wild boys in Harlem and other city slums which make a business of rolling drunks and "mugging" and robbing pedestrians on dark streets. Partly we were kept from taking that step because we all had been drilled from babyhood by decent middle-class parents in respecting other people's property and in actual revulsion for theft, but mostly it was lack of economic pressure. We either had small allowances or, like myself, opportunity to earn all the money that one actually needed to buy baseballs, bats, mitts, slingshot rubbers, twenty-two cartridges or even, if one had sufficient energy and determination, a bicycle.

The nearest I personally came to involvement in a larceny other than the chicken theft was with two older boys not members of our Swastika gang. I was out "junking" with my express wagon, which means I was prowling back alleys, picking up odd bits of discarded iron, bones and rags or, if very lucky, copper, brass, lead or zinc to sell to the junkyard, when I came across this pair on a similar mission.

Although I knew them as pretty tough boys, they were friendly, and one of them said, "Say, there's an old vacant house down the line that some folks just moved out of. Sometimes people leave good junk in a house when they move out. Let's see did they leave the back door open."

So the three of us went down the alley and in the back gate to a weed-grown lot behind a drab, gray saltbox house and the sagging screen door was unlatched and the battered door was unlocked, and we went into the hollow, echoing, sour-smelling kitchen. There was an oblong spot on the brown-painted floor where the kitchen range had been and another damp, blistered spot where the ice box had been and an old calendar hung on the wall with a colored picture of a plump-cheeked girl smirking over an armload of apple blossoms. In one corner were a couple of newspapers and a dirty rag that once had been a striped shirt. That was all.

We went from room to room and there was no salable junk—only fuzzy dirt that had been under the carpets and light rectangles on the walls where pictures had hung. The boys yelled up and down the empty staircase to enjoy the echoing resonance of their voices.

Then the larger boy squatted before the bathroom lavatory, took hold of the trap and shook it.

He spat on the floor. "That's God-damn good lead," he said. "We bust that off and maybe we get four bits for it."

I was horrified. "You can't do that," I said. "That'd be burglary to bust that off."

He looked up at me scornfully. "Hell we can't," he said. "That's an old wore-out pipe anyhow. If they want to rent this house again they got to put in a new one."

He sat on the floor and kicked at the soft lead trap with his heel. The pipe bent easily.

"See," he said, "see how rotten that is and wore-out? If they want to keep old junk like that, why don't they lock their door?"

"Well," I said, "if you're going to bust that off you need a hammer. Wait a minute and I'll get my hammer out of my wagon."

I went downstairs and out the kitchen door and ran away down the alley with my express wagon bumping behind me, very much afraid that some neighbor would see me making my exit and recognize me, and just as much afraid that the big boys would beat me up for deserting them.

If I was seen, however, I was not recognized. But a neighbor did hear the hammering in the vacant house and did see the boys passing the shadeless windows and did telephone Chief of Police Dorney who caught the pair as they were leaving with not only the bathroom trap but with the trap to the kitchen sink, a couple of brass faucets they had managed to wrench loose and one brass gas chandelier.

When I heard of the arrest I lived in terror for several days, expecting Chief Dorney to appear at any hour and take me as an accomplice.

It was logical to suppose the boys might suspect I had snitched on them and to involve me in the theft out of revenge. It was logical to suppose they would resent my deserting them and give my name to the police out of spite. I thought of telling my father the whole story, but I knew he would give me a thrashing for ever entering the vacant house in the first place and for keeping bad company, and that the whipping I'd get for complicity in vandalism would be no worse. So I kept my own counsel and sweat it out until the boys were taken to the state reform school at Boonville, showing, it seemed to me, surprising honor in not implicating me.

Although it was glorious fun, I can't defend the night life that Sliver and I in particular adopted. We simply lost too much sleep for the good of our health. I can remember women telling my mother that I didn't look well and asking if I got enough sleep. But as far as my mother knew, I was sleeping from ten to eleven hours every night and was still very difficult to wake up in the morning.

Sliver died of tuberculosis in Arizona just as he was entering manhood and I have little doubt that lack of sleep at eleven, twelve and thirteen was a contributing factor.

I believe that had Sliver and I and the rest of the gang been sent to a good boys' camp in summers we should have had even more fun and built up our health instead of tearing it down. But if it was a camp such as several I know about, I'm sure we'd have rebelled against restrictions just as we rebelled against the impossible restrictions of our homes.

Boys need very much to exercise their own initiative. Some camp directors seem so utterly unaware that their Cro-Magnon charges—and I mean normal boys from eight to going-on-fourteen—live in a different world. One cannot turn them into little gentlemen and if, through pressure, they act like little gentlemen in front of adults, they make up for it by being little heels when alone with other boys, or with girls for that matter. That is practically a law of boy psychology.

The strictly regimented day of some high-priced boys' camps can be as injurious to character as a reform school. It can turn the weaker boys into sniveling sneaks. It may only spoil the summer of the stronger ones. While I realize quite well the enormous difficulties in keeping a menagerie of young savages under something approaching control, that still only emphasizes the fact that a summer camp director should be an exceptionally well-integrated, understanding, shrewd character who is not disposed to take the easier, safer way.

It makes me sad to see a twelve-year-old cherish a sense of security over adventure.

Great progress has been made in the matter of summer camps, not only for well-to-do children, but for boys and girls whose parents have small or moderate incomes. In Chillicothe the Boy Scouts and Girl Scouts are leaders in this. They are sponsored by civic clubs such as Rotary and the churches.

Overnight camps are held near old Graham's Mill northwest of town on the river. The two weeks' summer camps are held at the Pony Express Council area near St. Joseph's, sixty miles away, which is distant enough to give a feeling of adventure.

One of the youth enterprises most popular in Chillicothe today is "Teen Town," now under leadership of Mrs. Ralph Wheeler, in which teen-age boys and girls learn the principles of democratic government by conducting a municipality of their own. Teen Town is a far cry from the romantic nonsense of the old NCK, because the youngsters run the organization on a basis of reality the way they want it to run. They believe in having fun and they have fun with parties and dances, large and small, and every manner of contest between intramural groups.

Teen Town is a going concern because it gets a minimum of interference from adults. It belongs to the boys and girls and depends on their unhampered initiative and energy for life. Given the framework in which to operate, teen-age youngsters never will run out of momentum, provided they are not made self-conscious by too much adult direction.

Chillicothe no longer has a town baseball team, and in a way I think that is too bad. But it does have something infinitely better in a junior league, which is *not* made up of young society misses and matrons. It is a league of junior baseball teams, each sponsored and outfitted by a business house or organization, and there is more excitement in Chillicothe—adult as well as adolescent—over the outcome of this pennant race than there is over the fortunes of the St. Louis Cardinals or Kansas City Blues. A league of this sort in a town the size of Chillicothe provides an opportunity for almost every boy with any baseball talent or inclination at all.

One bald, thick-middled contemporary of mine shook his head over the league, however. "They don't have the fun we did," he said. "They're too regimented."

Of course that is possible, but I still doubt its accuracy.

I once wrote a book called *Northend Wildcats,* which was a somewhat fictionalized account of our baseball team. In this story there was a happy ending when a businessman provided us with uniforms and equipment, and that was something we used to dream about but which never actually came to pass.

Our baseball team was a very haphazard organization and not more than two-thirds of us even owned baseball gloves. We had three bats, one of which was home-made from a section of broken wagon tongue, and most of us ordinarily played barefoot. Half the time at least, our ball would be a home-made string ball and too light even for boys in their early teens. With no advice from elders, I pitched nine-inning games with a light string ball or even a discarded tennis ball on chilly days without even the formality of warming up and consequently ruined my arm for serious pitching before I was fourteen years old.

A certain amount of supervision and training by competent

adults in this sort of activity is almost necessary and it can be accomplished without regimentation. Young boys and girls are happy to take the advice of elders provided they feel the elder is competent to give advice. But young boys and girls, being instinctual little animals, are uncannily quick in detecting a fraud and pretender.

There was a three-martini athlete who had no difficulty in convincing a credulous adult like myself that he had pitched two no-hit, no-run games for Princeton back in 1915 and 1916 and that several major league teams offered him a million dollars more or less to turn professional. But he didn't get by the boys of twelve or thirteen. When he essayed to show the youngsters how to throw his famous fadeaway, I was satisfied with his excuse of bursitis when it didn't quite come off. But the boys sensed immediately that he never had been a pitcher for anyone by the tentative manner in which he picked up the baseball and by his self-conscious stance. The way he walked also told them that here was a man whose feet never had felt at home in spiked shoes. While they listened to his glib exposition with simulated interest, they mimicked the faker behind his back and laughed at him.

One of the finest examples of this phony's opposite number is my old friend Judge Joseph E. Cook of Denver. For many years Judge Cook has been very actice in combating juvenile deliquency by promotion of junior sports. He has been a sponsor and coach in Denver's pony football league where teams are organized according to weight and age, where the building of health and physical condition is the first objective and where the Saturday games seem to be fully as exciting to the participants and spectators as our old gang fights and the hopping of freight trains in Chillicothe and infinitely better training toward good citizenship.

Judge Cook was too light to make the Varsity at Brown University but he was athletically inclined and was and is a student of sports. He has the knowledge and the poise which command respect of youngsters. And he is exhibit A toward proving that brains and a well-integrated personality are far more important for the perfect supervisor of youth activities than a record as All-American fullback.

As in most American rural communities, the 4-H clubs are of prime importance to Livingston County boys and girls.

Sponsored by the United States department of agriculture, these organizations give their members entertainment, social gatherings and contests, but their strong point is the fact that they give rural youngsters from ten to twenty-one a part in very real enterprises such as raising prize livestock and poultry. The 4-H clubs have local and state exhibitions from which the winners go each year to national conventions.

The idea behind the national organization, which now has more than two million members, is to improve farming and home-making practices as well as to provide recreation and social contacts for farm children.

Of course the 4-H program would have been well-nigh impossible fifty years ago before the motor car demanded all-weather roads. But the roads have been built and the cars and busses take the farm children to 4-H meetings where they learn what science has discovered about agriculture and animal husbandry and, perhaps of even greater importance, where the girls may find out that the American farm wife's skillet has probably killed more good men than all of the bullets of all the nation's enemies from the Revolution on.

A great deal of sentimental drivel has been drooled over the wonders of the cooking in the old-time farm kitchen, but the truth of it is that most of that cooking was frying—and not even in deep fat.

The traditional American farmer of fifty years ago was scrawny-necked, flat-chested and pot-bellied from flatulent indigestion.

In the first World War it was discovered—to the amazement of many medical men—that by and large the supposedly pale-faced and puny city boys were sounder in belly, wind and limb than their ruddy-cheeked country cousins and could stand up better under the rigors of warfare.

As a matter of cultural progress in the last fifty years, it should be noted that American rural cooking has improved immeasurably. And cooking is culture, by the narrowest definition you care to employ.

The 4-H girls learn not only cooking and how to organize a well-balanced meal, but every branch of home economics and whatever other angles of farm life they happen to be interested in. In short, both boys and girls are trained in the ideals of good citizenship while they're having fun.

There are nearly fifty 4-H clubs in Livingston County, Missouri, and the members include a good many boys and girls who live in Chillicothe instead of on farms.

The four-leaf clover insigne with the "H" on each leaf stands for improving the head, hands, heart and health. That may sound a little stuffy to an outsider, but there is nothing stuffy about the 4-H itself. It's one of the greatest assets existing for the future of these United States.

When I think of the obstacles and even parental opposition confronting sports and recreation for young boys in the first decade of the Twentieth Century, it seems almost impossible that such progress could be made in Chillicothe in the course of a generation.

We, in our district, had no place to play baseball, for instance, except a wholly inadequate and rutty lot down by the Milwaukee tracks. I and a good many of my associates were expressly forbidden to go to this place at any time and the fact that we went anyhow put our play outside parental law. My father, and many others, held baseball in low repute because it was a sport of "low characters" who made a practice of breaking the Sabbath.

There was no tennis or badminton or golf or basketball. There was not a gymnasium in town or anything approaching physical education even in high school.

Today Chillicothe has Simpson Park, one of the finest recreation centers I have ever seen in a comparable community. The land was donated to the town by the late Dr. Arthur J. Simpson and the improvements were installed and are maintained by the municipality. These improvements include extensive playground apparatus, picnic areas, a golf course, tennis courts, playing fields and the beautiful, big swimming pool.

In the spring, summer and autumn months Simpson Park is a place of perpetual activity. Organizations from far beyond the borders of Livingston County come to Simpson Park for outings in the rolling woodland, making use of the playgrounds and swimming pool.

Now one may ask the question, would we of the Swastika gang have been any happier or better-adjusted or healthier youngsters if we had had advantage of the facilities of Simpson Park? I say of course we would.

While the facilities of Simpson Park are, after all, material they still represent a tremendous change in mental attitude. Adults now recognize not only the right but the need of recreation for growing boys and girls. Adults pretty largely know now that the way to build character in future citizens depends not so much in laying down blue laws and flogging the violators but in encouraging and assisting children in developing initiative, sportsmanship and health with wholesome projects and games.

The Boy Scouts of Chillicothe, as well as elsewhere, are doing fine work. But I do believe firmly that there are serious defects in the Scout plan which militate against its doing the most good where it is most needed.

Scout uniforms and equipment are expensive. And while part of the enormous sum raised annually by the organization is supposed to go to provide this equipment for needy boys, it rarely is administered wisely. The boys know just which members of a troop are "objects of charity," largely because of the great amount of red tape which must be unwound before a poor boy is issued equipment free. The whole process has a certain amount of humiliation connected with it and I personally have known several instances where boys have committed thefts to gain money for Boy Scout uniforms. Many more don't join because their parents "can't afford it."

It would take no giant intellect to iron out that difficulty.

In Chillicothe few boys from the Levee district—those who need it worst—belong to the Scouts. There is a Negro troop, it is true, but it has only sixteen members.

The founders of the Boy Scouts realized well that a young boy is essentially a savage and they built their organization to appeal to Cro-Magnon gang instincts. I do believe, however, that the general management should consider the wise principle behind establishment of junior and senior high schools. If the Boy Scout executive council has not heard about puberty somebody really should tell them.

It seems to me that Scout age restrictions are quite wrong. A normal boy needs an organization like the Boy Scouts through his Cro-Magnon stage, or from about nine to approximately thirteen and a half. Yet he is not eligible for membership until he's twelve years old.

True, the little Cro-Magnon savage can join the Cub Scouts and that is good except for one rather important item; the Cub packs are directed by a pack "mother." In this period of their development the young bulls have been thoroughly weaned, psychologically as well as physically. It is the one period in their lives when they have no normal need or desire for female companionship, let alone female bossing.

I believe boys should be admitted to the regular scouts at nine years of age. And I believe they should be graduated at fifteen when a boy should have grown out of the Cro-Magnon stage and be developing interests beyond playing cave man and building fires by rubbing sticks. I think there should be another organization for boys of fifteen to eighteen.

A big moose of sixteen or seventeen is, or should be, living in a different anthroplogical era from a child of twelve.

Playing together is not good for either. The big boy is too old and not old enough. But when he reaches eighteen or so, if he is mature and virile and self-assured, and if he likes kids, he can take on the responsibility of camp counsellor and similar posts. Then he is boss and not playmate, and it's good for both.

Our Swastika gang had an enormous capacity for fun, and we had it largely outside parental law. Disregard for parental law naturally can graduate into disregard for all law, and it's not such a long step from burning a cop's bottom with a slingshot to letting him have it with a thirty-eight.

Again my point is that conditions have improved definitely for youngsters in the last forty or fifty years, that the boy of Cro-Magnon age today can have more fun than we had without breaking the liberalized parental laws, without injuring his health and without feeling the adult world is completely alien, hostile and cruel. Machinery has even helped in this, in facilitating transportation to modern swimming pools, playgrounds and woods.

Parents, by and large, have cast aside that late Nineteenth Century standard of stupendous silliness, and the young bulls have gained an important objective.

There is still room for improvement, however.

V

OUT OF THE MUD

THERE CAN BE little doubt that the automobile and its concomitant, the hard-surfaced road, brought about the most drastic change in our manner of life in the last half century. And to say that this change has not been almost completely for the good of the great majority of people, advancing culture according to any possible sane definition of culture, widening horizons, relieving tedium and promoting general happiness, is to close one's eyes completely to conditions in America at the beginning of the Twentieth Century.

Looking back, it seems to me that the automobile came upon us with startling suddenness. Men and women ten years my junior cannot remember the first motor car they ever saw. Many cannot remember their first ride in an automobile. But I, who turned six years old in 1900, have a clear recollection of the day when no one of my acquaintance had ever seen a horseless carriage and when, in fact, the idea in Chillicothe, Missouri, at least, was placed definitely on the fantastic side.

I remember a pleasant spring evening of that year when I, armed with a long switch, went to McNally's pasture with my brother Glen, and birds were singing and hurrying about last minute business before closing up shop for the night, and there was the scent of spring flowers and of newly mowed lawns and of back-houses and barnyards, and a sense of expectancy and of pride, too, at walking with my big brother who was a young man of nineteen. He was to help me perfect my technique of cow-driving (don't ever run a cow or you'll make her give bloody milk) so I could hold down my summer's job of driving two neighbor cows, night and morning, as well as our own Jersey.

That was an exciting prospect, to be practically an adult with a responsible job paying ten cents a week for each neighbor cow. Of course I should get nothing for driving our Jersey. A boy was not paid for working for his own family, and I well understood it was only through the great generosity of my father that I should be allowed to keep my twenty cents a week because he was legally entitled to everything I earned until I was twenty-one years old. But my father was generous and in only five weeks, if I saved every cent, I should have a whole dollar, and there weren't many boys my age who had earned and saved a dollar. But of course the Fourth of July would be coming.

Thinking of the Fourth of July made me think of my brother and my pride in walking with him, because Independence Day was a great day for Glen. And that naturally made me think of the Battleship *Oregon* and the Spanish-American War, which had closed a year before, and the great glory of being an American.

At that moment it was impossible to think of the Battleship *Oregon* without thinking of Glen or to think of Glen without thinking of the Battleship *Oregon,* for he had just finished making a gleaming white model of her, maybe fourteen inches long and complete down to the Union Jack at the stern. Now she rested proudly in the middle of the sitting room mantel and neighbors came from blocks away to admire the handiwork and hear Glen's lecture on the *Oregon*'s great run from Seattle around Cape Horn to take part in the destruction of the Spanish fleet at Santiago. I had a vivid picture (which I believe now was somewhat in error) of the counterpart of that beautiful white ship on the mantelpiece tearing in "with a bone in her teeth," orange flame darting from her smokestacks while her main battery of thirteen-inch guns blasted the fleeing *Cristobal Colon*.

In the lecture there were statistics—ten thousand tons displacement, seventeen knots, secondary battery of eight eight-inch rifles, cost more than three million dollars. People seemed impressed with these figures, though most of them, including my brother, had never seen a craft larger than a Missouri River steamboat. The thing that impressed me, however, was that three million dollars. I had just learned to count to a thousand and that was an arduous job, taking a long time, and my sister Una, also impressed with spending three million dollars for a "gunboat," had explained that I should have to count to a thousand one thousand times in order to count to one million.

Five weeks was a long time, especially when waiting for Christmas or the Fourth of July, and I should have to drive two neighbor cows night and morning for five weeks to earn just one dollar—which was obviously a lot of money. Consider then the immensity of a pile of one thousand silver dollars. And then one thousand piles, each pile containing one thousand silver dollars. The thought would, in the words of that greatest of men, William Jennings Bryan, "stagger the imagination." That would be a million dollars and the Battleship *Oregon* had cost more than *three* million.

The fact that my brother had made this beautifully perfect replica of the Battleship *Oregon* therefore connected him almost directly with the three million dollars, pile after pile of one thousand gleaming silver dollars each, stretching off past the blue horizon, up hill and down, and reaching perhaps clear to Graham's Mill.

I looked up admiringly at my brother, tall and slim in his maroon bicycle jersey that laced at the throat, his face set grimly as befitted one directly connected with the three million dollar Battleship *Oregon*. Though I tried desperately to lengthen my stride to meet his, that was impossible and I found it necessary to trot a few steps, every little bit, to keep from lagging behind. I wished that I dare take his hand but I was afraid he'd think I was a yellow-haired sissy. His own hair was as black and straight as an Indian's and I obviously could never win his respect until I developed enough strength and character to grow a manly head of straight black hair.

Near the pasture gate we met Earl Ridenour, Glen's best friend and hunting companion.

Glen spoke with great dignity. "Howdy, Ridenour."

Earl Ridenour spoke with equal dignity. "Howdy, Davis. How's your copperosity seem to sagiatiate this evenin'?"

Glen chuckled. "Pretty good, I guess. How's yours?"

"Middling."

Then Earl Ridenour noticed me, or rather he noticed the big red and white celluloid button on my jacket lapel. He slipped a forefinger under the button and bent over to examine it more closely. "Well," he said, "I thought it was just a buggy at first, but it's a horseless carriage, isn't it?"

"That's what they call it," said Glen, looking down at the button. I felt very important indeed at attracting the attention of both Earl Ridenour and my brother, and it seemed that the occasion called for a speech.

"It's got an engine in it," I said, "this horseless carriage, and that makes it go right along like a train without any horse."

"I heard," said Earl Ridenour, "that one of them was coming to Chillicothe this summer. Did you hear that?"

"Yes," said Glen, "I heard it but I don't know whether or not it's true."

"Well, I sure enough hope it does. I sure enough would like to see one. Do you think they're practical?"

Glen tightened his lips and frowned. "Well, sir, I just don't know. There's been a lot about 'em in *The Scientific American* and some people seem to think they're the coming thing but it seems to me they've got to get a new power. They've got 'em that run with a gasoline engine but sure as preaching I wouldn't want to go bouncing over a road with a tank full of naphtha right under my bottom. What's to keep it from slopping over? I know about gasoline engines. We had one in the elevator at Wheeling and you've got to have a hole in the lid of the tank so the gasoline will feed into the engine. Plug up that hole and pretty soon you've got a vacuum in the top of the tank and the gasoline won't feed.

Well, that's all right as long as your engine is stationary, but put it in a buggy and the gasoline's bound to slop out of the hole in the lid."

Earl Ridenour nodded gravely. "Wouldn't be very safe for the engineer to be smoking a cigar."

"Not only that," said Glen, "but you've got to have a lamp lit on the engine and that heats a rod red-hot and that explodes the gasoline vapor to make the engine run. Take a stationary gasoline engine and you have your naphtha tank quite a ways from the engine. But if you bolt the whole thing on the bottom of a buggy the tank has got to be pretty close to the engine. No siree, bob harry, I'll take a bicycle."

I could hear the cows bawling impatiently at the pasture gate but it was not up to me to interrupt this scientific discussion.

"How about a little steam engine?" asked Earl Ridenour.

Glen shook his head. "I can't see a steam engine at all, at all. In the first place how big a boiler could you bolt on the bottom of a buggy? Not very big, and it'd have to be a very high-pressure boiler, and you'd have to build a very hot fire—maybe with something like a double row of blow torches."

He tapped my celluloid button with a forefinger. "That's a steamer, that buggy. Look at the size of it. Where you going to carry a water tank to feed into the boiler?"

"Maybe," I suggested, "the engineer carries a canteen. You know, around his shoulder like a soldier."

They ignored me. "You take a little high-pressure boiler like that," said Glen, "and let your water level get too low before you dump in some cold water. Just do that and she'll blow you to bungie holler. Take a contraption like that." Again he tapped my celluloid button. "And you'd have to watch her like a hawk—steam pressure, water level, how your fires are burning, everything. No, I tell you they'll have to get a new power before horseless carriages are practical."

"How about compressed air?" Earl Ridenour asked. "I read about 'em having compressed air locomotives to pull coal cars back and forth in mines. Lot of power in compressed air. Look at the *Vesuvius* in the war with its big compressed air guns that threw torpedoes over into Santiago."

"Where you going to get your compressed air?"

"Shucks, there's plenty of air. All you got to do is compress it."

"Sure, and you've either got to have a steam engine and pump to compress it or put in all day pumping up enough air by hand to run you a couple miles. No, sir, I think they've got to get a new power."

The cows by the pasture gate were bawling in chorus now.

"Well," said Glen, "I expect we'd better go get the cows, bub."

"Well," said Earl Ridenour, "don't take in any wooden nickels. But I sure enough hope that horseless carriage does come to town this summer. I'd like to see one work."

"So would I," Glen admitted. "I'd like to see it, but I don't take any stock in it. A bicycle's good enough for me."

This conversation was brought back to me sharply the other day as I sat in the old Leeper House barbershop listening to the talk of a couple of lads in their late teens. They were sprawling in the aged arm chairs waiting their turn and one of them, who wore a leather jacket, obviously was doing some flying from Chillicothe's municipal airport. Both were long-legged, lean-hipped, ruddy, corn-fed youngsters and their accents were not quite of the South and not quite of the West but tinged with both.

The boy in the maroon jersey asked, "How fast will that kite step?"

"Oh, it's not any comet," leather jacket said. "It'll cruise maybe a hundred and ten."

"Um, I thought it'd step faster than that."

"Of course," leather jacket said, "a hundred and ten ain't so slow either."

"Not on a highway. But when you figure transports like DC Sixes and Connies make better than three hundred—"

"Sure. But they're long-haul ships. The thing is, Bud, you can't compare highway distance with air distance. I can take off, run over to St. Joe and down the river to K.C. and back in a little over two hours. How long it take you to do that in your Chev?"

"Oh, well. You can't compare planes with cars. You got to compare planes with planes. It's like if my Chev would only cruise twenty and the Burlington busses zip past me at sixty, and that's not saying anything about jet planes either. Did you see that in the *Constitution* about the Army guy, Yeager, I think, at Lake Muroc?"

"What'd he do?"

"What did he do? Well, they're not putting out exactly what he *did* do, but I reckon he went clean out of the transonic range and there was an unofficial guess he went twelve hundred miles an hour."

"Um, that's fast."

"You're telling me."

"Too fast for me."

"Well, if you're up there in a dogfight and the other guy's got something that'll step maybe seven hundred, it'd come in handy."

"Um, man. I don't know."

"Regular commercial jobs hauling forty passengers from New York to London in a little over nine hours and averaging three-eighty or so. Well, I can remember when they thought three-eighty was pretty good for a pursuit plane, so how do you know they won't pretty soon have jet transports running a thousand or twelve hundred?"

"Three, four hundred is fast enough for me."

"Well, look, Mac, I was just figuring about this twelve hundred an hour, and the earth turns a thousand an hour, doesn't it?"

Mac wrinkled his forehead. "A thousand an hour?"

"Sure. She's twenty-four thousand miles around the waist and she rolls over once every twenty-four hours."

"Sure."

"Well, I was just thinking—suppose a guy takes off from New York going west a thousand miles an hour and just for instance say it's an even three thousand miles from New York to Frisco.

Well, say he leaves New York at nine o'clock in the morning, he'll get in Frisco at nine o'clock in the morning."

"Huh?"

"Sure. He'll be going just as fast as the earth and keeping even with the sun. He'd pass over Chillicothe when it's nine o'clock here and it'd still be nine o'clock when he got to Frisco."

"Guess that's right. What do you know!"

"Well, here's what I was thinking. Suppose this guy's ship goes twelve hundred like Yeager's. Then he gains two hundred miles on the sun every hour when he's going west, and that would be twelve minutes. If he did that and left New York at nine o'clock he'd gain thirty-six minutes and be in Frisco at twenty-four minutes after eight."

"Oh, well, he couldn't carry that much fuel."

"Maybe not right now. But just say he could. Say he could carry enough fuel for twenty-four thousand miles, and then where're you getting into?"

"Higher mathematics."

"No, you're not. Just plain arithmetic. Say he can fly nonstop around the world and he gains twelve minutes on the sun every hour. Well, I figured it out and he gains damn near five hours—I think it was four hours and three-quarters. All right, Mac, now look. Here it is Wednesday and Yeager starts out at noon to fly around the world at twelve hundred miles per hour. He passes over Frisco at eleven, twenty-four, or thirty-six minutes before he started and keeps a-going around the world, and he gains two hundred miles or twelve minutes on the sun every hour he flies and when he reaches New York again he's gained four hours and three-quarters, so it's only a quarter after seven in the morning and of course still Wednesday."

"Nuts."

"All right. Figure it out for yourself. He goes around the world and lands four hours and three-quarters before he even started."

"Naw, it's tomorrow he lands."

"How can it be tomorrow when he's gaining twelve minutes

every hour he flies? He gets to Frisco thirty-six minutes before he started and is gaining on the sun all the time. I don't pretend I quite see how he does it because if he starts at noon today, he may still be in bed at a quarter after seven and there he is landing after flying around the world and is nearly five hours ahead of everybody else on earth."

"That explains it," said Mac. "He's still in bed and he just dreamed it."

"No," said Bud, "this is serious and kind of confusing. Because he's gained nearly five hours he finishes his trip nearly five hours before he started and that just don't make sense."

A barber called, "Next," and Mac stood up and stripped off his leather flying jacket. "That," he said, "is the first sensible thing you've said. Maybe I'm a stick-in-the-mud, but a hundred and ten is fast enough for me. What's all the hurry anyhow?"

So we still have conservative young men.

Well, my brother Glen and I went and got the three cows and I drove them back in the street while Glen, following on the sidewalk, pretended he wasn't aware of my existence except when no one was in sight. When fairly certain he wasn't being observed, he adopted the role of perfectionist, admonishing, castigating, expressing despairing disgust at my ineptitude.

"You know better than that! Keep 'em together, there! You got to watch that red cow. Watch her, I tell you. Give her a chance and she'll straggle back and eat weeds. Don't run her now. Don't let her run, I say. Now look at you. You've let old Fawny get up into the Doctor's yard. Oh, I knew it, I knew that would happen. Of all the—! Well, you'll just have to come back here with a shovel and clean that up. Get Fawny out of there. And there goes the shorthorn across the street. Keep 'em together. You've just *got* to keep 'em together or you'll have cows spread all over the country. Oh, my, my. You're letting the red cow straggle again. Well, I'm glad Pop isn't seeing this. He wouldn't let you take the job. He'd make you go tell 'em you haven't got enough sense to drive cows. And anybody that hasn't got sense enough to drive three cows hasn't got sense enough to pound sand in a rat hole. You're supposed to start to school next fall. What do you suppose they'll think of a boy in school that don't know enough to drive three milk cows?"

We were just turning into Calhoun Street and to my great relief two young women were walking down the hill. They wore enormous hats, leg-of-mutton shoulders and carried rolled parasols. Glen immediately dissociated himself from the cows and me, put one foot on Botts' stone wall and pretended to tie his shoelace. I giggled to myself about that because I knew he was wearing button shoes, and, perhaps even happier than he in the separation, I kept my cows in close formation, plodded on up the hill and delivered my charges safely to their respective barnyards.

Most barnyards in those days weren't kept very clean, especially in town where the owners felt they just didn't have time to be shoveling manure every few days. After all, they worked ten or twelve hours a day six days a week and it was a rare man who was heedless enough of neighbors' opinion to break the Sabbath by cleaning out his cowshed and barnyard on Sunday.

Generally speaking, milking was not regarded as women's work in that section of Missouri, so the chore usually was performed night and morning by one of the older sons or by the head of the family himself. In my family Glen had the job.

If the milker prided himself on cleanliness he made a perfunctory gesture of washing off the cow's udder, but that wasn't so important because the warm milk was strained anyhow when poured into the pans.

Those who owned cows and whose families were not large enough to consume the entire output usually sold a few quarts to families that had no cow. The price was five cents a quart.

Now bureaucracy and regimentation have extended so far that people are not allowed to keep cows within the town's corporate limits. Even more drastic is the city ordinance which requires all milk to be pasteurized and compels all milk dealers and dairy farmers to keep their barns and equipment spotless.

Of course there may be some compensation for this strict regulation in the fact that more Chillicothe babies live through their first two or three years now and that "cholera infantum" and similar complaints have virtually disappeared. I suppose it all depends on how you look at it.

Well, all summer I drove the cows and I kept inquiring about the arrival of the horseless carriage. The rumor persisted that it was coming but no one seemed to know exactly when. The Fourth of July came, however, and Glen and Earl Ridenour woke up the neighborhood at 4 A.M. with Glen's cannon and shotgun and revolver volleys while I spent at least a month's cow-driving wages for firecrackers. Dog days came and the blackbirds gasped for breath and the leaves withered and the ponds dried up to ellipses of green scum and the big boys quit playing baseball on the commons and lay under the willows listlessly playing mumblety-peg. But the horseless carriage didn't come.

One day we were all drawn in great excitement to the Milwaukee Railroad by a steam calliope screaming out, "Bill Bailey, Won't You Please Come Home," and here came a gorgeous train of flat cars filled with gleaming red threshing machines adorned with fluttering banners. The train stopped and by the time the steam calliope roared out, "Just Because She Made Dem Goo-Goo Eyes," practically the whole town was down to hear a dignified gentleman in frock coat and silk hat make a speech placing J. I. Case on a pedestal right alongside Admiral Dewey and William Jennings Bryan. Then they distributed celluloid buttons, some showing a red threshing machine and some showing an eagle sitting proudly atop the world. I got one of each to pin on my shirtwaist with the horseless carriage, and it was a day to be remembered forever. But the horseless carriage did not come.

That was the year 1900, which most people regarded as the very first year of the glorious new Twentieth Century, which would be marked by phenomenal progress, scientifically, spiritually, and culturally in America. Yes, and it was to be a century of great expansion for the United States for, thanks to the Spanish War,

I am sure that most midwesterners, at least, considered the Old World moribund and the people willing, if they had any sense, to put themselves under the inspired and virile leadership of the United States.

It may have been in the year 1900, and certainly no later than 1902, when I heard a visiting evangelist in fervent prayer urge the Almighty to hasten the day when "Old Glory shall fly over every nation in the world." And the prayer was interrupted by a quick spatter of applause, a sacrilege which shocked my father particularly because he was so violently opposed to the "Republican expansionists."

I suspect this was the period of greatest American chauvinism. The easy victory over Spain had been magnified in the press to ridiculous proportions. The Civil War (we in Missouri did not call it the War Between the States) was thirty-five years past and was being romanticized overpoweringly by sentimental novels and songs such as "Just Break the News to Mother." We were ludicrously proud of ourselves and intolerant of customs that departed from our customs; we had a chip on both shoulders; the majority of people in America, I am sure, were quite willing to teach a lesson to Germany, England, Russia, Japan or any other foreign power which failed to show us proper respect. Gloating over the achievements of Admiral Dewey and Teddy Roosevelt, we, as a people, felt there was something about American air and American soil which made the least American (although no doubt dyspeptic from an unbalanced diet of fried food) the mental and physical superior of anything Europe could produce. Look, for instance, at *Graustark*.

The refrain, "Underneath the starry flag, civilize 'em with a Krag," could well be extended from the Filipino insurrectos to the whole outside world and the whole outside world would profit. And there was nothing incongruous to the American mind in the fact that the "Krag," the Krag-Jörgensen rifle used by the United States Army, was invented by a couple of Norwegians.

It is interesting to look back over a half century and to analyze the source of that remarkable American pride. Why were Americans so decidedly superior to all Europeans? The answer would be American ingenuity and inventiveness under a political system that held all men equal. The average American in 1900 took it for granted that all great inventions of the period came from the fertile brains of Americans. He would have disputed a statement that the steam engine and locomotive and the dynamo and internal combustion engine and sewing machine and automobile, for instance, were not invented by Americans. Asked why the United States, with a polyglot population, happened to be so vastly superior to any European nation, the average American of 1900 would have replied sententiously, "We have drawn the best from all lands and welded them into the greatest unit the world has even seen."

That, of course, was scarcely true. The United States was not a unit. Also, successful individuals have little reason to emigrate. America drew Europeans whose situation under the intense competition of overcrowded cities and restrictions of discriminatory laws was so hopeless that they were willing to abandon the psychic security of familiar scenes, language and friends for a gamble amongst the unknown terrors of a new world; it drew fanatics and adventurers and debtors and criminals and congenital rebels. And the success of America seems to prove that the North American continent was singularly blessed with natural resources, that there isn't as much difference in races or individuals as people used to think, and that, as long as the natural resources hold out, the American form of government is still pretty good.

In any event, the traveling horseless carriage may have reached St. Louis in the year 1900 or Kansas City or even St. Joseph, but it did not come to Chillicothe. And it was not until the summer of 1902 that I saw a horseless carriage which by then was distinguished by the Frenchified term "Automobile" but dubbed by local wits as the "oughta-mow-hay." It was owned by Dr. Arthur J. Simpson and was, if memory serves, a one-lung Oldsmobile runabout. Strictly a fair-weather vehicle, it looked quite like a regular horse-drawn carriage, even to a whip-socket on the right side of the dash. Because it had no top at all, Mrs. Simpson when riding with the doctor would often hold a parasol over her head to protect her complexion. The runabout didn't go very fast and boys with bicycles had no difficulty following the automobile or even pulling alongside in the rough part of the street and shouting, "Hey, Doc, want to race? How about a race, Doc? Bet I can beat you to Elm Street."

I suspect Dr. Simpson may have enjoyed this retinue of bicycles and dogs, but he ignored all challenges as beneath his dignity or because he knew he wouldn't have a chance racing with a sturdy boy who probably could pedal up to twenty-five or thirty miles an hour for a short distance. I never followed Dr. Simpson because I had no bicycle yet, and wasn't big enough to keep up on foot. Besides, I fully expected the automobile to follow my brother's prediction and blow up when gasoline slopped from the tank into the lamp which heated the ignition rod, and I didn't want to be too close when that happened. I know I warned various big boys of that danger until I found out there was actually relatively little chance of that spectacle because there wasn't even any burning lamp in Dr. Simpson's machine. It seemed that some clever inventor had worked out a system whereby the gasoline vapor was exploded in the cylinder by electric spark much the same as the Battleship *Oregon*'s great thirteen-inch guns were fired. While this was disappointing in a way and branded me as a false prophet, it still was interesting.

It is doubtful whether ownership of Chillicothe's first automobile enhanced Dr. Simpson's popularity. I heard a good deal of adult grumbling about his "stink-buggy" frightening horses and causing runaways. I heard talk about passing an ordinance barring the thing from the streets, about threatened law suits, and also snide remarks such as, "I reckon we'll be having an epidemic of 'appendiseedus' now to pay for Doc Simpson's go-devil."

It was not for two or three years, however, that sentiment for and against the automobile really crystallized. By that time there were five or six machines in town, including the high-wheeled yellow skeleton owned by wholesale grocer Adams.

I doubt now whether Missouri automobile owners had an actual club at that time, but at least there was a loosely knit brotherhood that began to plant insidious seeds of progress where it would do the most good. For many years—long before I was born—the streets around the Square had been brick-paved, but despite their being graded periodically, the other streets in town were practically as bad as country roads, in spring, during summer rainy spells and most of the winter except in prolonged cold snaps. And at those times the country roads became impassable. Often farmers could not get to town for a month or more except on horseback, riding their strongest Percherons or Clydesdales, and passing our house smeared with mud to the withers. You could tell whether they were from the river bottom or the uplands by the color of the mud. Then as conditions improved, light wagons would appear, their wheels black or yellow discs of mud, without a spoke visible.

The automobile owners did not allow themselves to become identified with the movement, but talk began to grow that Chillicothe should get in step with the Twentieth Century and pave some of the important streets with good, reliable brick. Jack Newland, editor of the *Constitution,* believed in progress and he wrote editorials to that effect. Ike Hirsch, the Mayor, was in favor of paving at least one east-west street and one north-south street, probably Calhoun and Locust. Ode Grace, Second Ward Councilman and father of my pal Chester, was in favor of paving East Calhoun Street, which was in his jurisdiction. But there was bitter opposition. Some dissenting property-owners on Calhoun Street inquired plaintively why Ode Grace didn't come out to pave Polk Street where he lived if he wanted paving so dern bad, declared that Polk Street would be better than Calhoun anyhow because it led to the bridge over the Milwaukee tracks and to the road to Wheeling and Meadville. Others felt that Webster Street should be paved, if anything was, because it led directly to the Milwaukee depot and was traveled by the express wagons and the Leeper

House omnibus and the hacks. It made the obvious traffic artery. Hadn't the old horse car tracks been on Webster Street?

I remember one evening when the Widow Gordon, who lived a couple of blocks from us down Botts' hill on Calhoun Street, called on us, beseeching my father to fight this unholy scheme. She sat in the golden oak Sears, Roebuck rocker, rocking violently, fanning herself with a palm leaf fan in one hand while she dabbed at tears with a lacy handkerchief in the other. In her mind, it would be sheer piracy, a raid on a poor widow's bank account, to pave Calhoun Street just so the rich who owned those horrible, stinking, noisy horseless carriages could race up and down in all kinds of weather. If they must pave a street, let them pave Webster Street. Otherwise when it was muddy we'd have the noisy Adams Express wagon and the noisy Wells-Fargo Express wagon and the noisy American Express wagon clattering back and forth for every Milwaukee train, right past our houses instead of on Webster Street where they belonged, to say nothing of the percentage of farm wagons that now went in on Polk Street.

Well, my father turned down her plea. He said that he never would stand in the way of progress and if it was ruled that Calhoun Street was preferable to Polk or Webster Street he wouldn't oppose it, and he felt she needn't worry about the express wagons because it would be out of their way to take Calhoun Street and they never would do it except when the mud was deepest on Webster Street.

So it was decided that Calhoun Street, lying as it did between Polk Street on the north and Webster Street on the south, should be paved, and the contract was let to long-jawed J. E. Meek and in a surprisingly short time the street was graded smoothly, cement curbs were put in and neat vitrified bricks laid from east to west for nearly a mile. Likewise, Locust Street was paved south to the vicinity of the Burlington and the Wabash depots, which gave a nice side trip for the automobilists when they wanted a little variety. Mostly, however, they were content with the mile run on Calhoun—out to the west end, turn around and back to Woodward Street at the side of our house, where they'd execute a "Y," kill the engine, get out, crank it, adjust goggles and repeat the performance.

Poor Mrs. Gordon! She would scream imprecations from her front porch at the scorchers for wearing out the pavement which had cost her so dearly. She also was dead right about the traffic to the Milwaukee depot. During muddy periods on Webster Street they got in the habit of traveling Calhoun Street—the express wagons and the drays and the omnibus and the hacks and the private carriages—so when Webster Street was perfectly dry, although perhaps rather rutty, they all kept right on going out of their way to use Calhoun Street, and the clopping hooves and the steel tires of the express wagons and drays made a dreadful noise on the bricks, especially going to and coming from the Southwest Limited after nine o'clock at night when all decent people should be in bed.

Despite the annoyance of increased traffic, however, and despite the consternation of Mrs. Gordon and others at the paving assessment, most residents of Calhoun Street, east and west, were very proud of living on a paved street. I remember my mother and neighbor women talking about how much easier it was to keep the house clean during the hot, dusty days of summer and how much less mud was tracked in at other times.

It was more interesting also in the cool of the evening for the residents to sit on their front porches and watch not only the "stink-buggies," but the regular parade of horse-drawn carriages that started right after supper. It became a regular ritual, this parade back and forth on Calhoun Street and, because it was a parade on a paved street, the carriages must be clean and polished and the harness shiny and the horses groomed and gleaming. And because they felt they were under the scrutiny of the paraders, some of the housewives of Calhoun Street, both east and west, began to be self-conscious about the appearance of their property and to insist on their lawns being kept neat and their shrubbery trimmed. The Hoges got their big house repainted a glistening white and that made the Lees' house look dingy by comparison. So the Lees got their house repainted and that made the Tanners' house look dingy by comparison, and the Tanners were forced to follow suit. On our side of the street, the Sweeneys went for cream and green. We spruced up not only with robin's-egg blue and dark trim, but got rid of our eroded terrace and put in a neat concrete retaining wall and "granitoid" sidewalk.

And so it went over the mile length of Calhoun Street, east and west, and it became a mark of distinction to be a resident of Calhoun Street. Then the people of Polk Street and Webster Street and Jackson Street and Clay Street and of all the north-south streets, who had been chuckling about a handful of automobile fanatics putting one over on the property owners of Calhoun Street, began to wonder whether they had been so lucky after all.

So the inevitable happened and the property-owners of various streets began to form improvement associations and to volunteer themselves as subject to paving assessments and Mr. Meek found business booming and people punning at him about Meek inheriting the earth. By that time there were a dozen or fifteen automobiles in town and the feature of the next Fourth of July celebration at the Livingston County fair grounds was a five mile automobile race on the half-mile horse track, which was won hands down by wholesale grocer Adams in his high-wheeled yellow skeleton in something like fourteen minutes.

It was very nice indeed for the automobilists to have additional paved streets in town, but still it would be even nicer to get out into the country in the spring to see the orchards in bloom or in the fall to see the woodland's autumnal glory. The owner of an automobile was pretty well restricted to town except on the hot days of midsummer when it was no fun to go out on the dusty roads in any vehicle. Always the victim of his neighbor's hooraws, the automobilist was thick-skinned who would brave the odds-on chance of a breakdown on a muddy country road or of leaving his horseless carriage in the barn while he hired a horse and buggy.

Talk began to increase and the *Constitution*'s boiler plate contained an increasing number of articles about how dreadful it was for Missouri farmers to be marooned for such long periods by impassable roads. All-weather roads would be a blessing to farmers who could bring produce in to town when prices were high, augment their own monotonous winter diet with varieties of food shipped in by refrigerator car, buy needed articles of clothing and coal, and get to church Sunday. All-weather roads would be just as great a blessing to the merchants in town. They really were very simple to build by the McAdam process and ridiculously cheap, considering their value.

At this time roads generally followed section lines, up hill and down. What little work was given them came from farmers and others who preferred to spend otherwise profitless spare time working on the roads rather than pay cash for poll taxes.

But now came boom times for surveyors and for salesmen of road-building machinery. The Missouri farmer was about to climb out of the good old mud of the good old days.

In the first decade of the Twentieth Century this provincial, intensely chauvinistic American town of Chillicothe, Missouri, in company with hundreds and even thousands of similar American communities, stood on the brink of physical and psychic upheaval as potent as the industrial revolution. But it is not likely that one per cent of the population realized anything of the sort.

Now the Chamber of Commerce is pleased to call Chillicothe the "Highway City" because of the network of excellent roads converging upon the community. There can be no doubt that the highways have brought prosperity and caused the town to grow from what appeared to be a constant level of approximately seven thousand to something above ten thousand (called thirteen thousand by the Chamber of Commerce).

In the old days it was something of an adventure even in good weather for farmers in the vicinity of Wheeling, ten miles away, or Utica, five miles southwest, to hitch up and drive to Chillicothe on a shopping expedition. Now they run up on a moment's impulse from as far away as Carroll County, thirty miles south.

Because farmers can and do come to town any evening to go to a movie or other entertainment, many Chillicothe stores are staying open on weekday evenings to accommodate them. This makes for extra employment and it also makes for a "live town," although there is a local option law which forbids selling anything stronger than beer by the drink. Long forgotten is the old eight-thirty curfew and the traffic around Chillicothe's Square of a Saturday evening is well-nigh as congested as that in New York's Times Square. The pace is slower and the speech is slower and more concerned with squirrel dogs and coon dogs in Chillicothe, because they almost never discuss squirrel dogs on Times Square. But among the young folk there is the same talk about the same sports and the same movie idols and same dance bands.

Things seem a good deal less formal now than they did around the turn of the century because "going to town" isn't such a festive occasion. Farmers and their wives used to feel they had to spruce up in their Sunday clothes before going shopping. Now, because they go so much oftener, driving to town is like dropping in on a neighbor and unless it is for a special occasion they go as they are. On a Saturday afternoon probably the majority of farmers on the streets are wearing overalls—usually bibless levis.

Fashions in summer headgear have changed a little for Missouri farmers in the last fifty years. The broad-brimmed straw hat, plaything of sportive winds, is giving way to long-visored caps of light denim, something between a baseball player's and a railroad engineer's. People with any precious material under their skulls don't go out with uncovered heads beneath the Missouri summer sun. Before the first real frost, however, summer caps are retired in favor of the traditional broad-brimmed felt, more often than not black in color, which quickly assumes an individual shape to express the owner's personality.

Farm women, especially young farm women, dress better than they did fifty years ago. One reason for this, of course, is the fact that farming in Missouri is a much more profitable undertaking, thanks partly to legislation and partly to the farmers' knowing their business better. Probably a more potent reason is that farm women have examples set them by movie actresses and pictures in the magazines. In any event, Missouri farm women are inclined these days to bulge according to mode rather than as the wind listeth; their heads show effects of the hairdresser's art; their faces wear the conventional trim. Perhaps a majority of them not only have bathrooms in their houses but bathroom scales. In other words, corn-fed damsels are showing some discretion in their corn-feeding.

Of course a good many farm women now wear slacks to town for shopping, and that custom is not universally happy. But in any event the mother hubbard has vanished, and that is definitely a cultural advance.

The internal combustion engine has manumitted the Missouri farmer and consequently brought prosperity to hundreds of communities such as Chillicothe. And I fail to see how anyone can deny that with this prosperity has come wider perspectives, a lessening of provincialism, a sounder sense of fundamental values, better physical and mental health, more pleasant living conditions and, in short, an advancement of culture.

VI

DARKNESS OVER AMERICA

THIS BEING, AMONG other things, the story of the Twentieth Century's birth and the rebirth of America, I should like to tell a story about a Frenchwoman I used to know.

As a child this woman had lived in Paris across the street from a high board fence surrounding the very large store yard of a manufacturing plant, and she and other children used to slip through loose boards into the yard to play. It was a fascinating place inside the fence and strewn, apparently at random, with a collection of huge, weirdly shaped objects, some new and brightly copper-colored and others dull and weathered from lying in the yard a long time. There were openings in some of these objects that led to narrow tunnels through which a child could creep into dark caverns and never be found until he chose to reveal himself. It was a wonderful spot for hide-and-seek.

Usually of an afternoon no adult was in sight although sounds of activity came from the plant in front, but sometimes a singularly uncommunicative old veteran of the Prussian war would be sitting on a bench reading his newspaper, a fat gray tomcat sleeping on his lap, the yellow and green ribbon of the Medaille Militaire on his lapel. He paid the children no heed at their play and when one made bold to ask him the purpose of these huge copper abstractions, he would reply without looking up, "Zut! Some great nonsense which costs much money."

One day Yvonne's eye caught one of the objects in a different perspective. This was a minor object, perhaps five meters in length and half that in height, and it suddenly seemed to change form as a puzzle picture changes form when you look at it steadily. No longer was it a shapeless, meaningless part of the "great nonsense." Now it assumed an unearthly significance, a frightening significance.

"Regardez!" she cried. "C'est une main!"

The other children peered and they saw it also. Glancing about them in terror, the other objects seemed to the children to be changing and taking on life. The sun went under a cloud and the fenced-in yard became an unholy and perilous spot. Without a word they fled. They scrambled through the fence, tearing dresses and stockings in their haste, and Yvonne dashed across the street and breathlessly told her mother what she had seen—the great hand, the woman's head large almost as a house.

Her mother laughed. "My little cabbage," she said, "did you not know? M. Bartholdi is constructing the greatest statue in the world. It will be taken to America and set up in the harbor of New York because America is a place of cultural darkness, although the younger sister of France. This great statue is called 'Liberty Enlightening the World' and she will bear a great torch which will burn forever and the burning torch will represent France dispelling the cultural darkness which now rests so very heavy over benighted America. It is a beautiful gesture of France which will bind the friendship of France and young America closer. You should always remember that you were privileged to touch this wonderful work during its construction."

Well, it was pretty supercilious of this bourgeois French mother, living across the street from the metalworks of Frédéric Bartholdi to speak of cultural darkness covering America. About that time one of the greatest musical events in history occurred in the United States and it was advertised widely enough so that even an ignorant French woman should have known about it, if she read the newspapers. A brass band of one hundred pieces played the "Anvil

Chorus" from *Il Trovatore* accompanied by one hundred red-shirted firemen beating on one hundred anvils with one hundred square-faced hammers.

Of course this musical event took place in Boston, the center of American culture. You couldn't have scraped up more than fifteen per cent of a hundred anvils in all of Chillicothe, Missouri, and the attitude toward art was so apathetic that even after the turn of the century I can't remember the Silver Cornet Band ever having more than one anvil in the Elm Park bandstand when rendering the "Anvil Chorus" or the "Forge in the Forest." Also, the Silver Cornet Band in its interpretation of Tschaikovsky's "1812 Overture" seemed adequate only to those who had *not* been exposed in Kansas City to the higher culture of the Banda Rosa or Arthur Pryor's band which were equipped with church bells, gatling guns and brass cannon. The Chillicothe Silver Cornet Band had only a dinky dinner bell for the great climax when Napoleon flees Moscow and, while there were plenty of firearms available, the band's limited personnel were mighty busy about that time playing their parts, too busy for shooting.

So Barney Higby, the band-leader, got what seemed to be a practical idea about that "1812 Overture." Knowing my brother Glen liked to shoot he asked him and Earl Ridenour to post themselves at the side of the bandstand with their Winchester pump guns, revolvers and blank cartridges and to cut loose with a regular Fourth of July bombardment at the proper moment when he, Barney, waved his handkerchief. The trouble was, however, that Glen was so tone-deaf he couldn't tell "The Star-Spangled Banner" from "Hail to the Chief." And the inevitable happened.

Glen and Earl were on hand, fully accoutered, impatient to display their musical talents, and a little bored with waiting. Earl was busy flirting with a couple of pretty girls eating popcorn on a nearby bench and Glen was caressing his new shotgun and wondering how much longer it would be.

As an encore to the popular and antepenultimate "Cherry Intermezzo," Barney summoned the other cornet, the trombone, the alto, the baritone and the tuba to stand up with him and play the "Sextette" from *Lucia.*

It was a hot, muggy Wednesday night and halfway through the "Sextette," when there was a pause for the first cornet, Barney drew his handkerchief to wipe his perspiring face. That was enough for Glen. He didn't know this was an encore. He assumed it was the finale. "Come on, Ridenour!" he shouted and blasted at the stars with his pump gun. Earl, utterly oblivious to what the band had been doing above him, threw his shotgun to his shoulder and chimed in. The bombardment caught the musicians entirely off guard. The slow, emotional and quasi-barbershop harmony staggered and the trombone blooped out a two-foot glissando. A cornet shrieked a blue note years before its time. The tuba bawled despairingly, like a dying bull at the bottom of a cistern.

Well, a pump-gun magazine holds only five shells and Glen and Earl were shooting fast. When the last of the shots echoed back from the brick buildings around the Square, Barney Higby, his eyes bulging in desperation, tried to rescue the "Sextette" from utter ruin. Keeping time with his elbows and with lips drawn back tensely, Barney broke into the next measure and the five other horns valiantly but raggedly attempted to fall into line, but by that time Earl Ridenour had out his revolvers—a nickel-plated thirty-two in his left hand and a long-barreled forty-five in his right—bang-BOOM! bang-BOOM! bang-BOOM! And Glen was stuffing blank shotgun shells into his pump gun as fast as he could go and was whamming away again before Earl had exhausted his revolvers.

Fatty Putnam, the bass drummer, was the first bandsman to regain his poise. He stuck his sturdy right foot into the stirrup attached to the dinner bell and began to ring while the sad sweet notes of the "Sextette" dribbled away like the last few drops in a syrup pitcher. The trombonist caught on and, still standing in "Sextette" formation, blared out the measure of the "Marseilles" and Barney Higby, grasping despairingly at any straw, raised his silver cornet and burst into the climax of the "1812 Overture." Perhaps half of the band didn't know it well enough to play without the music, but they played anyhow, improvising or merely adding to the general cacophony while Fatty Putnam rang the bell steadily with his foot, clanged his cymbals and beat his drum and Glen and Earl Ridenour feverishly kept up their work with their four revolvers and two pump guns, one reloading while the other fired.

Never in the history of the Chillicothe Silver Cornet Band had there been such an ovation. The crowd massed around the bandstand cheering and applauding and the perspiring Barney Higby took bow after bow, presented his "Sextette" soloists, the entire band and finally called the powder-stained Glen and Earl to the stand with their pistol belts and shotguns where they received greater acclamation than all the rest of the musicians put together.

It would be difficult for one who did not live in that period and environment to appreciate how profoundly important were those weekly band concerts.

Music then in that region consisted of (1) the band; (2) church hymns; (3) amateur pianists, violinists, mandolin-players playing "In the Good Old Summertime" or, if they were really hot, such semi-classical items as the "Poet and Peasant Overture." Of the approximately fifteen thousand residents of Livingston County, I don't suppose more than a few hundred had ever been exposed to great symphonic music. People were starved for music—any kind of music, and the Wednesday evening band concert was a wonderful institution in more ways than one.

All the stores around the Square stayed open and farmers flocked in from every point of the compass to do their shopping and hear the band. Every hitching rack for blocks held its farm plug. Some families ate an early supper at home and augmented it later with bananas, popcorn and peanuts or ice cream sodas at Farrington's candy store or Swetland's or Clark's drug stores. Some flaunted their prosperity by eating at the Leeper House or the Henrietta Hotel or Hager's Bakery. Others brought picnic suppers in wicker baskets and ate on the grass of Elm Park where they could watch the marvel of the white ball dancing at the crest of the fountain's plume.

While the band was playing, mature and elderly folk sat on the park benches or on the grass and most children dashed here and there playing tag. Big boys and girls from the country as well as the sophisticated big town juniors walked around the Square, looking into windows and at each other, eating popcorn, peanuts and crackerjack and—after that confection had been invented—ice cream cones. Those boys and girls who were unattached usually traveled in twos or threes or more and, as I recall, the girls regularly traveled counter-clockwise and the boys clockwise. I can't be certain of all this because I left Chillicothe several years before I had much interest in that sort of thing, and it seems curiously similar to the custom in a Mexican plaza on Charanga night.

Of course the band concerts were held only in the summer and for a total of perhaps sixteen weeks. For the other thirty-six weeks of the year nine-tenths of the population, including my family, heard nothing approximating music except church hymns. If there were any organized amateur instrumental groups in town I never heard of them. I suspect I would have heard of them if they existed because music to me was much like catnip to an alley tom.

There were attempts to organize choral groups on several occasions, particularly by Ches Jordan, but our heterogeneous population did not seem to respond as would a like number of Germans, Poles, Welsh or Italians.

Ches Jordan was a big sandy-haired plasterer who went to Chicago to study harmony and composition and who wrote and published numerous hymns. He wasn't taken too seriously by the townfolk because it wasn't reasonable to suppose a mere plasterer could be much of a musician. Now I have little doubt that Ches knew more about music than anyone else in the community, and that the public's attitude hurt him and put him on the defensive. This could have been the cause of his developing a rather blunt, pompous manner which didn't help him much.

I got to know Ches pretty well after my brother Glen married his sister, and I also was prejudiced against him, not because there usually was plaster in his hair, but because his playing on the cabinet organ in the Jordan farmhouse lacked that thrilling four-four time sprightliness of the Silver Cornet Band or Mrs. Hornback playing her Kranich & Bach grand piano, and because I considered him a very inferior wing-shot despite his claims to the contrary. I went quail hunting with Ches once the fall after Glen's marriage. That was when I was eleven and owned no firearms except an old thirty-eight revolver and a Stevens' Favorite twenty-two with which I hoped to pick up a rabbit while Ches was filling his bag with quail. There were lots of quail around there and we hadn't gone far when a tremendous flock roared up in front of us. Ches emptied his pump gun at them and didn't get a feather.

There's a juvenile tendency, which a great many adults never discard, to assume that if a person is a dub in any line he'll be a dub in *all* lines; so, knowing full well the havoc Glen would have wreaked on that flock of quail in the same circumstances, I drew my own conclusions as to the height of Ches Jordan's musical talents.

Ches Jordan tried very hard to develop choral singing, especially in the First Christian Church, but one Eastertide his apathetic group sang Handel's *Messiah* while Ches, grim-faced and sweating, tried so desperately to keep his wandering sopranos and altos and tenors and basses out from under one another's feet that his burly plasterer's shoulders split the seams of his neat black cutaway, and in the magnificent Easter Hallelujah Chorus, instead of well-disciplined, overwhelming, concentric volleys, everyone seemed to be firing confused hallelujahs at will, louder and louder, and Ches Jordan's white carnation flew from its buttonhole as he waved his muscular arms in a vain attempt to rally his disintegrating forces as Sheridan, dashing in from Winchester, rallied his army at the Battle of Cedar Creek with his alleged cry, "Turn, boys, turn—we're going back!" But the First Christian Church's Choral Society was as wild-eyed and out of control as a remuda of spooked range horses in a thunderstorm, and Ches couldn't use the flat of his saber on them or swing his poncho because he had no saber or poncho but only an utterly impotent yellow lead pencil which he was using as a baton. Finally and at last, vocal cords became exhausted and Ches was able to rescue his group from that wild vortex of hallelujahs and restore some sort of order. That is, he did with all except one mild, bald-headed little bachelor named Adamantine Wainwright who clerked in the New York Store, and who had been so thoroughly swept away and who had so thoroughly lost his place that he continued to croak out a weak but fervent tenor hallelujah once in a while from then on out.

Ches Jordan fought that one through valiantly and with honor and at the end he delivered the package safely, even though a few minutes late and a little bit tattered.

Despite the dearth of music in Chillicothe, Missouri, at the beginning of the Twentieth Century, there still were a good many musical instruments around town—cabinet organs, violins, and especially pianos. The trouble was that so few learned to play them.

Clever salesmanship in the last years of the Nineteenth Century had convinced people it was a mark of distinction to have a piano in the home. And the quarter-sawed oak upright was a piece of furniture designed to hold framed tinted photographs, especially of deceased members of the family, bric-a-brac, sea shells, artificial flowers and relics of disasters such as the Johnstown flood.

Female children were forced to take lessons and the lessons apparently were formulated for the express purpose of putting music in the same pigeonhole with dish washing and furniture dusting. All over town of a Saturday morning one could hear the labored finger exercises of miserable little girls who were forced by threats, bribes, pleadings and actual application of the hairbrush to suffer on and on until they developed sufficient strength of character to beat maternal ambition into surrender. Mothers usually decided that "life is too short" about the time the little victim had mastered Ethelbert Nevin's "Narcissus," and given a couple of surly Sunday afternoon performances before a polite but unimpressed gathering of relatives and neighbors.

The teaching of music, like the teaching of almost everything else in those days, was based on the unspeakably stupid premise that "It's your duty. You've got to do it because I say so." Everyone knew the ancient English adage, "You can lead a horse to water but you can't make him drink," and believed it without giving a child credit for as much judgment as a horse. A music teacher with the intelligence, training, inclination and ability to open the door so a child might behold the exciting and glorious heaven beyond was almost unique. The witless worshippers of method, backed up by the sting of parental hair brushes, did too much psychic damage to be very funny even in retrospect. There are middle-aged women now who can't stand the ticking of a clock because it takes them back to the accursed metronome clacking away between the tinted photograph of dead Uncle Willie and the tinted photograph of dead Grandma Ross.

Well, one of my points is that it took inspired mechanics to rescue the latent culture of America from the little, uninspired, mechanical brains and souls of the pedants who learn mechanically and make a career of teaching mechanically. And these, incidentally, are not all dead yet.

I believe, however, that in 1900 it was more common among midwestern Americans to regard music as something which talented individuals just picked up. I believe the majority would no more have thought of paying for a child's music lessons than they would have thought of hiring someone to teach a boy to ride horseback or swing an axe.

My own passion for music, coupled with the fact that I could approximate tunes on a two-bit harmonica, made my own unmusical family suspect my no more than average talent might be something special and that I should be encouraged. I was in favor of that. I wanted to learn a horn so I could play in the Silver Cornet Band when I got big enough. My father, however, had a different idea. He may have realized there is no way on earth to housebreak a brass instrument, and he also was a man of very strong convictions.

"The fiddle," he said, "is the king of all musical instruments. If you want to learn to play something, it'll be the fiddle or nothing."

So he got out the Sears, Roebuck catalogue and he ordered a violin. The price was four dollars including a leatherette carrying case, a bow, four strings and a piece of rosin.

It was a beautiful violin, rich red in color, and through one of the sound holes you could see printing which read ANTONIO STRADIVARI (*model*) CREMONA.

My father said, "That's a very good make fiddle. Stradivari is a standard of fiddles like John Deere for plows or Studebaker for wagons. Now I want you to take as good care of that Stradivari fiddle as you would of a Seth Thomas clock or a Simmons saw and learn to play it good like your Uncle Sam."

Well, I didn't know how to put the strings on so my father sent me up Woodward Street to see Earl Blue, the mail carrier, who played a violin, and Earl Blue showed me how to string and tune the four dollar Stradivarius and he asked me who was going to teach me. I confessed I was going to learn by myself.

Earl Blue looked a little troubled and said he would go down with me and talk to my father. So I put the precious fiddle in its leatherette carrying case and I began to feel a little sorry for Earl Blue because I knew he was a shy and sensitive man, and I told him I didn't think there was much use of his going.

"We'll see," he said, and went down with me and confronted my father. "Mr. Davis," he said, "I'm glad you've got a violin for the boy and I—well, I wanted to say I'd be glad to give him lessons of evenings very reasonable."

My father shook his head. "No, Blue," he said, "that's kind of you, but music's something you've either got or haven't got. I couldn't carry a tune in a milk bucket myself, but some of my wife's family are musical. Don't know whether the boy inherited any of it yet for sure, but if he's got any music in him he can learn to play the fiddle without lessons. If he hasn't got it in him he wouldn't be a good fiddler even if I spent a hundred dollars on lessons."

Earl Blue tried to argue in his shy way, but my father wouldn't listen. "No," he said, "my wife's brother Sam Brion is a fine fiddler and plays at dances all around western Nebraska and never had a lesson in his life. Music lessons just make hack fiddlers out of people who haven't got any music in them and I'd rather have the boy give it up altogether than become a hack fiddler."

He looked very straight at Earl Blue and Earl Blue got the point and blushed and said, "Well, if you ever change your mind I'll be glad to give him some lessons reasonable." And my father said he would remember if he ever changed his mind, but I think Earl Blue knew as well as I by that time there was little chance of my father changing his mind.

I went to sawing at the four dollar Stradivarius and maybe I had an instinct for it because right away I developed that practice of amateur fiddlers of missing a note by a fraction and rectifying the near miss by hook-sliding into base. That gives a sort of wailing, Hawaiian steel guitar effect which the artist believes he can cover up with a constant tremolo.

Of course I could not read music and the things I knew were church hymns, choruses of a few popular songs and old ballads and snatches of Barney Higby's band music. The rhythm of Fatty Putnam's bass drum was deeply ingrained, but my sliding, wailing tremolo made everything sound sadly hymnlike no matter how diligently I stamped my foot in four-four time. It was so very melancholy that it even touched my tone-deaf father and he finally conceded that I had no music in me and ordered me to put the confounded fiddle away.

So I finally sold the four dollar Stradivarius to a tramp printer. He agreed to give me a dollar but when I refused to accept lead nickels which he molded nightly from stolen type metal, I got only fifty cents in good silver. I don't believe he ever learned to play very well either, because I doubt whether the government lets people take fiddles with them to Leavenworth.

As to machinery and music, Thomas A. Edison invented his "Mary-had-a-little-lamb" phonograph in 1877, but did not perfect the permanent wax cylinder record for commercial distribution until 1895, the year after my birth.

In our neighborhood was a little widow named Mrs. Parrish who lived in a drab, tree-sheltered, fence-enclosed cottage with her traveling-man son and one day, in 1901 or 1902, this son brought home from the city a "talking machine" and a big box full of cylindrical records.

On hot afternoons and evenings, Mrs. Parrish would play the phonograph and it was wonderful. Boys and girls would gather in droves and at first we draped ourselves along her front fence until she came to the door and called, "Please, children, don't break down my fence. If you want to hear the music, come inside the yard and sit quietly on the grass."

When we went in the gate and sat down under the trees she turned the phonograph horn to the open window so the music came out almost as loud as a band. Unfortunately, however, it frequently happened that some smart aleck would be in the group and he'd start horseplay. Then Mrs. Parrish would come to the door and say, "All right, children, if you can't behave yourselves you can go." Then she'd shut off the phonograph. That would make me very mad and I'd want to lick the miscreant, but it seemed almost a law of nature that the kids who deserved correction most were so big and tough they could handle me with one hand. I took this matter up with the Almighty in one of my nightly conferences, suggesting that if He wished me to continue as His agent in these affairs of music it was practically necessary for my fists to be endowed with at least a touch of supernatural power. But apparently my requisition was tabled because the bill of goods never was delivered.

Mrs. Parrish had twenty-five or thirty records—brass band marches, a humorous number called "Cohen at the Telephone," which didn't seem particularly funny after you had heard it ten or twelve times because you knew exactly what was coming next, but mostly they were vocal pieces. There were two or three comic songs such as "Please Go 'Way and Let Me Sleep," "Coon, Coon,

Coon, I Wish My Color Would Fade," and "All Coons Look Alike to Me," but the greater part of the records were sad songs such as "Sweet Alice, Ben Bolt," "Just Before the Battle, Mother," "A Bird in a Gilded Cage," "Hearts and Flowers," "Just as the Sun Went Down" and "Hello, Central, Give me Heaven."

It was years before anyone else in the neighborhood got a phonograph.

I wish I could report now that Chillicothe is another Lindsborg, Kansas—which is a community maybe one-fourth as large as Chillicothe in the Smoky Hill River valley and for the last forty years or so one of the musical centers of America, especially notable for its annual Easter festival of music. Chillicothe is no Lindsborg, but Chillicothe is making progress.

There is, for instance, the Chillicothe Civic Music Association, which brings artists of national and international reputation to the city for at least three concerts a year. Annual membership dues are five dollars a year for adults and two dollars and a half for students. As these dues are used to put on concerts, the steadily growing membership means more music each year.

For the majority of Americans classical music is "long-hair" and they don't like it. The reason they don't like it is that they don't understand it. And the reason they do not understand it is not because they are congenitally crude and stupid but because until recent years there has been no general opportunity for young Americans to become acquainted with the classics.

I think it could almost be said there is a reverse Gresham's law in music whereby good music drives out bad—almost, but not quite.

Forty to fifty years ago we had "music" in the Chillicothe grade schools. That is, we had class singing, and we were supposed to learn to read a simple score. I personally learned nothing because these sessions were insufferably boring and I, together with most of the other boys, assumed an antagonistic attitude.

This was a difficult situation for any teacher—attempting to sell music to a class without even the aid of a piano—but I do believe a smart approach could have broken down the oafish notion that singing is sissy.

They're showing wisdom in the Chillicothe schools now. Primarily they're trying to teach appreciation of serious music and they know it must be understood to be appreciated. In the junior high school, under direction of Miss Dorothy Snowday, they're teaching something of the history and theory and development of music from the ancient chants through Purcell and Handel to the great masters and up to the modern. Special phonographs records are used to acquaint the youngsters with various musical forms, ballad to concerto and symphony, and with the characteristics of different composers.

Such a course surely should hold the interest of any pupil with the faintest liking for music and if later he still prefers the white-hot rhythms of Hambone Schultz and his Dirty Dozen to Beethoven it's because he's built that way and no fault of Beethoven or the Chillicothe schools, but perhaps something in favor of Hambone Schultz.

As I understand it, the wish of the Chillicothe schools is first to expose the boys and girls to music, to explain its principles and its drama and glory. Then if the boys and girls want to go ahead and study further and to play, that door is open for them too.

Remembering my day when the sole equipment was teacher's tuning fork and the most ambitious enterprise was a ragged rendition of "Three Blind Mice," the situation now seems nothing short of remarkable.

It must be kept in mind that Chillicothe is a very much down-to-earth, practical, midwestern community without cultural tradition and that Raymond E. Houston, superintendent of schools, is a husky, energetic extrovert who demands and gets efficiency and who believes that the first purpose of a public high school is to direct each student according to his aptitudes toward the special training which will enable him to become a successful citizen and good American. George P. Newbolt, high school principal, also gives the impression of a business executive, primarily interested in production records, reduction of overhead expense and up-curves on sales graphs. And it is quite true that the schools now do emphasize efficiency, discipline and the teaching of sciences and the "practical" arts more than is common in some eastern schools.

Nevertheless the Chillicothe High School does have something of a record in music under the leadership of Earle Dillinger and has won numerous regional awards for bands, orchestras, choral and instrumental groups.

There is a school band averaging sixty pieces. There is an orchestra of thirty pieces, a mixed chorus of ninety-three voices, a girls' glee club of ninety-seven, a boys' glee club of thirty-four, besides a mixed quartet and boys' quartet, an instrumental sextette, a double quartet, a woodwind quartet, another clarinet quartet and string groups.

The school owns a magnificent library of music and supplies instruments, so no boy or girl can complain of lack of opportunity to develop musical talents. Naturally all candidates do not have the native ability or willingness to work necessary to make the first team, but the fact that so many do find a place with some musical group speaks highly for Mr. Dillinger's method of teaching.

These student musicians are not kept cloistered in the music rooms and school auditorium. They play at all athletic contests, at public celebrations and festivals, and any organization which feels the need of some music, from a fanfare of trumpets to chamber music, usually can get it by calling Mr. Dillinger. The square-jawed Mr. Dillinger is very generous that way.

One boy member of the band said wryly, "If you ask me he's too *dern* generous with our time." But two girls made it plain that this boy's was very much a minority report, that they found playing outside "very thrilling."

As with any athletic director, graduation is the saddest time of the year for Mr. Dillinger. "Just when they're getting really good," he says mournfully, "graduation comes and takes away your stars."

There is some satisfaction to Mr. Dillinger, however, in the thought that perhaps a majority of his lost stars will continue with their music after graduation. Of course not many will take up music as a career, but they do know the difference between Mozart and Sibelius and they are able to listen to a great symphony or operatic program with intelligent appreciation instead of boredom. And many of these members of choral or instrumental groups will keep up their old high school association and will be getting together twenty years from now to sing or play. There must be a great deal of pleasure to Mr. Dillinger in that thought.

Speaking of the nation at large, it seems obvious to me that the radio has stimulated and spread culture by bringing great music to the average American home. Of course it is true that most radio programs are vulgar and even degrading. But there are many fine programs available for those who have learned to love serious music. An even greater boon to the advancement of culture has been the electric phonograph and high fidelity reproduction although it must be admitted that today many more jazz records are circulated than classical. Twenty-five years ago, however, the manufacturers weren't even producing symphonic albums.

Fifty years ago you could count the American symphony orchestras off on the fingers of one hand. Today you'd need an abacus.

Thousands of fine musicians fled Europe to the United States during the regimes of Hitler and Mussolini and they formed the backbones of many community orchestras during the Depression in the days of WPA "boondoggling."

These orchestras gave concerts, usually "pops" which were made up of selections from light opera and other semi-classical popular numbers, but oozing in some Mozart and vigorous Wagner. Before they knew it, hinterland audiences were listening to Debussy and Brahms and Bach and feeling proud of themselves because they were enjoying "long hair" stuff.

I am not going to claim that Chillicothe or St. Joseph or even Kansas City are world centers of musical culture. I don't have to do that. All I have to say is that things are better now than they were in 1900, and I believe I have shown that is so.

VII

THE BUDDING OF ART

To THE BEST of my knowledge fine art did not exist in Chillicothe, Missouri, or in comparable Midwestern towns at the beginning of the Twentieth Century. Although I suspect oil paintings of a sort did hang on the walls of such mansions as the Mansurs' and the Miners' and in the better saloons, I am sure I never saw one until I went to Kansas City in 1908.

Pictures on the walls of most middle-class homes consisted of (1) big, bad crayon portraits of slightly cross-eyed bewhiskered men with pink cheeks, and slightly cross-eyed women with pink cheeks (those copiers of photographs seemed to have difficulty in making eyes match); (2) steel engravings of sentimental subjects, historical events and portraits of great men and Frances Willard; (3) bright lithographs, usually of German origin, of lakes and trees and hills and a waterfall and a small boat with or without sail and a humble cottage and lowing kine and birds in the sky; (4) religious chromos.

Frequently the pictures were enhanced by a spray of gilded cattails or peacock feathers arching from behind the frames.

It's my opinion that the series of world's fairs—Philadelphia, 1876; Chicago, 1893; Buffalo, 1901; St. Louis, 1904—threw the first gleam of artistic light into the cultural darkness of America.

My father and mother spent ten days or so at the Chicago fair and were fascinated by the Hall of Art—or whatever they called it. Whether the selections in the main were good, bad or indifferent, this art exhibition made them conscious at least of a wonderful world which had lain unknown beyond their horizon. The fact that my mother preferred the German section above all others is not particularly significant. The German's traditional obsession with detail would have its appeal to a meticulous housewife. I believe they both absorbed a good deal and I doubt whether it was entirely accidental that the two big French etchings my father purchased in Chicago turned out to be sound art.

Assuredly there must have been some fine American art available in 1893 and I take it for granted it was represented at the World's Columbian Exposition. But there also was some atrocious American art available and I suspect that was even better represented.

I used to know a Japanese diplomatist named Yakashira Suma who was Japanese minister to Spain in 1941. Dr. Suma came from a wealthy old family and he had with him a stack of portfolios containing photographs of his inherited art collection. Most of this extensive collection was Oriental, of course—ceramics as well as pictorial—and wonderful. There were portfolios of French, Italian, Spanish, English and German art, each example very good and representative and picked with the skill of a shrewd connoisseur.

Suma brought out his American portfolio last. "This," he said solemnly, "is our representative collection of American art purchased by my Grandfather Suma at the Chicago World's Fair in 1893."

The portfolio contained perhaps twenty photographic prints, about eleven by fourteen, of paintings which must have been perpetrated by the dunce class of the Hudson River school. They were primitive but not primitives. They were pompous, pretentious, sentimental and awful.

"Surely," I said, "your Grandpa Suma could have found better things than these."

"Oh, no doubt," he said, "but you see my grandfather was not looking for the best. He wished our collection to be representative of American art as the others are representative."

"So," I said, "he picked the worst damn daubs he could find. I don't believe, Dr. Suma, that your grandfather liked the United States very well."

He smiled and licked his lips. This, incidentally, was a few months before Pearl Harbor. "Oh," he said, "on the contrary. He often told me as a child of his visit to America with a great deal of pleasure. He enjoyed himself in America very much, and especially the Chicago World's Fair. You see, my Grandfather Suma had a great sense of humor."

I suppose it's too much to hope that the precision bombing of Tokyo and Yokohama was precise enough to destroy Suma's American collection and to spare the rest.

Well, "art" was taught in the Chillicothe public schools in the early nineteen hundreds. We had drawing books and we were supposed to copy spheres, cubes, triangles and the like. Then, as the class advanced, we would draw apples and cats.

You drew an apple by grasping the pencil backwards, resting your thumb knuckle firmly on the paper and, with this makeshift compass established, you turned the paper on the thumb pivot until the pencil drew a circle. Then, free hand, you drew a reclining parenthesis near the top of the circle with a sprig emerging from the reclining parenthesis. That was an apple. You made a cat with a big circle for the body and a smaller circle joining it at the top for the head and then drew in the ears and tail.

Being clumsy at this procedure, I thought it silly, and I didn't believe the apples looked like apples or the cats like cats. So I tried to be smart and draw free-hand apples that looked like apples and free-hand cats that looked like cats, and Miss Vivian Evans, the third grade teacher, was appalled at my rebellious stupidity. She assigned Jennie Carr, a bright little girl in pigtails, to move over with me and give me special instructions. Jennie tried and I tried, but it was no use. My thumb would slip and the pencil would cant and the running line, trying desperately to dock against adverse winds and tide, always floundered in on the wrong side of the river. I tried a slideslip and I tried a hook-slide, but Jennie would stand for neither and finally she held up her hand and spoke with exasperation, "Miss Evans, it's just hopeless. I just don't think he can learn *anything.*"

Because I admired Jennie Carr, that hurt me. I realized there was justification, but I felt she could have been more gentle in her pronouncement.

In any event, Jennie's judgment was accepted and thereafter I was ignored during "art" period, being awarded an automatic "F," and I put in the art class period drawing pictures of locomotives complete with all current appurtenances.

Later we had a teacher named Miss Belle Lowe, a slim, grave country girl who had ideas of her own. Somehow, some way, she either got permission or took it on her own initiative to have us get cheap water color outfits that came with a limp camel's-hair brush in the box. We were to try to paint still lifes—flowers and such.

My first one was a purple iris and, though I tried very hard, I simply could not achieve the impeccable neatness that my pal Chester, sitting next to me, got so easily. I was ashamed of my picture but I knew there was no way to avoid turning it in.

Miss Lowe came down our aisle, picking up the damp papers, occasionally commenting, "That's nice, Jennie," "Good, Fred."

Then she picked up mine and my face began to burn as she paused to look at it. There was a shuffling sound as the boys and girls turned in their seats waiting for the fun. Miss Lowe didn't know my "art" work, but they did.

"Clyde," she said gravely, "I think that's wonderful."

The class roared. She looked around her but didn't change expression as she held up my painting. "This," she said, "is very close to real art, I think. He's captured the spirit of the iris."

I slumped lower in my seat, burning with humiliation while the laughter beat upon me in waves. The class was delighted. They hadn't expected such delightful humor from the solemn Miss Lowe. I hated her venomously. I hated everyone. I even hated my pal next to me. At least Chester, I thought, in view of our close comradeship, might have restrained his laughter.

When she had gone Chester whispered from the side of his mouth, "Spirit of the iris."

I punched him on the thigh as hard as I could in the cramped quarters. He punched my thigh. I punched him back. He punched me back and Miss Lowe turned and called sharply, "Boys!"

We stopped punching but I whispered, "All right for you."

Realizing that things were getting on dangerous ground, we didn't follow it up after school, even though Chester's mouth did quirk when other boys called me "Iris."

I didn't even try at the next painting session, but Miss Lowe shook her head and said, "That's fine. I thought yesterday it might be an accident, but this has got something too."

There was a little laughter at that, but not much, and I began to wonder if perhaps, if just *possibly* Miss Lowe was not making fun of me after all.

I know that Chester was puzzled as well as amused, as also, no doubt, was the whole class. I was astonished but very, very pleased when it developed that Belle Lowe was actually finding merit in my lack of manual skill, in my clumsy inability to delineate detail as well as the average youngster. Maybe everyone else thought Belle Lowe was silly, but I didn't. All along I had felt there must be a deep-lying vein of superiority of some obscure sort in me, and Belle Lowe was the first to sense the latent riches which lay so well-hidden beneath the surface.

Working, apparently, on the premise that if a person is bad enough to be outstanding, he had potentials for outstanding goodness, Miss Lowe declared before the class that I might become a real artist if I wanted to badly enough and worked at it and went away to art school when old enough.

Well, I didn't know that I wanted to be an artist. From what I had read of them they were a bunch of dern sissies, except, of course, Ernest Thompson Seton. While taking it for granted that when I grew older great purple talents would blossom from me like springtime violets in the graveyard, I had not decided whether I wanted to be Ty Cobb, Thomas A. Edison, Napoleon Bonaparte or Admiral Dewey; and there always was a specter lurking in the background in the thought that perhaps God would take heed of my father's suggestions and demand that I become a preacher. Being an artist assuredly was preferable to the life of a preacher and I was grateful to Belle Lowe for the suggestion. Maybe, in a pinch, God could be talked into a compromise.

There was another point to be considered, also. Not a soul except myself ever had remarked any similarity between me and Ty Cobb on the baseball field. As yet I had invented nothing of importance except the caterpillar tractor and a few minor things like that. And if I were to become a great military chief I'd have to develop a more dominating personality. Of course a sword at my side and a lot of gold braid would be of considerable assistance, as would a prancing charger, but attempts to be a Napoleon so far had brought me nothing better than a black eye and cut lip.

Yes, I was grateful to Belle Lowe for the suggestion. I was more than grateful because it was my first recognition of any sort. Maybe Miss Vivian Evans and all the rest were right and Miss Belle Lowe was silly in giving me public praise, but I loved her for giving it. I loved her dearly. Perhaps I should become a great artist just to prove to the world that Miss Lowe's faith in me was not misplaced. At least I wanted to do *something* for her to show my appreciation. But I didn't know how. All I ever did was virtually a betrayal.

That came about through my inordinate love for marbles, and it happened I know while my principal income still came from selling *The Saturday Evening Post,* which averaged twenty cents a week.

Through some obscure tradition the boys of Chillicothe called agate marbles "flints," and a flint was the best possible taw or shooter. At that time I was far from being an expert player, and my only flint was a miserable gray thing with a flaw, two bad nicks and numerous "moons." It was too small for a proper taw.

One spring day at the height of the marble season a new consignment of marbles appeared in the window of Clark's Pharmacy and among them was a small box in which a dozen agates rested like precious jewels on a bed of cotton. Among these was one perfect gem of rich wine color, ringed with cream, just the exact size, I thought, for my hand. Brazenly, I entered the store and asked to see it, and it was more beautiful even than it had seemed from the outside. Utterly flawless, it glowed in my hand, just the proper weight, just the proper size.

"How much is it?" I asked.

"Twenty cents," said the clerk.

Most flints of adequate beauty and utility cost a nickel. Mine, for which I had traded a handful of ordinary marbles, had probably cost three cents. Some exceptional flints cost a dime and Harry Hayden claimed he had paid fifteen cents for his tawny beauty which had won him such a weight in marbles. I never had even heard of a marble selling for twenty cents, but I admitted in my heart that this one was worth it. It was the most gorgeously voluptuous thing I had ever seen in my life.

"Well," I said to the clerk, "I'll have to think it over."

The clerk carefully replaced the magnificent agate marble on its cotton. "Don't think too long," he advised, "or somebody else will get it."

I didn't really need to think it over at all. That was merely a phrase I had picked up from adults and employed because I had only two pennies in my pocket. But I should get my *Saturday Evening Posts* Thursday evening and, if I were lucky, could sell them by Saturday noon. That would give me the necessary twenty cents, but, alas, I should be compelled to give a nickel to Sunday School.

However, with Saturday afternoon free, I could scurry around back alleys with my express wagon, picking up bits of iron and bone and rags and no doubt find enough before Rupp's junkyard closed for the night to get three cents or perhaps even a nickel.

Each day then until Saturday I checked Clark's window and the lovely thing was still there. But Saturday afternoon after the magazines were sold my plans to raise three cents were thwarted by my mother's antipathy to plantain weeds in the lawn. There was a little argument, but not much. I stayed home and cut plantain weeds from the lawn.

Monday morning I ran to Clark's before school, seething with a plan which might work in the remote event that the marble had not been sold. Steeling myself for the disappointment, I glanced at the window and the flint was still there. For a moment I stood grinning at it and that beautiful marble grinned back at me.

Then I went into the store and Mr. Clark himself was up front. I approached him and said, "Howdy, Mr. Clark-you-know-that-twenty-cent-flint-you've-got-in-the-window?"

"That what?"

So I explained and more slowly, and he went to the window and took out the box and lifted the treasure from among its poor relations.

"Mean this one?"

"Yes, sir, Mr. Clark. Well, what I wanted to say, Mr. Clark, I want to buy that flint but I haven't got enough money right now and I'm afraid somebody else will come and buy it and I wanted to say I'd be much obliged if you'd let me pay you seventeen cents right now and you take the flint out of the window so it's not for sale any more and I'll have the other three cents next Thursday and come in and pay it and take the flint."

He looked down at me solemnly and then at the agate in his hand.

"You kind of like that marble?"

"Yes, sir."

"And you've got just seventeen cents?"

"Yes, sir. But I'll have more Thursday."

Mr. Clark smiled. "Well, son, here's a curious coincidence that's going to interest you. The price of this marble was just reduced this morning from twenty cents to seventeen cents. You give me the seventeen cents and the marble is yours right now without waiting till Thursday."

So I ran to school, but was forced to stop every block or so to take out the marble and gaze at it and fondle it and rub it against my cheek—a smoothness beyond description—and to tell myself this was the most wonderful thing that ever happened to me because it was the most beautiful flint in town and maybe in the world.

I plopped panting into my seat perhaps half a minute late but Miss Lowe did not look up from her desk. Fred Black, however, ostentatiously took out his watch and held it up at me, hoping, I thought, that Miss Lowe would look up as he did it and catch the implication.

I did not like Fred Black. He was everything I was not. He was bright and alert and knew all the answers. When a question was asked Fred Black's hand was always the first to be raised. When another pupil was wrong Fred Black always shook his head violently, groaned audibly and thrust his clean, white hand upward. He was always neat and wore a stiff, white linen collar. His hair was always combed. He assuredly was the boy most likely to succeed.

"All right," I said to myself, "you've got a watch and ain't that fine. It keeps you from ever being late to school. But I've got something I like better than any derned old watch."

I touched Chester Grace at my side and whispered, "Lookit."

Drawing the flint from my pocket, I held it in shooting position against my thumb knuckle with my forefinger and it glowed there richer than any ruby that ever adorned a potentate's crown.

"Gosh!" Chester whispered and reached for it. But as I glanced up to see that Miss Belle Lowe was still occupied, the wondrous smoothness of my treasure betrayed me. It slipped from my grasp, banging like the crack of doom on the floor and it rolled, horribly, horribly across the worn old boards. Miss Lowe looked up. Everyone looked up. And Fred Black, with his neat hair and linen collar and watch in his pocket, leaned over quickly and then held up his hand.

"Here it is, Miss Lowe," he cried triumphantly.

"Bring it up, please," said Miss Lowe.

So Fred Black walked to the desk and gracefully handed my lovely flint to Miss Lowe and Miss Lowe, without even looking at it to admire its beauty, placed it like any ordinary old marble in the corner of her desk and Fred Black with his fool watch that nobody else would want ticking in his pocket and probably a clean handkerchief in another pocket—yes, and probably perfume on the handkerchief—went back to his seat and shot his cuffs and smoothed his hair and sat down with the air of one who has simply done his duty, but well.

Oh, I knew the rule that any marble dropped on the floor was confiscated. My treasure of treasures was gone before I had ever plumped from a taw-line with it, before I had ever banged it with back-spin against another taw with the shout, "vent-takin's and everetts!"

I sat in my seat and died. But I managed somehow to keep from bursting into tears.

Miss Lowe opened her book and started calling the roll.

"Fred Black."

"Present," said Fred, in a pleased, clear voice.

Then there was a knock on the door and Miss Lowe went to answer it. She stood with the door half-open, her back to the room. Instantly I was out of my seat and on my hands and knees, moving swiftly but softly forward. I knew I could do it because the sympathies of almost everyone would be with me, and I *did* do it. I reached around the side of Miss Lowe's desk, found my flint, grabbed it and crawled quickly back to my own seat long before Belle Lowe left the door.

Because I was living in approximately the Cro-Magnon period of my development, I was inclined to see signs, portents and omens in the most innocent things about me. So it was very easy for me to attribute mystic properties to my beautiful new agate marble. I made a chamois bag to carry her in and I named her "Vashti the Magic Taw." When I took Vashti out of her bag, blew on her and rubbed her between my palms, the other kid was half-licked before we ever lagged for taws. She won me a fortune in marbles.

Miss Lowe never mentioned the marble, but of course she knew what happened. Of course she knew who dropped it and recovered it. She couldn't possibly have known what Vashti meant to me and it would have been logical for her to think of me as a despicable little sneak.

Perhaps it was only my imagination, perhaps it was because a guilty conscience did something to my work, but after my deliverance of Vashti a cool, intangible barrier seemed to rise between Miss Belle Lowe and me. From then on she gave my "art work" no more than perfunctory praise when she noticed it at all. Perhaps it was my imagination, but the contempt I sensed in her eyes shriveled my soul and the lonesome little flame of ambition fluttered and retreated into a weak smoulder.

For many years now Miss Lowe has been at Iowa State College teaching not art but science. She says the only reason she ever taught "art" in Chillicothe was that "I had had two or three courses in college, whereas the other teachers had none."

Miss Lowe has attained national distinction in the field of foods and nutrition and is the author of a widely used textbook. She not only has no recollection of the marble incident, but doesn't remember me.

What became of Fred Black, the boy most likely to succeed? The last I heard about him he was a major general in the United States Army. He *would* be.

Well, I have said fine art did not exist in Chillicothe in those days, but that was only objectively true. It did exist—in a latent form. It was exemplified by a yearning for mystic, unknown things and it found a partial outlet in religion, needlework and maybe political oratory. Despite her denials that she ever was an artist, I believe Miss Lowe did carry the innate sense of proportion and fitness of things and rightness which could be called the spirit of art.

The law of averages being what it is, and people being what they are, so fundamentally alike whether they live and die in Tiflis or Topeka, who can say what mute inglorious Miltons or unsung

Cézannes lived out their lives in Chillicothe, Missouri, trying to assuage the misinterpreted pangs of unrealized ambition with calomel and quinine?

After all, there is bound to be talent in any region. We only know of this talent when the proprietors are lucky enough or strong enough to emerge from the wilderness and find opportunity to develop their talents. In 1905 there were, for instance, such small boys as Thomas Hart Benton, Grant Wood and John Steuart Curry in Missouri, Iowa and Kansas who escaped their native environments to paint their native environments.

It is interesting to compare the careers of these three great American artists, all born where a map of the United States folds in the middle, within eight years of each other. All found it necessary not only to go far from home for necessary training, but felt they had to go to Europe for it.

Benton, the eldest of the three, was born in Neosho, Missouri, in 1889, the son of a lawyer and politician and named for his great-uncle, Thomas Hart "Old Bullion" Benton, Missouri's first United States Senator.

Neosho was only about half the size of Chillicothe, but I gather the school systems were about the same in all of those Missouri towns and that young Thomas proved adept at drawing apples and cats by thumb-circle. At any event he could draw at an early age. But he didn't like going to school in Neosho and quit altogether in 1906 to take a job with some surveyors around the lead mines of Joplin. Shortly afterward he talked the Joplin *American* into giving him a job as cartoonist, using, I suppose, the chalk-plate process which was usually employed in those days by small-city papers. Inasmuch as I never saw a chalk-plate cartoon that wasn't pretty crude, I suspect young Benton's also looked as if they had been carved out of wood with a jackknife.

The father, Colonel Maecenus Benton, still wasn't convinced that his son shouldn't have an education and that fall the boy was sent to the Western Military Academy in Alton, Illinois. But by that time young Benton was certain he wanted to be an artist. In a couple of months he left the military school and went to Chicago to enroll in the Chicago Art Institute where within a year he convinced an instructor that his talent was exceptional and moreover persuaded the instructor to persuade Colonel Benton to send him to Paris to study.

In Paris from 1908 to 1911 Benton "wallowed in every ism that came along." He went to Italy and studied the Italian masters. Then back in New York and without his father's support, he worked as a stevedore and anything else that came his way until the first World War when he entered the Navy, as an architectural draftsman. It was there, apparently, that what he had learned in Paris and Chicago crystallized. There, he says, he was forced to observe for the first time the objective character of things and to "forget my esthetic drivelings."

With the Navy Benton discovered himself and also discovered America. Following the war Benton had a successful exhibition in New York and became an instructor at the Art Students' League. Then he married and moved back to Missouri to achieve a world reputation.

Grant Wood, born in 1892 near Anamosa, Jones County, Iowa, had no father to back him in going where he could gain the art education he desired. The boy was only nine when his father died and, because he and his mother and younger sister were unable to operate the farm, it was foreclosed and they moved to the city of Cedar Rapids. Grant worked his way through high school and helped support mother and sister, partly as a metalworker and partly as night watchman in the morgue.

I don't know whether Iowa schools taught drawing then by the thumb-circle cat and apple method, but at least young Grant Wood was skilled with his hands. He loved to draw and he wanted to paint.

At twenty-three, however, he was still a handyman around Cedar Rapids, trying to save enough money some way to go to art school. For a dollar down and a dollar a month, he bought a lot in a brush-grown thicket on the edge of town and built there a ten-by-sixteen shack. He and his mother and sister lived in this shack for two years while he continued with his odd jobs, trapped rabbits and cooked them on an outdoor fireplace and drew pictures on every scrap of paper he could pick up. He actually learned to draw by drawing—and without instruction.

The first World War interrupted this program when Wood went into the Army. There he picked up extra money (and hoarded it) by drawing portraits of other soldiers.

These pencil portraits attracted attention, enough attention so that after the war the Cedar Rapids schools gave him a job as art teacher, which he kept seven years.

Grant Wood may not have known too much about art at that time. But he could draw, and in the minds of the school board anyone who could draw was a fine artist. Grant Wood knew well that he was no fine artist then, but he also knew this job would give him opportunity to get the training and study he needed to *become* a fine artist.

Each summer for those seven years he went to Europe, studying like Benton in Paris and Italy. He learned principles and he learned technique. But it was in Munich, under the fascination of early German masters, that he discovered himself and discovered Iowa. It was in Munich that he found the rhythm of Iowa and his own individual interpretation.

He went back to Iowa, became artist in residence at the University of Iowa, a fine artist and without doubt a great artist.

John Steuart Curry was born in 1897 on a farm near the hamlet of Dunavant in the hills of Jefferson County in eastern Kansas.

Curiously enough, Margaret Steuart Curry, a Kansas farm wife, mother of four children besides John Steuart, working from dawn until late at night, still had the time and inclination to make a collection of reproductions of the old masters. And when John, the eldest child, showed the common love of children for drawing, she encouraged him to make copies of reproductions. From that he graduated to sketching farm animals.

Young Curry attended high school briefly in nearby Winchester, a village of less than five hundred, but there was nothing in the curriculum to interest him. He quit and got a job as section hand on the Kansas City, Northwestern Railroad, saved his money and went to Kansas City to attend classes of the Kansas City Art Institute.

At this time I also was attending night classes of the Kansas City Art Institute, and it quite definitely was fast enough company for one of my meager talents. Destiny, an acute sense of discrimination or something prodded young Curry out of Kansas City quickly, however. He went to Chicago where he financed a couple of years at the Art Institute by working as a restaurant busboy and janitor. Following that, he discovered he could make a living illustrating western story magazines, but that still didn't give him what he wanted.

Borrowing a thousand dollars, he, like Benton and Wood, went to Paris. And in Paris he discovered Kansas—and John Steuart Curry.

His "Baptism in Kansas," which he painted from memory, was purchased by Gertrude Vanderbilt Whitney, who also subsidized him for two years at fifty dollars a week. That was all he needed to gain international fame.

These three—and particularly Wood and Curry—might be called the bootstrap boys. They lifted themselves by the bootstraps. They succeeded in the face of impossible obstacles.

Well, no reasonable claim can be made that Missouri, Iowa and Kansas are ideal spots today for the talented youngster. But I am positive that it no longer is necessary for a boy or girl to go to Europe to find himself or herself in art.

Even the Kansas City Art Institute has grown tremendously and, although Thomas Hart Benton quit as director after saying some harsh words, Mr. Benton is not known for his tolerance of things which fail to measure up to his conception of perfection.

Chillicothe is still no art center. As yet there isn't even much amateur painting going on in the region. But there is one marked improvement, and that is in the quality of pictures hanging on the walls of middle-class homes.

There has been practically a revolution in the buying of fine art in the last thirty-five years.

Up until the first World War the big New York galleries counted on only a few sales a year, but those sales would be to wealthy collectors at fabulous prices. There was little market for anything short of an old master.

Now the income tax has made it necessary for the wealthy collectors to dip into principal if they want to pay a fortune for a famous painting, and not many are willing to dip into principal.

The typical purchaser of art today on New York's Fifty-Seventh Street is from the Midwest or Southwest and is a college graduate in his early thirties. He has had a course in art appreciation and knows more than the affluent merchant prince collectors did in 1900. He isn't buying names. He is buying art and buying it on his own surprisingly good judgment. His top price is about three hundred dollars.

This is a wonderful development from the viewpoint of the comparatively unknown contemporary artist. It's all right, also, from the viewpoint of the galleries whose volume of sales has multiplied to the extent that a number of them have opened branch galleries in midwestern cities.

I don't want to give the impression that any large proportion of midwesterners are buying good original oils and water colors because that would not be true at all. But there is a definite trend in that direction and many more are buying and hanging gelatine process reproductions of good art, modern as well as the old masters.

What is the cause of this growth in good taste? I think there are several answers.

For one thing, mechanical developments which not only have made those gelatine prints possible but have advanced photo-engraving and color printing to a point where popular magazines and book publishers can put marvelous reproductions of real art into general circulation together with dissertations by competent critics, explaining just *why* these pictures are real art. After all, a corn-fed Missourian can tell an emerald from a piece of beer bottle glass once he has the opportunity to hold them together. And, given his choice, he'll almost invariably select the emerald.

Just as important is the fact that educators in these days are better educated. They have been exposed to culture, more or less, in college. Many midwestern colleges and universities are finding places on their faculties for competent "artists in residence." And a good many educators realize what I think Miss Belle Lowe sensed, that drawing is not art although it may be *part* of art.

Teaching art in the Chillicothe High School now is Mrs. Honor Israel, a gentle and soft-spoken woman, who concentrates on teaching appreciation of art rather than on drawing. Her equipment is largely a number of books of art prints together with portfolios of color reproductions of art from Giotto through the Impressionists to the non-objective moderns, which she has clipped from various magazines over the years. She uses as a text *Art Appreciation for Junior and Senior High Schools* by Collins and Riley, and she lectures on the history and development and meaning of art over the centuries.

Mrs. Israel's students also draw and paint, of course, and while I saw little evidence of great budding talent, the work at least was quite uninhibited. The principle of the thumb-circle cat has been thrown overboard completely, even in the elementary grades.

The point is that these boys and girls are learning *appreciation* of art, and that is true advancement of culture by any definition you can dig up. The point is that Susie comes home from school and talks. And Susie says, "Mother, *when* are you going to get rid of that *dreadful* old picture over the mantel? It just makes me cringe every time I go into the living room." And Mother says, "Why, darling, I always kind of liked that picture of the sunset on the millpond." And Susie says, "Oh, *Mother*—it's pure corn.

The composition is terrible for one thing, and mostly it's crude and, well, really, Mother, it's in poor *taste* and I feel just humiliated when the Spencers come in because I know they're looking at that *thing* and smiling to themselves and pitying us because we don't know any better. Mother, the Spencers have got two Van Goghs and a Cézanne." And Mother says, "Well, darling, you know we couldn't afford to buy any real fine oil paintings." And Susie says, "But they're *not* originals, Mother. The originals would cost thousands and thousands of dollars, but there are beautiful reproductions that look just like originals." And, of course, the net result is that finally some new pictures are bought. Probably they're not Van Goghs, but perhaps a reproduction of something by Edward Hopper or Charles Burchfield and a good still life by some capable but not very renowned artist. And after the family has lived with the new pictures for a while they begin to see what Susie was talking about and appreciation of art has budded in the home.

After all, in my humble opinion, the principal thing Benton and Wood and Curry learned in Europe was not painting technique (although they probably learned some of that too) but a deep understanding of what art is about. That, in their day and in mine, they could not do at home or in Kansas City or Cedar Rapids or very much in Chicago or even New York.

As far as the creation of art is concerned, the WPA art projects during the early days of Franklin Roosevelt's presidency really started things. Those projects put paint brushes into the hands of thousands of young men and women who produced acre upon acre of very bad canvases, but an astonishing number of very good pictures, and to almost all of the participants came an inevitable joy of creation and an awakening to the beauties which lie so unexpectedly in line and light and shadow wherever you may be—under the old L in the Bowery or in the Great Salt Desert, above the clouds in an airplane or in a Livingston County barnyard.

I have heard that Franklin Roosevelt didn't know a hawk from a handsaw as far as art is concerned and that in approving these "boondoggling" projects he remarked merely that he supposed an artist had to eat the same as anyone else. Yet I suspect those boondoggling art projects in the long run could prove to be of as great importance in the cultural development of America as any other governmental act in the first half of the Twentieth Century.

VIII

SEX

FROM LONG YEARS as a newspaper reporter over the country I have found three prime sources of information about what is going on in a neighborhood. One of these is a friendly barber, another a female gossip and the last is an alert boy around fourteen. Of the three the boy will prove the most reticent (almost as reticent as a shrewd bartender), but his information, if he gives it, is usually more reliable. I have found this particularly true in gang shootings and other underworld activities.

Now I was a boy of fourteen when I left Chillicothe, Missouri, and for several years I had been convinced that there was such a thing as sex in the world, not only among livestock but among humans on the lower level of our highly stratified society.

This may come as a surprise to some of the yearners for the good old decent days who feel that interest in sex is a comparatively recent development foisted upon a reluctant America by Hollywood and pornographic publications.

In our family and in the families of most of my boy associates, Protestant and Catholic, obscure euphemisms were employed whenever absolutely necessary to refer to the body and its functions. Even these euphemisms were strictly avoided in mixed company and often a small boy was required to suffer long periods in silence in the interest of "decency."

My mother and sister were especially circumspect, and I can

remember my mother speaking with some embarrassment of a "gentleman cow" frightening a picnic party. I don't know why she did not feel it necessary to call a rooster a gentleman chicken.

On several pre-school occasions when I repeated some vigorous-sounding word I had picked up, my mother washed out my mouth with laundry soap so I never, never, would say such a thing again. But she didn't explain why except that the word was "nasty." Sex, of course, was the ultimate in nasty subjects, and it remained so with me until I was nearly grown and able to reason things out for myself.

My first initiation in the difference between male and female came when I was five or six under the tutelage of a big girl of fourteen or so.

One day this big girl lured me and several other small boys and girls into her woodshed and shut the door. Then she explained, with crude pedantry, the male and female function.

At the close of the lecture I fled, feeling sick and defiled, but I presently convinced myself that I didn't believe a word of it, any more than I had believed her when she told me there was no Santa Claus.

The girl, however, had used a number of terms from the vulgar language and they stuck in my memory and I began to understand expressions and allusions made by big boys which heretofore had been obscure. But I still didn't believe and neither did my associates —most of them. We had been told that the doctor brought babies in his black bag. We had seen the doctor visit homes with his black bag on the advent of a new infant, which certainly was corroborative evidence. Whose testimony should you believe—your parents or dirty kids?

It was plain enough where the dirty kids got their curious idea. We learned that at the stud horse barn. The dirty kids were crediting human beings, who (with the exception of Negroes and Highview people) were made in the image of God, with the same practices and reproductive system as the lower animals. That thought would be revolting if it weren't so ridiculous.

But one day a boy friend came to our house looking grim and a little pale. He asked me to go home with him. He wanted to show me something. His mother was away and had his younger brother and sister with her and the boy, doing a little prowling, had found a small key in his mother's bureau which fitted a locked section of the bookcase.

I went home with him and the boy opened the bookcase and took out a large book. In it were colored plates showing the development of the human foetus in the womb.

That was a shocking thing. The dirty kids had been telling the truth after all. Our parents had lied. Women were no different essentially from mares and cows. Men were no different from stallions and bulls. It was a horrid situation, a sickening situation, and what could God have been thinking of?

Well, we couldn't hold it against our parents too much. They were merely trying to shield us from a very nasty, disgusting fact which they could not help.

Then this boy's ingenious mind came up with a comforting idea. Probably low people, dirty white trash and such, engaged in sexual actions no different from animals. But clean, respectable men and women never would be guilty of such a thing.

We had learned about artificial insemination at the studhorse barn. We knew how the seed of a fine stallion or bull could be prepared and sent miles away to impregnate a mare or cow by remote control. And that, of course, was the procedure employed by genteel people. When a man and wife decided they wanted a new baby the prospective father prepared a syringe which he presented to the prospective mother or left where she could find it. She took care of the intimate details in retirement.

This was a very convincing theory and we took comfort from it. After all, decent people could be ladies and gentleman even though God had seemed to put embarrassing obstacles in their path.

I relayed this information and theory to my other associates, the "tough" Catholic boys, and most of them also were convinced but comforted. Science and culture had joined to lift respectable people above the status of animals.

Some learned psychiatrists have said lack of frankness in the home causes small boys to scrawl dirty words on fences and walls, and there would seem to be some logic in the hypothesis. The practice could be part of the revolt of the young bulls against conventions and restrictions imposed by adults. But, on the other hand, I should think it could also be a result of young minds being encouraged to dwell and enlarge on subjects which overexcite immature imaginations.

The trouble with the large generalities upon which many psychiatrists love to oraculate is that the experience of psychiatrists is mostly with abnormal persons.

Assuredly I believe in treating sex with frankness. But I do not believe in making a children's circus of it. I feel that the attitude of the average American parent toward sex at the turn of the Century was not only incredibly silly but dangerous. But I must say also that I am convinced there are grave dangers in going too far in the other direction.

It was a sad thing, of course, that I and my pre-puberty associates of the Swastika gang considered sex the ultimate of nastiness. But that conception at least had the advantage of keeping our minds pretty well away from the subject. The physical drive was still latent. There were too many intensely interesting things in the world to allow our minds to run wild on subjects we considered filthy. And there were the usual number of town imbeciles who were pointed out as horrible examples of "playing with yourself," which at least kept that practice secret and down to a minimum.

I know that I personally never had an inclination to write four-letter words where they would assault the eyes of grownups, or any other place for that matter. To the best of my knowledge, neither did any of my friends, and I was a member of a fighting gang which, I suspect, could have held its own fairly well with any juvenile court's steady customers.

We knew boys whose talk and practices caused us to catalogue them as "dirty kids" and we ostracized them. It seemed to be a general rule that these boys were under par physically, poor baseball players and quitters in a fight. We held them in contempt.

As to the calls of nature, the rest of us relieved ourselves casually and naturally in the woods in front of others. We swam and ran around naked together at the river or lakes with utterly no self-consciousness unless some giggling neurotic showed up and by word or gesture earned for himself a gob of mud in the face and the order, "All right, Filthy McNasty, cut that out or get the hell away from here."

By the time we were twelve or so we knew vaguely that there was such a thing as homosexuality because word spread from railroad men to avoid tramps. A couple of years previously a hobo pervert had murdered a boy up the Milwaukee line, so we avoided hobo jungles unless there were four or five of us in a group. But I never actually knew of but one case of homosexuality among boys in Chillicothe. That concerned a simpering behemoth of a boy about fourteen who was the son of whistle-stop entertainers wintering in Chillicothe to take advantage of our reputedly excellent schools.

At the river this fellow attempted an assault upon a small, chubby boy and, through intervention of another younger boy, was beaten to a whimpering pulp. Of course parents could not be told of the incident but other boys were, and for the remainder of his stay in town the pervert was the Number One pariah. We considered him a loathsome monster.

There are now many so-called experts on human behavior who would say we were boorishly intolerant of a poor lad who was only following a "normal instinct for erotic play." I believe it was the *perversion* of a normal instinct. I believe this boy had been forced to lead an unnatural life and had seen and heard too many things which inflamed his immature imagination to the bursting point when there was no possible normal outlet for his precocious drive.

I first made the acquaintance of commercialized vice at eleven when I became a carrier boy for the *Constitution*. One of my customers was a lady well past the first bloom of youth, who lived in a secluded cottage near the Wabash tracks, and she was the most prominent of the town's whores. Somewhat before that, I had vague knowledge of a drab frame building known variously as a disorderly house and house of ill fame, and I knew evil things were taking place inside because I often heard raucous female laughter blending with loud, rough male voices as I passed. I had assumed the reason they called this tawdry hotel a disorderly house was because they drank beer in there. In my youthful training no thing was more evil than drinking beer.

As a matter of fact, my first impression of evil about my notorious customer's place was a vine-grown pavilion or arbor attached to the rear of her yellow-painted cottage where I imagined she and her callers sat and grew maudlin over bottled beer. But the big boys soon made it plain to me that other things were supposed to be going on in my customer's home.

The fact that I delivered the paper there made me a person of some importance to big boys of fourteen to sixteen, and presently I found myself capitalizing on my position. They assumed that I rang the doorbell every Saturday morning to collect the weekly dime for the paper and I saw no reason to disillusion them. Actually, however, my customer subscribed by the year, paying at the office or perhaps mailing in a check; so virtually my only contact with this lady of awful fascination was throwing the rolled-up newspaper to her front porch. In three years I probably caught sight of her no more than a couple of dozen times. Only once did she speak to me. Then she was out by her front gate when I came along, a small, thin woman with brick-colored hair who revealed a bright golden tooth when she smiled. She was wearing a homely gingham house dress.

"Good evening," she spoke pleasantly.

"Howdy, Miss," I said, grateful for the picket gate between us as I passed the paper over to her beringed hand. That was protection against her seizing me and dragging me into her evil yellow house where she might force me to drink a bottle of beer or heaven knew what.

"Look," the big boys would ask, "how does she act when you see her?"

I had to appear nonchalant and a little bored by their questions or come out and admit she was a yearly subscriber and sacrifice a great part of my distinction.

"How does she *act*?" I would say with a touch of annoyance. "How would you expect she'd act? No different than anybody else."

"She ever ask you to come in the house?"

"Gee, I don't remember. How can I remember every little thing about all my subscribers? Gosh, I've got over a hundred subscribers, and in the winter when I'm collecting, some of 'em take me into the hall while they're getting their chink and some of 'em don't."

"Well, look, Davis, when she gets her money does she lift her dress and take it out of her stocking? Does she show her garters?"

"Gosh, no. You make me tired, asking things like that. If you want to know so much about her, why don't you go and see her yourself? She's a customer of mine and I ain't going to tell everybody all about her."

One dark winter evening when I was making a short cut along the Wabash tracks I met a couple of men who seemed halfway between tramps and railroad brakemen on the loose.

"Hey, kid," one of them said, "can you tell us where there's a honky-tonk in this town?"

"A what?"

"A honky-tonk. Don't you know what a honky-tonk is?"

"I don't know any honky-tonk."

"Well, a whore-house. Do you know what a whore-house is?"

"Oh, sure," I said. "I know a good whore-house."

We weren't far from my customer's yellow house and I gave them directions. They chuckled, thanked me and started away. Then I turned and called, "Say, tell her that her paper-carrier sent you."

One of the men snorted. "Pimps start out early in these parts," he said.

I didn't know that word, but it had a bad sound and I thought it pretty poor return for a courtesy. "Well," I said to myself, "what can you expect from white trash looking for a whore-house? Be polite to a beer drinker and that's what you get."

There is a little professional prostitution going on now in Chillicothe, but it doesn't seem to be very profitable and civic leaders attach little importance to it.

One leader said, "Why should a young man go to such a place when there's so much amateur competition? Even the high school girls are in competition now."

I asked him how he knew the high school girls were offering such spirited competition and he said he knew it by the increase in juvenile delinquency.

Police and school officials, however, deny there is any increase in delinquency among actual students. They say it is among girls of high school age.

One official said, "Of course there's sex trouble in the schools occasionally, and I suppose that's inevitable. As far as I know there's no increase."

In that connection I recall a scandal in my own class when a mousy girl of about fourteen became pregnant and three boys chipped in to buy her an abortion. The girl died and the physician was sentenced to life in prison for second degree murder. There was talk of expelling the boys from school, but political influence saved them after nominal suspensions.

Nothing like that has happened in Chillicothe in a long time. Those who are completely convinced that the younger generation is going to the dogs (just as many elders were convinced that my generation was going to the dogs) say the young girls can bitch around with comparative impunity because they all are acquainted with contraceptive methods.

In advancing any sort of sensible conjecture as to whether extra-marital sexual adventures have increased in America in the last half century, one should consider every possible factor, and it must be admitted that the potency of old-time deterrents has been lessened since 1900.

The Protestant church's control over the morals of its communicants has been weakened materially by its virtual abandonment of hell-fire and brimstone. An increase in public education was making it more and more difficult to keep parishioners convinced that they certainly would sizzle through eternity in payment for mundane peccadilloes. So gradually ministers of the Gospel ceased fanning the flames until hell has become a fairly innocuous smoulder which could be forgotten entirely in a moment of passion.

Medical science has done much toward mitigating the terrors of a maiden's misadventures. Again, two major wars have had their effect in lowering public opinion toward sexual morality. Virginity no longer is regarded as quite the priceless jewel it was fifty or even twenty-five years ago. Now it has approximately the status of a semi-precious gem.

In some quarters today an unmarried girl is not even considered ruined because she has undergone a sex experience, and I doubt whether many juries now would accept without question the premise that a female witness' testimony is automatically impeached if opposing counsel can prove she has been guilty of a liaison. A promiscuous woman, in the eyes of the law, is a liar per se, and one established "misstep" used to be enough to brand the witness with promiscuity. Lawyers have scrapped that preposterous weapon, as a general practice, however, with the advent of women on juries. Any counsellor would have an understandable reluctance about asking a lady of the venire whether she had ever bedded with a man not her husband, and, with several women on a jury, no lawyer above the grade of imbecile would think of attacking a witness' credibility on grounds of a flexible love-life.

Pornographic, or at least sexually stimulating literature, plays, movies and advertisements certainly have had their effect, as has the concomitant lowering of old barriers in mixed-company conversation. Most important of all, indubitably, is the increase of opportunity offered by the automobile and its attendant motor courts.

With all this, it must be said that certain situations which existed in 1900 have well-nigh disappeared today.

To the best of my information, obtained largely from old-time physicians, an appalling number of brides went to their turn of Century nuptial couches utterly ignorant of the facts of life and were so thoroughly shocked out of their gossamer dreams as to be psychologically incapable of a normal sex life from then on. From those whose experience entitles them to some opinion, I have heard that men who won dainty, carefully shielded Victorian brides, and never got more than a reluctant acquiescence at home, totaled up to a thundering minority of the respectable American citizens of that time.

In other families, a decade of too rapid childbearing almost inevitably left the wife a semi-invalid and a firm advocate of continence for the rest of her life.

In many more families economic pressure either called a halt after the birth of two or three children or, lacking in restraint, the man and wife went on, with each additional little gift from heaven taking them deeper into the hell of destitution. The commonest end to that tragedy was the woman bursting her boiler in a glorious final pregnancy and leaving her husband with nine or a dozen motherless children to rear.

Some wealthy men then, even as always, relieved their domestic situations with mistresses. Others got involved—often with the finesse and shrewd judgment of a gold-star idiot—with some buxom maid and reaped the whirlwind. Others paid surreptitious visits to houses of prostitution. More took refuge in prayer and cold baths.

At the turn of the century practically every American city had its red light district, some of which were enormous in comparison to the population. Most cities had ordinances strictly prohibiting prostitution, and these allowed them to arrest and fine the madams and girls regularly in what amounted to unofficial licensing. In addition to this regular unofficial fee, the entrepreneurs were required to pay extra tribute to the cops on the beat, to the heads of vice squads, to the district captains and to political ward bosses. In exchange the girls were given police protection from obstreperous customers and from men who made outrageous claims that they had been given knockout drops and robbed. If such a man were foolish enough to press his charge he could be arrested himself on charges of disorderly conduct, vagrancy and contributing to a house of ill fame. The rococo parlor houses and squalid one-room cribs usually were severely segregated and kept from spreading to respectable business or residential sections.

Arguments in favor of red-light districts started off with the premise that they protected our own pure daughters from the lust of unprincipled men. Reformers, however, protested that houses of prostitution constantly were in need of recruits and that suave procurers were employed to lure or even kidnap gentle girls into a life of sin. There was also talk about teen-age boys with a dollar in their pockets buying themselves what was known as a "social disease."

Police and crooked politicians were heartily in favor of segregated districts not only because of the considerable cash tribute they were able to exact, but because they always had a good idea which houses were frequented by which criminals, making it comparatively easy to pick up non-elect thugs for questioning after a burglary or stickup.

These authorities also argued that with a nicely segregated red-light district, well regulated by systematic shakedowns, the girls could be compelled to submit to frequent physical examinations, thus reducing the spread of disease, but if the segregated districts were eliminated the girls would spread over the city, into hotels and apartments and private houses, making regulation almost impossible and confronting decent people with the danger of having a brothel established next door. It was pointed out that man's lusty nature could not be changed and that, after all, the majority of bordello customers were not criminals and low characters but respectable married men purchasing a few moments' simulated enthusiasm to carry them over cold refusal or frightened submission at home.

One of the auxiliaries of the red-light district was the "medical museum," for men only. These, presided over by quack physicians, exhibited wax models showing the horrors of venereal diseases, and glib attendants were capable of convincing a terrified country boy that his acne or hangnails revealed an infection which, if not treated immediately, would leave him in the awful state of this or that model. Of course the treatment for an imaginary malady could be almost as prolonged and expensive as for a real infection. If a bumpkin, sick with fright though otherwise healthy, sought to break away from the treatment while he still had a dollar or a job, he was threatened with exposure as a danger to his associates. Medical museums operated, of course, under the same protection as the segregated districts.

To be at all consistent, the yearners for the good old days of fifty years ago should welcome a return of the red-light houses. Perhaps they do. At least there has been an effort on the part of the nostalgia merchants, both Hollywood and literary, to gild with glamor a condition which was the shabbiest, most sordid breeder of crime, disease, drug-addiction, civic corruption and general moral breakdown that the geniuses of hell could devise.

Those shrewd, witty, wise madams with hearts of gold and tremendous political influence frequently were not only fences for stolen goods but actual accessories before the fact in burglaries and stickups. Jobs were mapped out in madam's parlor with madam supplying necessary information.

Madam, as a rule, held her girls under virtual peonage until they began to fade under the strain and then tossed them out to become streetwalkers. Madam paid cash tribute to the police authorities all right, but the police knew she must not be pushed too far because madam kept a horseshoe in her lavender glove, in the shape of blackmail material.

In fact, one of the principal by-products of the red-light system was blackmail. Let a tension-ridden citizen of some reputation or position seek relief in madam's palace of sin as an anonymous guy merely wanting to gain comfort from an anonymous blonde or brunette after placing his anonymous fee on the dresser, and, likely as not, madam had a dossier on him within twenty-four hours. Likely as not, madam was, with complete police knowledge, operating a "panel joint" and, while the customer's interest was engaged, a staff creep would enter through a sliding panel and obtain all the facts possible to obtain through examination of a man's pockets and wallet—which would be sufficient for an investigator to work on. If the customer seemed important the creep would steal only some token as a souvenir of his visit just in case madam ever saw fit to extort cash or political support or both. Yes, madam was a honey.

The red-light district was a product of its time. Being filthy in itself, it could batten only on men who had been convinced as children of the essential filthiness of sex and who had never outgrown the conviction.

I presume from the evidence that there has been some increase in extra-marital sex activity in the last fifty years. Considering the enormous advance in knowledge of contraceptive methods, I should guess that this increase among unmarried women has been substantial. I have not had the advantage of reports from a group of college students out seriously recording the sexual daydreams of other college students, so I can provide no charts nor graphs, but from perhaps wider than average experience with human beings plus an ability to add two and two without a lead pencil, I hold a suspicion that the increase is not as large as many lads of college age and some older mental libertines try to pretend. These chaps are inclined to chalk up a near miss as a fait accompli.

Yes, I am ingenuous enough to believe we as a people still retain a few ideals. I do not believe Americans are quite minks yet, although I know some pundits solemnly declare otherwise.

I am inclined to agree in part at least with H. L. Mencken when in a footnote to his contention "it is, indeed, the secret scandal of Christendom, at least in the Protestant regions, that most men are faithful to their wives," he says: "I see nothing in the Kinsey Report to change my conclusions here. All that humorless document really proves is (a) that all men lie when they are asked about their adventures in amour, and (b) that pedagogues are singularly naive and credulous creatures."

Moreover, it seems to me there is anthropological and historical evidence that homo sapiens actually has an instinct for monogamy—even if the monogamy is a little ragged around the fringes. And it seems to me that the biblical Ten Commandments, the old common law and the various prohibitory ukases of Christendom, both secular and ecclesiastical, did not evolve entirely from the mean spirits of some prostatic blue-noses, but actually resulted from the experiences of tribes that succeeded and tribes that failed, and were compiled with an actuary's care.

Recognizing that the human race has passed through various historical periods of licentiousness and reform, and that the Nineteen-Twenties were a fairly good representative of the former, I feel there is a great deal to be said for the present.

At the turn of the century we were attempting to hide sex under a bushel, but it just didn't work. The light shone through; the masked turmoil came bouncing out at inopportune moments and almost everybody knew it was there all the time anyhow.

In the last fifty years we have come to accept sex as a matter of course, largely without a blush or a leer. We are more natural and less hypocritical. Who can say that is bad?

I know there are those who feel so strongly about the growing divorce rate that they believe American family life was better fifty years ago. I don't agree.

Of course a broken family is to be deplored, especially when there are children, but surely "it is better to dwell in a corner of the housetop, than with a brawling woman in a wide house." Granting that serious defects in character or personality may be indicated when a husband and wife cannot live together without constant quarreling, granting that one or both may be immature and self-centered, these cases of extreme incompatibility have always existed, but there would seem to be less reason for them now than ever before.

Because of the wide dissemination of birth control information, few wives now live in terror of sexual relations. It has been said that amateur competition of late has driven countless numbers of poor prostitutes out of business. But, inasmuch as the prostitutes themselves, the police, the whore-mongers, the tribute-taking politicians, and everyone connected with the old-time booming commercialized vice used to be agreed that most of the business came from married men, I should suspect that a large part of this dire competition is coming from legal wives, finally unshackled from their fears.

There would seem to be reason to believe the ratio of incompatibility among married people has declined since 1900. Why, then, have divorces become so common? Simply because we have adopted a more common-sense attitude in that direction also. No longer is a woman eternally disgraced because she is a divorcee. No longer is her status only a short half step above that of a "fallen woman."

I remember well when a first cousin of mine was divorced. The shame of it spread for hundreds of miles, crossed state lines and settled sickeningly over our home. It was spoken of in whispers lest the neighbors overhear, and my mother remarked smugly to my father that nothing of the kind had ever happened in *her* family.

Around the corner from us lived a high-minded Christian couple who had worked out their problem of incompatibility without disgrace. They simply didn't speak and hadn't spoken directly to each other for a dozen years. On the rare occasions when it became necessary for one to communicate with the other it was done through a third party. They occupied separate rooms in their house and the husband had constructed a spite-fence partition three feet high in the middle of the dining table so he would not be compelled to look at his wife during meals.

Nevertheless the couple went to church together every Sunday and sat together and prayed together and sang hymns together (using separate hymn books) and walked home together after services.

When the husband finally sickened and died there was a big church funeral and the widow, veiled and in deepest mourning, wept audibly from beginning to end. For the rest of her days she wore nothing but black, holding the sympathy and respect of those who believed a weaker vessel would have succumbed and accepted the eternal disgrace of divorce.

At this time there lived in our neighborhood a shy little widow and her two tall, dark, equally shy sons. Floyd, the elder son, was a brakeman on the Milwaukee, and Paul was a fireman.

I did not know why then, but the family didn't seem to fit into the neighborhood. It was almost as if the small house was not there. You'd see the widow out puttering around the garden and the young men mowing the rutty lawn; you'd meet them on the street and tip your cap and say, "Howdy," and that was all.

I never knew my mother or any of the neighbor women to call on the widow and I'm sure I never saw her in our house or in any of the other houses I frequented. I don't remember seeing Floyd or Paul talking with any of the other young men or women in the neighborhood or taking part in their activities. They were not members of our church and I am not sure they attended any church at all. If they were ever discussed in any way by adults I never heard it. Floyd and Paul and their mother were very quiet and polite, but they just didn't seem to matter.

The spring of the hot summer of 1901 Paul's freight train was wrecked somewhere up the line and he was terribly scalded by escaping steam. They brought him home swathed in cotton. I saw them carry him into the house on a folding cot and you couldn't see Paul—just the white cotton.

He was quiet when they carried him in, but within an hour he began to scream. For the first time Paul began to attract attention in the neighborhood. He screamed all the rest of that afternoon and evening until the Southwest Limited had come and chuffed away into the night, and the three express wagons had rattled past and I went to sleep. He was screaming when I woke up in the morning and a ghastly pall had settled over the neighborhood. My mother and sister couldn't eat breakfast and everyone spoke in hushed tones as if a normal voice might disturb Paul.

There was no baseball, or marbles or kite-flying. There was nothing but Paul's screams. The boys huddled together on corners whispering and they looked strange and frightened. Big Everett Scott said Dr. Gordon had shot enough morphine into Paul to kill two ordinary men but the pain just ate it up. The spring sunshine was curiously veiled as if freighted with Paul's screams.

While I was asleep that night Paul quit screaming and died.

They held the funeral from the house with the minister of the North Methodist Church officiating. Most of those attending were railroad people and strangers, but all of the other women watched from their windows.

Mrs. Watson was over at our house watching and she pointed out a tall, bearded man in black suit and derby hat as Paul's father who had come from St. Louis before his son died, but Paul had been too far gone to recognize him.

"He married the other woman, didn't he?" my mother asked.

"Yes," Mrs. Watson said. "I hear they have a little girl."

This puzzled me and I said, "I thought she was a widow."

"Hush," my mother said, "she's a *grass* widow."

So then I understood why the family had never seemed to belong.

Well, I am willing to let them sing of the good old days; the days when O. Henry said proudly that he'd "never written a word which would bring the blush of shame to the daintiest cheek"; the good old "gentleman cow" days when a young gentleman might be married for years with only the most vague idea of what a woman really looked like; when many a man felt the weight of a chivalrous fist because he said "damn" or "hell" within a woman's hearing; when legs were "limbs" and a woman could be arrested for showing half a calf in public; when a pregnant woman was in a "delicate condition," and kept strictly out of sight for six months, but ordinarily padded her hips and buttocks to extraordinary proportions, squeezed her vital organs out of place to give the appearance of a tiny waist and Holstein bosom; when a lady never in the world would say she was "hot" because of the implication, fainted sweetly on occasion and believed that babies came to brides because of the holy words spoken over them by a minister of God.

But, by and large, I think things are better now.

IX

THE FIGHTING WORD

Of course it's only my personal opinion, but I feel the decline in pistol-toting among respectable citizens is a sign that culture has advanced in the last fifty years. One might argue contrariwise, pointing out that a well-dressed gentleman who neglects to carry a neat revolver in his hip pocket is no fit escort for a gentle lady, that he surely can't cherish his own honor because he is in no position to rebuff insult, and therefore he's a mollycoddle. But again it's my opinion that the argument, like the custom, is out of date.

For the first decade of the Twentieth Century, and somewhat later, every popular magazine carried advertisements for pocket guns, using a fear technique similar to that employed so successfully in 1950 by insurance companies and manufacturers of preparations to make the human body smell nice. Some of these old advertisements depicted dramatic scenes wherein two unshaven thugs were slinking away and probably hissing, "Zounds!" and "Foiled!" before the small, nickel-plated revolver in the hand of a gentleman in derby hat and striped trousers, while a wasp-waisted lady in picture hat stood admiringly by.

Most advertisers, however, were content to publish pictures of their fascinating products. Both Smith & Wesson and Colt, being traditionally the manufacturers of quality merchandise, made little effort to capture the popular market with cheap hip-pocket firearms, at the turn of the Century. With the advent of the automatic pistol a few years later, however, Colt and the Savage Arms Company were advertising pocket-size pistols which, in the hand of an expert, could deliver eight or ten steel-jacketed bullets in a couple of seconds. But these vicious little weapons were rather expensive for the average non-professional gunman of the time.

Every crossroads general store and town pawnshop carried its display of cheap, unreliable and dangerous thirty-twos and thirty-eights, from Belgian and Spanish exports costing ten or twelve dollars a dozen wholesale to the slightly superior Iver-Johnson "Owl's Head" and Harrington and Richardson "belly-gun" retailing at about five dollars, except to special customers. The American Bulldog thirty-eight was a good murder gun at ranges not exceeding ten feet. Any half-witted white man could buy one of these weapons without question in a town like Chillicothe, Missouri, if he had three to five dollars or credit at the store, and many a boy who wouldn't need a razor for half a dozen years owned and, on occasion, carried a cheap revolver in his pocket. A Negro usually had more difficulty in buying a new revolver but there were always second-hand guns for sale or barter.

The first gunfight in my experience came when I was about five years old. I was still forbidden to go "uptown" without adult escort, but Forrest Walters, whose parents were somewhat more liberal toward him, was being sent to Schultz's butcher shop for a quarter's worth of round steak (about three pounds) and he begged me to go with him. His special inducement was this: Because he was making such a substantial purchase, Mr. Schultz would give a "wienie" not only to him but to his company. That temptation was too great for my feeble will power so I disobeyed orders and went with Forrest.

As we approached Locust Street on the east side of the Square there were loud, excited voices from half a dozen men in the street and a long-legged Negro broke away and started running south down the brick pavement. Immediately a white man in a white shirt, red suspenders and straw hat drew a shiny revolver from his hip pocket and started firing at the fleeing Negro. The

Negro stopped short and turned, pulling a revolver from his own pocket. I don't believe he had covered more than fifty or sixty feet and the white man was standing with feet far apart, firing very deliberately four or five times. The Negro shot twice, very fast from a crouching position, and the white man's revolver flashed as it fell from his hand to the red bricks and the white man hugged himself with both arms and turned his back to the Negro and folded up on the pavement with knees drawn up to his chin. When the white man fell the big Negro turned and ran very fast on south, his feet clopping rapidly on the pavement. No one followed him.

I don't remember that there was any yelling. But instantly a crowd was on hand and they picked up the fallen warrior and carried him a few feet to the grass of Elm Park where they laid him on his back. At once he was surrounded by a thicket of adult legs which Forrest and I could not penetrate. We kept asking if he was dead and what the shooting was about and whether they would hang the Negro, but no one paid us any attention. At last we gave up and went on to Schultz's butcher shop where Forrest bought his two-bits' worth of round steak and then asked if we could have a couple of wienies. Mr. Schultz grumpily broke two wieners from a chain and we bit off small pieces and then pretended the frankfurters were cigars, holding them jauntily between middle and index fingers as we sauntered toward home, taking little bites now and then and flicking off imaginary ash.

The man in the white shirt was gone when we reached the park and so was most of the crowd. Two loafers were standing gloomily on the curb and we approached them.

"Mister," I said to one of them, "is that man dead?"

He spat tobacco juice into the street and grunted something. I repeated the question and he ignored me.

There was a small spot of blood on the pavement bricks and Forrest made as if to stick his bare toe into it, then changed his mind. We walked slowly on toward home, nibbling our cigars. We discussed the shooting but, as I recall, with no great excitement. We did, however, consider it disgraceful marksmanship on the white man's part. After all, he had fired at least three times before the Negro had his revolver out.

Naturally I could not tell my family what I had seen, without confessing disobedience and suffering a whipping. I assume that my family certainly must have heard about the affair, but they did not believe in discussing that sort of thing in front of children.

To this day I do not know what the shooting was about, whether the white man was killed or what happened to the Negro.

While I do not mean to imply that this kind of thing was common in peaceful, midwestern communities at the turn of the century, I do believe there were few homes in those days without a revolver of some sort and that possibly a majority of citizens carried a pocket revolver when going on a journey or when they were to be out late at night. And before I was fourteen in gang fights with clods and brickbats I had heard bullets pass over my head, fired by rival boys with the purpose, I suppose, of frightening us. At least, that result was achieved.

Chillicothe had an ordinance forbidding the carrying of concealed weapons as did most similar communities. But the ordinance was invoked mostly against suspicious persons and vagrants.

Well, I believe the pistol situation, generally speaking, has improved considerably in the last fifty years and I believe that is a sign of advancing civilization and consequently a cultural victory. I say this although quite convinced that certain areas such as New York City have gone too far the other way. New York City, in my opinion, has carried the already too-stringent Sullivan Law to ridiculous lengths, when a citizen of good character cannot obtain a pistol permit without affidavits that he is a bank messenger or otherwise protecting large sums of money; when it can happen and has happened that a good citizen with an unlicensed revolver has captured an unarmed burglar and suffered a more severe penalty than the burglar; when anyone with underworld connections can buy anything from a "stingaree" finger pistol to a sub-machine gun; when the police know from tracing serial numbers of captured weapons that a thriving export business exists between manufacturers and Cuban concerns which smuggle Tommy guns right back to the United States; and when the situation is the Volstead Act all over again, only infinitely more hazardous to the police. This, however, is relatively unimportant to the whole picture. No longer is it possible for an irresponsible boy to send to a mail-order house for a pocket revolver, no longer are the magazines and newspapers filled with advertisements for cheap pistols that are worthless for any legitimate purpose although pretty effective for suicide, the close-range murder of unsuspecting persons and the accidental killing of children. In few American areas is it now possible to buy a five dollar revolver as one might buy a claw hammer.

I suspect few of those nickel-plated abominations are in existence now, but they turned up with diminishing regularity until a dozen or so years ago. One of the first occasions in my memory was in the Southwest about 1915. A woman reported she had shot a prowler and we found her in near hysterics with a nickel-plated thirty-two in her hand. She said she had fired through the window glass at an evil-looking man and felt sure she had killed him.

There were tracks outside in the light snow, all right, moving away in what appeared to be a stumbling run, and we followed the tracks to the Santa Fe railroad and down to the old brewery warehouse, where they stopped. Flashlights revealed a man under the warehouse, and we hauled him out from where he had crawled to die and took him to the station to examine his wound. Groaning in what he considered his last moments on earth, the man unbuttoned his coat and vest and the thirty-two bullet dropped to the station-house floor. His only injury was a small red spot on his hairy solar plexus where the little missile, turning end for end, had smote him a breath-taking blow. It turned out that this wretch was not a burglar but a lover, that the woman shot him inside the house instead of outside and broke the window later to make her story of the prowler good. The man, it appeared, had been neglecting the lady and obviously deserved killing.

Some time later I was witness to another case where a shiny

little pearl-handled "Owl's Head" betrayed a lady in a critical emergency. Her husband was everything a husband ought not to be. He not only did not make enough money to provide a motor car and a fur coat but he simply refused to give her proper grounds for divorce. At last, in desperation, she emptied the contents of her weapon at his back while he bent over the kitchen sink doing the dinner dishes, three of the bullets, as they say, taking effect. But they didn't take sufficient effect. They only served to rouse in him the great rage which comes sometimes to the male animal on sudden realization of misplaced confidence. Abandoning his dish-washing, disregarding the fact that the little woman was helpless before him now that her pearl-handled pistol was quite empty, this man so far forgot love and chivalry in the selfish fury of his stinging back that he broke his wife's neck right there in the kitchen. She looked very pretty even in death on the kitchen floor, and pitiful too, with the shiny little revolver that betrayed her held in her dainty hand. Far, far better for her to have owned no gun at all than this pot-metal gaud which let her down in her hour of need.

Ordinarily one could hit nothing at a distance of ten feet with one of those black-powder thirty-two caliber protectors of home and person. But let one fall from a man's hip pocket and it invariably went off and the bullet invariably picked out the most amiable person in the vicinity, usually a child, and killed him dead. Or if a citizen fired at a burglar and, of course, missed, that bullet which might come to a halt after passing through a suit coat and vest at a range of six feet, would pass out a window, carry a quarter of a mile and strike down a visiting nurse on an errand of mercy. In other words, the popular pocket guns of the turn of the Century usually were quite selective, preferring to kill innocent bystanders rather than mad dogs and thugs.

When I was eleven years old my brother Glen got married and put, for the time being, childish things behind him. So he gave me his Stevens' Favorite twenty-two rifle, his Fourth of July cannon and an American Bulldog thirty-eight caliber revolver, which was a more formidable weapon than the conventional thirty-two hip pocket gun. Later, when I got into mild trouble over the revolver, Glen explained himself to our father by saying the action was so stiff he didn't believe I had strong enough fingers to fire it and he didn't believe I could get cartridges. He forgot that I had two hands and could either use two thumbs to cock the hammer or hook two or three fingers over the trigger to fire it double-action. And it so happened that Max Blanchard had a box of thirty-eight cartridges, gangrened with age, which he had found in his attic and I traded him a spare jackknife for them. The Bulldog had a frightening recoil which would throw my hands over my head and it spoke with a satisfactory bellow. But I couldn't even touch a tree when close enough to hit it with a paving brick.

As I understand it, there was a sort of code among toters of five-dollar revolvers. In an altercation with a social equal and acquaintance, it was almost unforgivable to draw your weapon and fire at him. If you were a white man of position it was even more unforgivable *not* to draw and fire your revolver if a recalcitrant Negro threatened violence. To strike a Negro with your fist was putting yourself on the Negro's social level and you probably would never live it down—especially if the Negro gave you a licking.

White men of equal social status could and did engage in violent fist fights and never even think of the pistols in their pockets unless one landed painfully on his "Owl's Head" when knocked down.

I remember very well the first fist fight I ever saw between men and it was on the Fourth of July, probably in 1899. We had gone to the Livingston County fair grounds in the family surrey for the celebration, and my father was maneuvering the team toward a parking place or hitching rack when this altercation began right in front of us. A small, curly-haired man was accusing a paunchy, middle-aged man of being an anarchist. I knew what an anarchist was because we had a book with a picture of the anarchist bomb exploding at the Haymarket riots in Chicago and I didn't like it when my father pulled up the horses. If there was going to be bomb-throwing, it seemed sensible to me to move elsewhere.

"This man," cried the little fellow in a quavering, oratorical voice, "on this Independence Day, this birthday of our glorious nation, has insulted our flag, has insulted the heroes of Bunker Hill and Gettysburg, George Washington, Abraham Lincoln and Admiral Dewey, and hanging to a sour apple tree is too good for him."

"What he do, bub?" an old man in the gathering crowd asked.

"He's an ungrateful dog that bites the hand what's feeding him and I'm going to lick him until he takes and gets down on his knees and kisses Old Glory and begs her pardon."

The fat man half turned, looking for a convenient exit, but the crowd had closed him in and a burly farmer blocked him. "Just a minute, mister," the farmer said. "Don't be so fast until we see what this is all about."

The little man pointed a quivering forefinger at the fat fellow who looked very sick indeed by this time. "What did he do? Well, I'll tell you what he did. On this morning when every decent American was hanging out the Star-Spangled Banner and blessing God for his heritage, this fat sow, this worse than a dog, this *anarchist,* hung out a *red flag*!"

A groan of horror swept up from the crowd, and we in the surrey had a grandstand seat for everything.

"Let me hold your coat, bub," said the old man who first asked the question. "Go learn 'im a lesson."

The little man took off his straw sailor and his coat, and his shirt was striped red, white and blue. Protruding from his right hip pocket was the butt of a revolver.

"I didn't either hang out any red flag," the fat man cried, but the curly-haired fellow in the red, white and blue shirt was upon him swinging vicious punches into his body and face. The fat man struck out awkwardly, hitting downward like an old woman beating a rug, and then he was knocked flat on his back.

Men grabbed the curly-headed patriot by his striped arms, calling out self-righteously, "Let him up. Got to fight fair here."

When the middle-aged man showed reluctance to rise, he was helped to his feet and stripped of his coat. The straw hat had tumbled from his bald head when he went down and now blood was trickling from his bulbous nose. I noted that he also carried a revolver in his right hip pocket and that its stock was brown wood while the patriot's was black rubber.

With a desperate, frightened expression on his fat face, the accused anarchist assumed a position similar to that of John L. Sullivan in the sporting prints but it stood him no stead. He gasped in pain when the little man swung resoundingly into his plump belly and, as he lowered his guard, he caught a rain of vicious blows in the face that sent him into the dust again, blood-smeared and blubbering hopelessly.

The patriot stood over him with fists still doubled.

"You got enough?" the patriot demanded.

"Yes," the fat man moaned and spat out a tooth. "Yes, I got enough."

"You willing to kiss the Star-Spangled Banner now?"

"I'm always willing to kiss my country's flag."

"Somebody bring a flag!" the patriot called and a spectator took a small, starchy American flag from the hand of a little girl and passed it forward.

"Thanks," said the patriot. "Now, you anarchist, get on your knees."

"I'm not any anarchist, but I'll get on my knees."

"All right. Now wipe off your face so you won't stain Old Glory with your stinking traitor's blood."

The beaten man, now looking deplorably old instead of middle-aged, got out a handkerchief with a palsied hand and wiped his face. The patriot held the small flag by the stick and pushed it at his kneeling adversary who took hold of a stiff corner with each hand and kissed the cloth with a smack which could not be misunderstood.

"All right. Now swear you'll never hang out another red flag as long as you live."

"Of course I swear. I love the American flag."

Tears were running down his bloodstained plump cheeks and,

still on his knees, he sobbed, "So help me God, I never *did* hang out any red flag."

"You call me a liar?" The patriot drew back a fist hip-high.

"No, but look." The kneeling man ripped open his right shirt sleeve and pulled it up, revealing a bright red undershirt. "I got to wear red flannel underwear for my rheumatism even in summer, see? This morning I washed one of my red undershirts and hung it out to dry. So help me God and may He strike me dead, that was what you saw—not any red flag but just my red undershirt hanging out to dry."

The patriot spat into the dust, reached around and recovered his coat and straw sailor.

"All I got to say," he said, and spat into the dust once more, "you better not let me catch you hanging out anything red again on the Fourth of July and I mean not even a red handkerchief."

The fat man wiped the blood from his face once more and one eye now was puffy and discolored. Then he pulled himself painfully to his feet and brushed the dust from his knees.

Several men helped the patriot into his coat and slapped him on the back. "You're a dandy, Joe," one of them said. "Yes, siree, bob-harry," said another, "a regular *jim*-dandy. Let's go have a drink."

No one offered to help the fat man with his coat. He stood holding it and his straw hat, the picture of despair, mumbling over and over, "Folks, I *never* hung out any red flag. I never did. Look here, it was just a red undershirt like this one." But nobody paid any attention to him and the crowd dispersed and my father drove the team on to the hitching rack.

Details of this sorrowful affair were carved so deeply into my memory not only because it was the first adult fist fight I ever saw but because of other implications. While cleanliness was a virtue without question and while the fat man was deserving of praise rather than censure for washing his red undershirt, he still was guilty of outrageous stupidity or of blatant disregard for convention in hanging out on the Fourth of July a thing of scarlet which, at a distance at least, might be sufficiently ambiguous to attract attention.

I was *beginning* to realize, young as I was, that failure to conform was one of the most heinous of crimes in that region and day. I was to learn painfully that even suspicion of non-conformity was subject to cruel punishment and that, in those days of rugged individualism, nothing was more abhorrent than individualism. Men, women, girls and boys were severely regimented by public opinion, and public opinion was the greatest despot of all dictators. A working man must dress himself and his family somewhat more expensively than he could afford or public opinion held him lacking in self-respect. And who could respect a man who failed to respect himself?

A woman or girl who failed to conform exactly to public opinion's dictates in dress or manners or activities got herself "talked about." Then, if the male members of her family had any self-respect, they were required to defend her "honor" either with fists or firearms.

And a self-respecting man not only was required to defend his own honor and that of his family by direct action, but also he must defend the honor of his dog.

I remember an occasion in Chillicothe's Elm Park, where the Livingston County Court House now stands, when a relaxing citizen threw away a cigar butt and another relaxing citizen's bird dog, eager to exhibit his retrieving talents, dashed out and seized up the hot butt. He did not, however, bring it back to the smoker nor to his master. He let go the cigar butt and cried piteously, as much, I suspect, from the humiliating realization that he was a very stupid bird dog as from his burnt tongue, and his master, taking only a moment to soothe him with a pat on the head, stalked stiff-legged to the bench where the butt-thrower relaxed.

"That," said the dog-owner, "was the meanest, lowest, orneriest damn thing I ever see—throwing a hot cigar for a poor dog to burn hisself on."

"Mister," said the butt-thrower, "you want to watch your mouth about that kind of talk. I was through with my cigar and I just simply pitched it away. I didn't even know you or your dog was around. I got better things on my mind."

"Any kind of a man," said the dog-owner, "knows what he's doing before he throws hot cigars. Here you was and there I was and there was my dog that's trained to bring things back and you couldn't help seeing us and you couldn't help knowing a fine bird dog would run and get your cigar and burn hisself and seeing you done it I say you couldn't help doing it on purpose and I say it's the lowest—"

"Just a minute, mister," said the butt-thrower, "you're talking pretty high and mighty unless you're ready to back up your talk."

"I can back it up, all right enough."

"And when I say I didn't see your dog and didn't burn him on purpose you're practically calling me a liar and besides all that a fine bird dog is a one-man dog and don't go running after things total strangers throw and it seems like to me that's a pretty poor specimen of a bird dog that'll run and grab up a cigar butt thrown away by somebody he never laid eyes on before."

There it was. The honor and intelligence of his bird dog were libeled and there was no alternative but to hurl the fighting word.

"Why, you son-of-a-bitch," said the dog-owner.

They fought clear around the fountain with its white ball dancing innocently atop its plume of sepia-toned water; they fought as country men fight, with wide-swinging lefts and rights, and the dog-owner got a bloody nose and they grappled and went down in the grass, pummeling each other, and by then there were half a hundred spectators, making it difficult for a small boy to see well without climbing a tree—which I did—and the spectators got them to their feet and they fought northeast toward Webster and Locust Streets and the butt-thrower was knocked down and got up and was knocked down twice more, and then Judge Arch Davis showed up in a plug hat and ordered Policeman Purdy to stop the fight.

Then the blood-smeared butt-thrower said he was sorry the bird dog burnt his tongue and the blood-smeared dog-owner said he'd apologize for his fighting words if the butt-thrower would swear he didn't burn the dog on purpose and they finally shook hands and went to wash their bruised faces in the fountain.

Considering the number of physical combats between grown men I either saw or knew about, and considering the fact that I did not frequent barrooms between the ages of five and fourteen, and that a barroom is the native habitat of brawls, I should judge that fist fighting was very common indeed in that day and region.

Jack Newland, editor of the *Constitution* and superintendent of our Sunday School, must have been engaged in scores of battles. He was a small, handsome, dapper man who wore rimless nose glasses attached to a fine gold chain that clipped around his right ear. He always had a spare pair of glasses and Crelland's were ready to supply new ones at moment's notice because those nose glasses always seemed to be the first casualty in a fight.

Mr. Newland was a crusader at heart and a brave man. He could, as the saying is, "take it." If he suffered a bloody nose and broken glasses as the result of a trenchant editorial assailing Republican political corruption, he came back the next day with a blow-by-blow account of the fight and with an even more bitter attack on his enemies. If he was beaten up again the next day and his spare glasses broken, he delayed writing the third diatribe only until Crelland's delivered another pair of glasses.

As I look back it seems that almost always Mr. Newland had cuts about his eyes and puffed lips as he led the Sunday School in singing "Let the Little Sunshine In," or "Bringing in the Sheaves." I used to wonder why Mr. Newland didn't hire Charley Ludwig or some other rugged young athlete to walk with him and do the *Constitution*'s fist fighting. I personally was craven enough to refuse to fight Mack Woods, for instance, because I knew I had no chance against him; so I was unable to understand Mr. Newland's strength of character, determination, ideals and boundless optimism in the face of physical improbabilities.

One day, however, it happened. Mr. Newland *won* a fight. Accosted on a street corner by a ruffian who began the old verbal build-up which inevitably was to end with bruises and broken glasses, Mr. Newland did not wait for the preliminaries to run their course. Instead he smote the fellow on the nose and followed it up with a succession of fast punches to salient points of the face and body, and he won a complete victory.

So elated was Mr. Newland over this encounter that he gave it prominence on page one in substantially these words:

"Should passers-by at the corner of Vine and Jackson Streets notice blood on the granitoid sidewalk, let them know it is, for once, not editorial blood but the gore of an unidentified thug, no doubt in the employ of the corrupt Republican liquor interests, who to his sorrow accosted your editor at that point with intent to do bodily injury.

"Let this be a lesson to the forces of evil in Chillicothe who seem reluctant to realize that your editor cannot be intimidated by physical violence or any other means and that he will continue the good fight with pen and fists until complete victory has been won for Christianity, prohibition and the Democratic Party."

Journalism was one glorious battle for Jack Newland in Chillicothe for some years and he loved it. Then, after he had been largely instrumental in closing the town's thirteen saloons with local option and Woodrow Wilson was in the White House and the Democrats in complete control at Jefferson City as well as in Chillicothe, a whole drab year went by without a fight and Crelland's, with a couple pair of nose glasses ready and waiting for him, were having to pay cash for their advertising and were wondering whether Mr. Newland was taking his trade elsewhere and the little editor grew morose and preoccupied and he finally sold out his interest in the *Constitution* and bought a paper in Oklahoma where there was some call for biting editorials and opponents might take issue with their fists. I suspect he may not have felt he was doing his duty to his community unless he was collecting occasional cuts and bruises.

Perhaps some (although I am sure not the esthetes) may argue that the decline in fist fighting among men is a sure sign of our decadence. I feel it is a sign of growing civilization and that it gives hope for the human race.

There are still men who feel that mob violence is justified when legal processes fail to punish, but happily this minority is diminishing rapidly.

In the old West members of vigilante groups and of stockmen's protective associations felt they were patriotic citizens indeed when they stretched a rope around some wretch's neck without bothering with a jury trial. Usually they worked on the principle that property rights were superior to a man's life, provided it was *their* property and the life of someone without money or influence.

It is the custom in these days to think of lynching in terms of white mobs killing Negroes, but in America's shameful record of mob violence, this is far from the rule. For instance, in the year 1884 when 211 persons were killed by mobs, 160 were white men and only 51 Negroes. Arizona has a record of 29 lynchings, all of them whites. Montana mobs have slain 84, only two of them Negroes.

In southern and border states, of course, the ratio is different. Missouri, with a total of 121 recorded mob slayings, killed 51 white men and 70 Negroes.

No records have been kept of instances where the moral sense of a highly Christian community has been outraged but the resulting mob substituted tar and feathers for the rope or fire.

My father once halted such a party. A man had deserted his wife and children and had gone to live with another woman which, of course, was an affront to every decent citizen for miles around, especially to the good women. So a group of moral citizens, steaming with indignation, armed themselves, appropriated a barrel of tar, procured an old feather bed and marched upon the cottage where the sinning couple slept.

When my father heard of the proceedings, he hurried to the scene where the mob surrounded the naked culprits, who were shivering from terror and chill night air despite the fact that a roaring fire already had been built to heat the tar. Mounting a wagon, my father delivered an impassioned oration on forgiveness, telling about Christ and "He that is without sin among you, let him first cast a stone at her," and he finally shamed the mob into letting the man and woman go on promise that they'd leave the community immediately, which they did by dawn.

I thought it pretty good of my father to get up before that armed mob and to talk them out of their violence and I told him so. He shook his head. "No," he said, "cattle like that don't deserve being called men and women. Tarring and feathering was probably too good for them. The thing that concerned me wasn't that man and woman. But the mob had *my* barrel of tar."

There is no record of an actual lynching in Livingston County, Missouri, as far as I can find. But they did ride a preacher on a rail.

This was a Methodist minister, the Reverend J. E. Gardner, and it was a result of the 1860 presidential election wherein the county voted 578 for Bell, 470 for Breckenridge, 401 for Douglas and 20 for Lincoln.

In the village of Utica, just across the river southwest of Chillicothe, where the population was and is about six hundred, the citizens were scandalized on counting the votes to find one ballot for Lincoln. The question was who among them had cast this black Republican ballot and suspicions smouldered and citizens began looking askance at neighbors and wondering and the tension grew as days passed into weeks. Then a whisper began to circulate about the Reverend Mr. Gardner, practically the last man in town to be suspected. It seemed incredible that the pious and Christ-like Methodist minister could be the guilty man, but the rumors persisted until a committee of his parishioners was appointed to call upon their pastor and to put the question to him boldly and bluntly.

The committee was diffident and hesitant, but they finally did blurt out what they wanted to know. They hated to ask it, but was it true that the Reverend Mr. Gardner was the man who voted for that Rail Splitter?

The Reverend Mr. Gardner drew himself up straight. "Gentlemen," he said, "under the Constitution of the United States, we all vote a secret ballot. When an American citizen enters the voting booth to mark his ballot he is alone with his God and his own conscience. How he marks it is his own business and concerns no other living man. You, gentlemen, have no legal or moral right to ask such a question of me. I have nothing to be ashamed of. Being a servant of the Lord's, being a follower of our Saviour, Jesus Christ, I cannot condone slavery. Gentlemen, I will answer your question. I am proud to state that I was the man who voted for Abraham Lincoln. Now you can make the most of it."

So the committee went away and made their report, and not only the town of Utica but the whole county was sickened by the revelation. A man of God, a man whom they had taken into their hearts and respected and loved, had betrayed them.

A petition (at least they called it a petition) was written and signed by the leading citizens of Utica, ordering the Reverend Mr. Gardner to move himself and family out of Livingston County immediately.

It stated: "You are the only man in our community who voted for Lincoln, and you have publicly declared that you would glory in making yourself a martyr in the cause of abolition."

This was on January 2, 1861. On the following day when the minister went to the business district he was surrounded by a crowd who wanted to know when he was leaving. The Reverend Mr. Gardner made an evasive answer.

"All right," someone shouted, "if he likes the Rail Splitter so well, somebody get a Lincoln rail."

So someone came up with a fence rail and the shouting, jeering mob rode the preacher through the village streets while he sang at the top of his voice:

> "Children of the heavenly king,
> As we journey let us sing."

While they bounced him along on the rail he then preached an impromptu sermon, assuring them the Almighty would not overlook this treatment of a man of God and that their punishment would be dreadful and swift because the Day of Wrath was just around the corner.

At the termination of this parade, which lasted an hour or so, the Reverend Mr. Gardner took his wife and children to Chillicothe and filed suit against the leaders of his Utica tormentors. The story of his disgrace had preceded him to the county seat, however, and a mob followed him into the old court house.

A spokesman addressed Judge Hughes to this effect: "Judge, we just held a meeting and the sense of the meeting is, your honor, that we reckon it'd be a good idea for you to bring them papers outside right away and make a little bonfire of 'em in the yard."

So the judge took the papers outside and was cheered when he set them afire, and the man who voted for Lincoln and his family were escorted gently but firmly to the county line.

There is no record of what became of them.

As to the reduction of mob violence in the United States since the beginning of the Twentieth Century, there were 130 fatal lynchings reported in 1901. For the last seven or eight years, American mobs have killed only from one to three persons annually. At least, that's all that have been officially reported.

In the matter of personal physical combat, I have not seen a single punch thrown by a grown man in fifteen years, except in the prize ring, and in that time I have lived in several cities and three small towns. Once in New York I did witness an altercation between two burly truck drivers which seemed destined to blossom into physical violence, and I loitered nearby for five minutes while they discussed their differences with faces close together and with many eloquent gestures. While I entertain a normal interest in exciting events and a pair of two hundred pound male animals slugging it out can be very exciting indeed, I am happy to report that the only casualty in this encounter was the English language. When hairy-chested truck drivers can settle marked differences of opinion regarding personal habits, alleged torts, motor skills, mental alertness, possible miscegenation and intimate peculiarities by mere discussion, however vehement, a step has been taken away from the jungle. Thirty years ago, I feel certain, this exercise in dialectics never would have progressed beyond the first of a hundred fighting words.

While I must admit that in late years I have not frequented waterfront barrooms habitually or lived in a bunkhouse with what used to be called he-men, I still get around a little and I hear a lot, and it is my impression that the fighting word has lost a great deal of its pristine potency. I think that is fine. Speaking the fighting word used to be tantamount to throwing down the gauntlet. It was a crude relic of knight errantry and compounded complete silliness with vulgarity.

There may be some significance in the fact that in America the more common of the small arsenal of fighting words reflected on the morality of the mother and in the Latin countries on the faithfulness of the wife. However, the words themselves carried only academic meaning. A young Mexican, for instance, would leap furiously into the fray at the word "cabrón," even though not married or thinking of marriage.

The challenge was the thing, not the words. One could call a man a son-of-a-gun with impunity; it probably would be taken as a vigorous compliment meaning he was an extraordinary fellow. Yet the word "gun" in that sense meant thief in early Nineteenth Century slang, possibly deriving from the Yiddish *gonoph*. Then, although a man might love his female dog more dearly than his own mother and with much more reason if his mother happened to be a low and selfish character and his bitch a faithful, gentle creature, he would throw off his coat and fight to the finish at the words "son-of-a-bitch." Any able-bodied man or boy who failed to fight in those circumstances was held beneath contempt. His fellows never would forget and he would be forever conscious of their scorn when they ignored his opinions on politics, Ty Cobb or the best way to catch channel catfish.

There were, of course, a few exceptions. If some lout hurled fighting words at an elderly man or a cripple or invalid or minister of the Gospel, the shoe was on the other foot, and some champion among the witnesses would rise and demand retraction and apology. Unless given quickly, the champion, full of self-righteousness, would at least attempt to give the ill-advised lout a beating.

Among boys some fights resulted from quarrels, but mostly they were part of a perpetual tournament to determine one's standing. Thus, if both Higgins and Moriarity had whipped Duboise, it was inevitable that Higgins and Moriarity should fight and other boys saw to it that they met and fought at the earliest opportunity. There was a sort of loose, esoteric seeding among boys according to size, age and class in school but there was nothing rigid or official about it. A smaller boy could challenge a larger boy and win glory if successful. A larger boy might not enhance his batting average ordinarily by whipping a smaller boy, but there were circumstances in which his reputation might suffer unless he took action.

As an example, there was Julius Meinershagen who was a handsome, gentlemanly lad a year or so older than I, and I was annoyed by my father's continually holding Julius up as an example. I habitually traveled at a loose-jointed dogtrot, "rooster-fighting" with other boys from one side of the street to another, and conversing in a well-modulated bellow. Julius walked with the dignity of a gentleman, kept himself neat and was a favorite with the girls.

One day when Chester Grace and I were working on some project in our barn, Julius came to pay a formal visit to Maurine Sweeney. They played at tea party in Maurine's back yard, across narrow Woodward Street from our barn and to me it was a disgusting spectacle.

I yelled out the barn window:

"Meinershagen is a fool
Because he plays with girls in school."

I remember Maurine's saying, "Pay no attention to him. Just consider the source." That was a popular phrase with grownups then—"consider the source."

So every once in a while I'd yell out the barn window:

> "Meinershagen is a fool
> Because he plays with girls in school."

He pretended to ignore me, but the next day I met Julius and he walked up to me with great dignity and said, "Davis, you have insulted me and I'm going to teach you a lesson."

This was an astonishing thing. I had considered Julius a complete sissy who wouldn't think of fighting. But more astonishing was the discovery that someone had been giving Julius boxing lessons. He didn't even lose his calm dignity or self-confident smile in giving me a drubbing complete with black eye.

The usual system for a boy who wished to fatten his batting average was to appraise the physical assets and liabilities of available boys reasonably near his size and pick out one who seemed the frailest and most inoffensive. Then there were two routes to follow. First was to inform another boy that he was "laying for" the intended victim, knowing that the word would be passed on and possibly lessen the morale of the lad so he would default. If it was commonly known that Johnny was laying for Tommy and that Tommy was consistently going around the block to avoid a clash, after a week or so, Johnny was tacitly recognized as the conquerer of Tommy without even swinging a fist. The other method was more direct. The aggressor would walk stiff-legged up to the unsuspecting victim, spit on the ground and speak from the corner of his mouth: "D'you want to fight?"

In this case if Tommy were apprehensive of the result or just naturally didn't like fighting, he'd make an inconclusive reply or say frankly that he did not care for combat right then. Then Johnny would spit on the ground again and say, "I can lick you."

If Tommy didn't accept that challenge immediately, Johnny would jerk Tommy's cap over his eyes or snatch it off and throw it on the ground. That was a mortal insult and if it didn't bring action it meant that Tommy was craven and Johnny might give him a contemptuous shove and walk off or twist his arm a little, just to emphasize his victory and the elevation of his social standing a degree.

This curious performance was probably an everyday occurrence somewhere in town. It was my misfortune as a small boy to look like a big-eyed innocent and consequently was selected as a soft touch by ambitious lads too often to be fun. No matter how the thing resulted, I never did come to enjoy particularly the feel of a fist against my nose.

Well, Missouri has no Sullivan Law, but gun-toting has simply gone out of favor. Except for non-resident thugs, no one has been arrested in Chillicothe with a gun on his hip in years. There have been no shooting scrapes, except in the Levee district, in years. Chief of Police Barrett can't remember a fist fight between men in the business or residential areas since he's been in the department. Again, there have been drunken brawls on the Levee, but they're not taken seriously.

Even the boys seem to have grown civilized or effete. According to school officials and leaders of youth activities, boys just don't fight much any more.

This fact is a little puzzling to me. In the movies, and especially in those pictures shown on Friday evenings and Saturdays for edification of youngsters, it's a rare reel without a fist fight. In the "comic" strips, the hero is always slugging someone out. And even in the slick paper magazines such as the *Saturday Evening Post* it's a dull issue without at least one graphic illustration of a muscular citizen clouting another.

It would seem boys would get the idea from these things that fist fighting is a normal way of life, that everyone except drips and lilies throws left hooks on the slightest provocation.

But the teachers and directors of sports and the kids themselves say that a real fist fight between boys is a rare thing indeed in Chillicothe these days.

Have modern boys gone soft? I don't believe so. I'm sure modern Chillicothe boys look sturdier and healthier than my generation did. A comparison of the interscholastic and intercollegiate athletic records of today with those of 1910 or 1912 would seem to indicate the improvement is not all in appearance. Part of this, I think, is in training, but I believe also that boys today eat better balanced meals and sleep more than we did. Consequently they, as a rule, are not as hot-tempered because their nerves are not as taut.

The school and Scout people in Chillicothe feel there is less fighting among boys now because basketball, baseball and other sports provide a more wholesome outlet for the normal competitive instinct.

As a rule, I believe, there is something wrong emotionally or physically or both with the man or boy who carries a chip on his shoulder. A well-adjusted, happy fellow is not naturally quarrelsome; he doesn't feel it necessary to prove something.

From about the middle of the first decade of the Twentieth Century until after the first World War, at least, a curious aberration simmered in the brains of perhaps a majority of young American males; it still exists to some extent in Hollywood and in the strange imaginations of some magazine writers, and it boils down to the stark proposition that a man's sexual attraction is in direct ratio to his physical strength and fighting ability.

I think I know where this came from. I think it stemmed from Charles Darwin's "natural selection" and Herbert Spencer's "survival of the fittest," but not directly, of course, because not many of the victims ever heard of Darwin or Spencer. The general idea was picked up and spread by that idol of the people, Theodore Roosevelt, with his *Strenuous Life,* and popularized by that voice of the period, Jack London, and other writers following the trail he broke.

The male animals fought to a gory finish while the gentle female stood by with parted lips, dilated nostrils and sparkling eyes, ready to give herself to the victor. It was all very elemental and red-blooded, and also pretty much nonsense.

Muscular young oafs used to fight it out over some lass and then be flabbergasted when she failed to follow fundamentals, and dropped the two of them for some entertaining lad with more common sense. Perhaps if she were a Ubangi maiden or Apache Squaw, she'd follow the script, but I'm not even sure of that.

It's been my observation that most girls prefer boys who know how to make themselves agreeable, who are poised and self-assured, but not *overly* self-assured, who can be gay or sympathetic, who show an ability to cope with the situation immediately surrounding them rather than the situation of 10,000 B.C.; and part of the situation immediately surrounding him is making the girl feel that she is very important indeed.

The hairy-chest school of writers, both Hollywood and magazine, to the contrary notwithstanding, I don't believe a normal Twentieth-Century girl ever got much of a thrill out of seeing a young man chin himself with one hand, lift a bale of cotton or leap twenty feet. I seriously doubt whether many young American women, in the throes of deepest love, could tell whether their sweetheart's biceps measure eleven inches or sixteen. Moreover, although she might have a particular reason for hating some individual violently and be especially happy if her Number One Hero beat the stuffing out of the odious fellow, I still think most girls would just as soon have the beating take place offstage and out of her sight.

I'll admit I have changed my own mind completely about all this since, say, 1917.

Perhaps much of this narrows down to the young folk taking a more realistic view of themselves than they did back in the good old days. Maybe they have a better sense of humor now. A sense of humor is a splendid preventive for fist fights, just as is a sense of proper perspective. The latter, at least, is largely a matter of education.

Even more important, probably, is the change in the American ideal from he-man to good joe. The pompous, swaggering, patronizing he-man, for all his nobility of character, hairy chest and flashing eye, could be pretty boring, and also, if the light struck him just right, more than a little ridiculous. The good joe is a reaction and antidote.

I think Will Rogers may have been the first public good joe—the ideal American whose laconic good humor could not be shaken, who was personally unassuming and always considerate of others, who could slay dragons with a gentle wit, who could stand on his own two feet with enormous calm in the face of potentate, catastrophe or personal insult; an effective champion of good causes but never shrill about it—sane, shyly self-possessed, genial and unexcited. Will Rogers himself was no exceptional phenomenon. But the American public's adulation of him was.

Although superficially quite unlike Will Rogers, Bing Crosby probably is Rogers' successor as the archetype good joe.

Mechancial developments—the movies and the radio—were responsible for a large part of the popularity of both Rogers and Crosby. Each had only one role to play—himself. And neither, by any stretch of the imagination, could ever have been romantic or dramatic. Their naturalness made the chesty posturing of "heroes" seem silly, yet they both became heroes to the American public in spite of themselves.

This, I believe, is very important. No people with the good joe ideal could go overboard for any totalitarian ideology or dictator.

The good joe doesn't take himself too seriously. He doesn't dramatize himself. He neither boasts nor whimpers. He plays the game and he knows the score, but he also is quite conscious that the game is a game and he has fun playing it. He does the best he can, but if he loses, tomorrow is still another day.

The good joe principle has captured the world of sports. The most popular figures in all lines of sport are good joes. If they are not good joes they're not popular, no matter how skilled they may be. The principle has been carried into factories, business houses, college campuses, high schools and, to some extent, into politics. The chest-beating demagogue doesn't impress the American people as he did at the turn of the century, and I suspect the success of Harry S. Truman in the 1948 election might be attributed to the fact that he went to the public with a minimum of theatrics and impressed people as a pretty good joe trying to do a job of work.

Having a sane sense of humor, the good joe naturally regards duels and fist fighting as infantile and ridiculous. Of course the archetype Crosby does find himself forced to swing a fist in some movies, but even then he avoids dramatics and keeps the thing in its proper sphere by combining the knockout with a game of patty-cake.

As far as I know there is no Society for the Advancement of Good Joeism to be credited for this development. As far as I know, it just grew by itself as a reaction to the Strenuous Life and demagogy in general, with assists to Will Rogers, Bing Crosby, Robert Benchley and a few others. In any event it is a very real element in American life today.

There is infinitely less downright churlishness among Americans now than there was forty years or so ago. When I was a young man and traveling around, one had to expect to be met with a certain amount of ill-bred rudeness. That was the lot of the stranger. As a snarl warrants a snarl in return, the exchange could bring a fighting word and fisticuffs.

I believe the enormous volume of motor travel these days, reaching the most remote sections of the country, has had much to do with improving American manners. Business people—gasoline filling stations, hotels, motor courts, restaurants—have learned that courtesy pays dividends. Their experience is absorbed by other members of their community. Good Joeism pays material dividends.

Yes, our manners have improved immensely in the last half century, and manners are a decidedly important part of culture.

X

KNIGHTS OF THE CADUCEUS

IN THE NARROWEST sense of the word, perhaps one wouldn't call medical science "culture."

But if you take the definition of Webster's New International Dictionary—"Conversance with and taste in fine arts, humanities, and broad aspects of science . . ."—medical science *is* culture, just as it will qualify under T. S. Eliot's "Culture may even be described simply as that which makes life worth living."

So if your family physician longs for the good old days when the Twentieth Century was aborning, you'd better hunt up a new doctor—a younger one.

In 1900 the medical profession was not longing for the good old days. It was looking back with satisfaction at a century of progress—probably the greatest one hundred years of progress since Claudius Galen invented the anodyne necklace sometime before A.D. 200.

In 1900 physicians not only had ceased trepanning to expel demons, but many had advanced far enough to smile at the medical theory current in 1800 that epidemics were caused by a "pestilential diathesis" of the atmosphere, often induced by a nearby comet or by a shower of meteors.

Competent doctors in 1900 knew epidemic diseases were contagious or infectious and that many of them had better be quarantined. They had learned that, despite the 1815 pronunciamento of Joseph A. Gallup, M.D., LLD., specialist in epidemic diseases and leader in the New England Medical Society. Dr. Gallup wrote of his twenty-five years' experience with epidemics and stated with some warmth, "Not in a single instance could the disease be traced to contagion. Diseases of the epidemic character cannot be propagated except under certain states of the air which favor their spreading. . . . Tedious and oppressive quarantines have been established to the great injury of commerce and annoyance of individuals, and these restrictions have their origin in a profound ignorance of the laws and principles that govern epidemic diseases."

The states of air causing epidemics, according to Dr. Gallup, were "mephitis" and "miasmata." Mephitis was the noxious exhalation from the bowels of the earth. Miasmata consisted of the "production of corrupting materials on or near the surface of the earth, whether vegetable or animal . . . in a state of slow or rapid decomposition."

By 1900 practically all practitioners had discarded mephitis as a cause of disease. But many were still clinging to miasmata as the cause of such diseases as malaria and typhoid fever. In 1900 the more enlightened medical men knew malaria was contracted by the sting of the anopheles mosquito, but to the public at large and to at least one of the leading physicians of Chillicothe, Missouri, it was the result of breathing "miasmic mists," especially at night. Thousands of general practitioners had learned it that way at medical school, and they were not going to be quick to pick up new fads.

In 1900 practitioners generally had ceased to regard bleeding as mandatory treatment for such maladies as tuberculosis, diphtheria and typhoid fever, although failure to bleed a patient and bleed him copiously, seventy-five or eighty years earlier, could and did brand some well-meaning physicians with the damning appellation of "quack."

Dr. John C. Warren, a noted physician of the early Nineteenth Century, writing in the *New England Journal of Medicine and Surgery* for July, 1813, was caustic in his scorn of practitioners who showed timidity in bleeding pneumonia patients. After relating numerous instances where patients died because they were not bled sufficiently, Dr. Warren quoted a happier instance by a Dr. Gredley: "One patient, who had apparently a moderate attack of pneumonia, was bled once and took a cathartic. The disease changed to the bowels, resembling enteritis [typhoid]. On the eighth day of the illness, I drew about three quarts of blood at two bleedings, which relieved him. About twenty-four hours later he sent for me in haste and said he must be bled again. He now lost twenty-four ounces of sizy blood, which again relieved him. The bowels now became pervious, and the patient recovered."

This patient of Dr. Gredley's was obviously quite a man.

One of our great national heroes, especially to nostalgia merchants, is "Old Doc," plowing indomitably through storm and snowdrift to draw three quarts of blood from a gasping patient and thus drive death from the door of some remote farmhouse.

Well, Dr. Gredley was very sure of himself and Dr. Warren was very sure of himself and Dr. Gallup was very sure of himself.

Likewise, good Old Doc, the family physician in 1900, was very sure of himself on any subject confronting him, and able to pontificate in learned double-talk to impress the patient and his family. Precisely because of this act, Old Doc of 1900 was sometimes a pretty good faith healer or witch doctor but as far as being a scientific practitioner is concerned, any pink-cheeked, reasonably bright interne today is ten times the physician Old Doc was in his palmiest days.

Not that Old Doc of 1900, as well as Old Doc of any time in the Nineteenth Century, wasn't frequently a self-sacrificing hero. He was subject to call at any hour of day or night with no thought of weather or road conditions. A large proportion of his work was frankly charity work for which he had no hope of pay. Many other patients were charged just enough to give Old Doc day-laborer's wages for his time.

Yet Old Doc usually did manage to own about the best house in town.

While he probably had no access to an x-ray machine and certainly not to a fluoroscope, Old Doc could set and splint a broken bone with dispatch. He could administer cathartics with enthusiasm, for in the medical theory of the time a purging was indicated as the first order of the day in treatment of almost any malady under the sun. He carried on his clothing the scent of iodoform, in his black bag a portable pharmacy ranging from morphine sulphate through quinine and nux vomica to soda-mint tablets, in his manly beard whatever microorganisms his last patient had coughed into it, and under his fingernails a reasonable cargo of tetanus bacilli from old Bess' stable.

In his heart Old Doc carried the Oath of Hippocrates, which he regarded as sacred and which he lived about as closely to as humanly possible:

"To please no one will I prescribe a deadly drug, nor give advice which might cause death.

"I will not administer to a woman to perform abortion.

"I will preserve the purity of my life and art.

"In every house I enter, I will come for good only, keeping myself from ill-doing and seduction.

"All that may come before my knowledge in the exercise of my profession or outside which ought not to be spread abroad, I will keep secret and never reveal."

Old Doc, by and large, was a pretty sincere, honest and admirable citizen. He also was a good, practical psychologist, and the beard and black-ribboned pince-nez and grave dignity and bedside manner and scientific double-talk were all part of a routine deemed necessary to make his people accept his guesses as Gospel.

It is not my purpose to detract from the honors lavished on Old Doc. It is my purpose only to give an inkling of the tremendous advances made by medical science in the last half century, advances which not only save countless lives but relieve suffering and prevent disease.

The general use of diphtheria toxin-antitoxin together with the Bela Schick test is a case in point.

Before the turn of the Century diphtheria or, as it was sometimes called, membranous croup, was a national scourge. Epidemics, like the Pied Piper, would sweep away children, killing more than fifty per cent of those it touched. In one such epidemic three of my cousins died in two days. A young neighbor girl was strangling to death and their particular Old Doc, lacking proper surgical instruments, took out his jackknife and, without wasting time to sterilize it, performed a tracheotomy then and there. The child recovered with nothing worse than a bad scar on her throat possibly because Old Doc ordinarily used the knife to cut his chewing tobacco.

Although the diphtheria bacillus was first recognized by Edwin Klebs in 1883 and experiments with antitoxins began in 1884, Dr. William H. Welch, professor of pathology at Johns Hopkins, could write a monograph on diphtheria in 1900 which was distinguished mostly for its vague assumption that the disease was infectious rather than contagious and that it "may occur as a complication of scarlet fever, measles and other infectious diseases." But Dr. Welch himself did great work in the development of toxin-antitoxin as well as in revolutionary discoveries in treating gas gangrene.

In the last fifty years medical science—utilizing public health programs and Schick tests in the schools—has cornered the once fearsome ogre of diphtheria and whittled him down to a shadow.

Old Doc in 1900 never had heard of an allergy and his best information on asthma was "a disturbance of the function of breathing, usually a neurotic affection, but sometimes due to heart or kidney disease." Old Doc had little patience with hypochondriacs and was inclined to believe asthma came from a run-down condition and uncontrolled nervousness. So he tried to build up asthmatics with cod-liver oil, malt extract, milk and eggs, iron and nux vomica. This treatment was so completely logical that Old Doc was inclined to be disgusted with a patient if he failed to co-operate and get well. Of course not many asthmatics did respond, unless the disturbing element—ragweed, horses or whatever—was removed.

But asthma never killed many people. It merely made them

miserable and tore down their resistance so they fell prey to any virulent bug that came their way.

Tuberculosis was the great killer at the turn of the Century, and the work of the various public health agencies in education and in the prevention and cure of the old "white plague" is too well known to need emphasis here. Enough that the death rate from tuberculosis in the United States, as a whole, for the year 1900 was 202 per 100,000 population. For the year 1947 that figure had been reduced to 33.4 per 100,000 population, according to U. S. Public Health Service figures.

This tremendous improvement does not mean tuberculosis has been whipped yet. Considering the fact that the victims are almost all young, the death rate is still shockingly high, although only one-sixth of the 1900 toll. The remarkable reduction in fifty years has been effected largely through preventive measures, although an early diagnosis is of paramount importance.

In 1900 Old Doc simply was incapable of making an early diagnosis. Practically his only method was listening for rales with his stethoscope and guessing. Usually his patient was spitting blood before Old Doc pronounced the dire word, "consumption," and he believed that form of nephritis called "Bright's Disease" was consumption of the kidneys.

While the bacillus had been discovered by Koch in 1882, Old Doc wasn't quite certain of the nature or cause of the "tubercles," except that he took it for granted the disease could be inherited from either mother or father just as syphilis could be inherited. And Old Doc was positive of the latter.

As to treatment for consumption, Old Doc had just one prescription—go to a dry, invigorating climate. If the patient couldn't do that, he'd better make his peace with God.

In 1900 Old Doc often was reluctant to treat that syphilis thing, regarding it as a judgment of God and believing it might be presumptuous of him to interfere. If a stranger came to him suffering from gonorrhea Old Doc was inclined to blurt out that he was no "clap doctor" and send the fellow into the hands of the quack "specialists."

While Fritz Schaudinn did not discover the *Spirocheta* until 1905, medical science had definite ideas about syphilis in 1900. So had the general public.

One conviction was: "The wages of sin is death. . . ."

Another conviction, widely quoted, was: "The sins of the father shall be visited upon the children unto the third and fourth generations."

That first conviction was from Romans VI, 23. I don't know the source of the second conviction, although it always was credited confidently to the Holy Writ. It seems to be a combination of Euripides: "The gods visit the sins of the fathers upon the children," and Exodus XX, 5—". . . I the Lord thy God am a jealous God, visiting the iniquity of the fathers upon the children unto the third and fourth generation of them that hate me."

In any event, it was taken to mean that the "unmentionable" disease, which was called the "old ral" in vulgar circles, could be inherited and passed down in the blood of grandchildren and great-grandchildren. Of course August Wassermann did not perfect his blood test until after Dr. Schaudinn discovered the corkscrew microbe, but five years earlier Dr. Prince A. Morrow, author of *Relations of Social Disease and Marriage,* could write authoritatively that "syphilis may be transmitted directly from the father, the mother remaining healthy." And "Syphilis may be transmitted by direct inheritance through the specifically infected sperm or ovule at the time of impregnation."

Dr. Morrow also wrote what now seems to be a scientific non sequitur: "Absolute proof of the curability of syphilis is furnished by the fact that an individual may have a second attack of the disease, showing that he has recovered from the first."

This all was some ten years before Paul Ehrlich's laboratory developed salvarsan in its six hundred and sixth experiment, the first practical specific for syphilis. Before that the treatment consisted of a mercury preparation and the Old Docs had a punning wisecrack about it: "Ten minutes with Venus and ten months with Mercury."

Whether mercury ever actually cured a syphilitic would seem decidedly questionable. There was no way of knowing without an adequate blood test.

Syphilis is known as the "Great Simulator," because it may assume the appearance of any number of other maladies and, without a reliable blood test, diagnosis was mostly guesswork. Old Doc of 1900 had a natural reluctance to brand a friend syphilitic on mere suspicion, and countless thousands died of syphilis under the more respectable aegis of heart disease, cerebral hemorrhage or whatnot.

The earliest possible accurate figure on the toll of syphilis in the United States is for 1910 when the U.S. Public Health Service published it as 13.5 per 100,000 population. It can be assumed that if the truth were known this figure would be much higher. In 1947 the published toll was 8.9 per 100,000 population. Without a doubt the later figure is nearer the truth, but probably a lot of syphilis fatalities still find their way into the heart and circulatory departments.

Of course, we know now, while infants may be infected by mothers, that syphilis is no more inherited than a broken leg may be inherited, that the unborn baby's blood stream is independent of the mother's. So it is quite fortunate that the new "magic" drugs will cure the disease quicker and even more definitely than salvarsan, if taken in reasonable time, because the victim no longer has a creditable alibi.

About the time the *Spirocheta* was being discovered we had a God-fearing neighbor who was far along with locomotor ataxia. I discovered I could imitate Mr. Brillig's loose-kneed, slap-footed gait, which the other boys thought was very funny indeed. But when my father caught me in my act he whipped me so I would remember never to mock a poor Christian gentleman who was only suffering for the sins of his grandfather. In a hushed voice my father explained to me that Grandfather Brillig was reputed to have been a sinful man and that God visited the sins of the fathers upon the children unto the third and fourth generations. He did not specify Grandfather Brillig's sins, but I assumed they were drinking beer and playing cards and I felt sorry for Mr. Brillig and never walked like him again.

If anyone feels that diagnosis, treatment and prevention of syphilis has not improved in the last fifty years, that legislation of progressive states requiring a blood test before issuance of a marriage license is not a good thing, that the public attitude toward venereal disease in general is not wiser now than it was in 1900, and that these things do not make for better living conditions and, in short, for advancement of culture, then that person is convinced that syphilis is a visitation from God which must not be denied and he isn't subject to argument.

The 1900 Old Doc's medical library probably dated mostly from the time he was graduated from medical school and he was far too busy to keep up with all the ephemeral fads of the day. There's a good chance that the 1900 Old Doc classed syphilis as blood poisoning along with a whole array of mysterious and apparently incurable maladies.

Old Doc realized the importance of the blood, just as did the ancients. He knew human blood consisted of plasma, red cells, leucocytes, "blood plates" and some other mysterious things. He knew what the red cells and leucocytes were for, and if he had a 1900 book, it described the platelets (whose disintegration when exposed to air or foreign matter causes clotting) in this manner: "Little is known of their function. They are thought to be globulin-like in nature, and of use in the phenomenon of coagulation; others claim them as nucleo-proteids, made from the white blood cells."

The *American Cyclopaedia,* edited by George Ripley and Charles A. Dana and published in 1881, contains an article by an unidentified medical scientist which presumably holds the sum of 1881 human knowledge concerning the blood.

This article devoted a good deal of space to a comparative analysis of men's blood and women's. A table, compiled by Becquerel and Rodier, is provided showing the difference in fibrine content, phosphorized fatty matter, cholesterine and animal soap and, while both sexes were identical in fibrine, it appeared that man had the edge in phosphorized fatty matter and woman was clearly the superior in cholesterine and animal soap. These findings seem to have been regarded as of considerable scientific importance.

Perhaps of even greater significance was the discovery of a certain Dr. Barruel that if he added sulphuric acid to human blood he could detect immediately from the resulting odor whether the blood was male or female. The *Cyclopaedia* writer observed regretfully that this discovery had its limitations because "very few have the organ of smell sensitive enough for this purpose."

Well, Old Doc was a sensitive man and he felt his educated fingertips were all the sphygmomanometer he needed in detecting high or low blood pressure. He also knew how to determine the sex of a patient without going to the trouble of adding sulphuric acid to the blood and sniffing it.

He knew about attempts at blood transfusion and the fatal results. But it was not until 1907 that Dr. George W. Crile, the endocrinology pioneer, was successful in avoiding clotting by making direct transfusions between the donor's artery and the patient's vein and not until 1914 that the Argentine, L. Agote, found that sodium citrate added to the donor's blood was an effective anti-coagulant. Development of the dehydrated plasma system and discovery of the RH factor later reduced the patient's unfavorable reaction to an insignificant minimum.

For Old Doc in 1900 the whole vast field of endocrinology and biologicals was unexplored territory, a mysterious realm only half suspected by imaginative pioneers.

The first hormone, adrenalin, was isolated in 1901 by the Japanese-American, Dr. Jokichi Takamine, but a generation was to pass before anything much was done about it.

It was not until 1923 that Dr. Frederick G. Banting of Toronto discovered insulin, the hormone which allows diabetics to live long, useful and practically normal lives instead of wasting away to certain death.

A curious thing about diabetes mellitus is that it was considered a rare disease in America in 1900, although more common in Europe. I don't know whether that was a matter of faulty diagnosis.

In 1900 typhoid fever was one of the great killers in America. Although the bacillus was discovered in 1880 by the German, Karl Eberth, little was known in the United States twenty years later of how the disease was transmitted.

In 1903 Dr. Jerome Walker, author of *Walker's Physiology,* wrote that among the causes of typhoid fever were "excess in eating, drinking, want of sleep and too much mental work. . . . It is believed that the blood of such persons has undergone some chemical change which has diminished its bacterial quality and so lowered its inherent power of resistance to disease."

He added: "Some believe that the bacilli are conveyed by air to the respiratory mucous membrane, and that their initial colonization takes place there rather than in the gastro-intestinal tract."

And of course any grade school physiology pupil knows better than that today.

Partial immunity, at least, may be gained by inoculation, but the greatest progress in prevention of typhoid and para-typhoid has been in matters of sanitation and avoidance of contaminated drinking water. Typhoid, of course, is not contagious but infectious and the bacilli must gain entrance to the intestinal tract.

In about 1904 a neighbor of ours died of typhoid fever and his particular Old Doc, puzzled why this hardy gentleman should have been struck down in his early middle life, sought the cause. Mr. Rawlins was not given to excesses in eating or drinking. He had not been losing sleep nor engaging in too much mental work. But Old Doc, prowling around, discovered the family ice box was on the back porch, and that Mr. Rawlins, annoyed at the necessity of emptying the ice-box drip pan night and morning, had bored a hole in the porch floor, inserted a big tin funnel and allowed the melting ice to run under the latticed-in porch. This ingenious device, said Old Doc, cost Mr. Rawlins his life. Beneath the porch he had found a mass of slime, and emanations from that slime must have found their way into the house to be breathed by their victim. Why the wife and three sons, who were home a great deal more than the husband and father, were not stricken also did not bother Old Doc. He had learned in his youth of the dangers of miasma and he had been far too busy to learn that that old myth had been exploded.

He and most of the rest of the Old Docs of the day also believed firmly that the typhoid patient must have nothing to eat and virtually nothing to drink until "the roses disappeared from his belly."

Instead of keeping the patient's strength up and protecting the typhoid ulcers from the digestive juices with bland food, Old Doc turned the case into a table-stakes game between the bacilli and the patient's vitality. The cards were stacked slightly in favor of the bacilli. If he survived, it was common for a rugged, average-sized man to come out of typhoid fever a feeble skeleton weighing less than one hundred pounds.

At the turn of the Century typhoid epidemics could be expected somewhere in the United States every few years. Thousands died in the great epidemics of 1890 and 1900 in Chicago and Philadelphia, and in Ithaca in 1903.

By 1910 the patient had a somewhat better chance because it had been discovered it wasn't fatal to allow the feverish sufferer something to drink.

In 1910, according to U.S. Public Health Service figures, the typhoid death rate was 22.5 per 100,000 population. By 1947 that figure had been reduced to .3 per 100,000 population. In other words, for every typhoid fatality in 1947 there were approximately sixty-nine in 1910, on, of course, a per capita basis.

Likewise the death toll from pneumonia was 141.7 per 100,000 population in 1910 and 38 in 1947; from scarlet fever 11.4 in 1910 and .1 in 1947; and whooping cough's fatalities had been cut from 11.6 to 1.2.

In 1946 a child born in America had more than three and a half times better chance of living past its first year than one born in

1900, for the death rate of infants had been reduced from 162.4 per 1,000 births to 45.3.

The mother in 1946 had four times as good a chance of surviving childbirth as she had in 1912, as the maternal death rate had been reduced in those thirty-four years from 15 per 100,000 population to 3.7.

Surgery probably has advanced as much or more in the last fifty years than any other branch of medical science.

While there are seemingly authentic accounts of remarkable surgical operations hundreds of years before Christ in Egypt, India and Greece, superstitious prejudices caused virtual abandonment of the art. Reverence for the dead created such public abhorrence of dissection that surgeons could learn their trade only in secret and at considerable personal peril.

Even as late as 1788, when word got out that a dissection was being performed in New York Hospital, a mob stormed the building and in the ensuing riot seven were killed. The physicians and medical students were jailed.

The first famous American surgical operation came in 1831 when Dr. Philip Syng Physick at Philadelphia removed something like a hatful of stones from the bladder of Chief Justice John Marshall. Marshall lived four years after the operation, but didn't feel very well.

In 1849 Ignatz Semmelweiss was driven from Vienna by antagonistic colleagues and he died insane. In charge of the Vienna maternity hospital, he had insisted that physicians and other attendants wash their hands in chlorinated lime water instead of plain soap and water, and had reduced the maternity mortality rate from 16 per cent to 1.7 per cent.

In 1867 Joseph Lister first published the result of his experiments in vivisection and, in the Glasgow hospital, of his use of the first antiseptic catgut sutures (which virtually eliminated secondary hemorrhages from most operations) and of his performing the first aseptic surgery through use of carbolic acid.

While even the ancients had used opium and cannabis indica for relief of pain, and while nitrous oxide gas and ether were tried in 1844 and 1846 respectively by the dentists, Horace Wells of Hartford and W. T. G. Morton of Boston, hundreds of thousands of amputations and other major surgical operations were performed during the American Civil War without anesthetics and with no antiseptic care whatever. Some of the patients recovered—those with remarkably belligerent leucocytes.

Even with the foundations laid, it took more than a generation of experiments, many of them fatal, for safe methods of anesthesia to be developed. And the technique of antiseptic surgery had to be learned, tested, argued and finally taught to a new crop of medical students who in turn experimented, failed, succeeded and passed on their findings and skills.

At the turn of the century most of the Old Docs of America, never quick to seize upon innovations, were decades behind their times. Old Doc usually listed himself as "Physician and Surgeon," but, viewed by modern standards, his fingers were too fumbling and clumsy for anything except the most elementary scalpel work. More likely than not he never had a pair of rubber gloves on his hands, he certainly never wore a gauze mask over his mouth, nose and beard while operating. To him the methods of suturing blood vessels developed by George W. Crile and Alexis Carrel would have seemed humanly impossible.

In fact, while surgery was just starting its incredible advance in 1900, Old Doc, by and large, was little better fitted to perform a major operation than was Gus the corner butcher. I suppose Old Doc's surgery saved lives. But I fear it also took them.

During the first decade of the Twentieth Century appendicitis became practically a fad. To the public it was append*iseed*is and it was popularly believed to be caused by grape seeds or berry seeds working their way into the vermiform appendix and sprouting there.

Even today it is my understanding that the best of surgeons cannot be certain in diagnosing appendicitis. Although there may be an abnormally high white blood count, fever, boardlike rigidity of the abdomen and extreme tenderness in the right lower quadrant of the belly in the classic symptoms of acute appendicitis, the appendix itself still may prove to be perfectly normal and white.

But during the appendi*seed*is uproar at the beginning of the Century a lot of the country-town Old Docs were going into peritoneums with all the confidence of a farm wife cutting a cake.

I don't know whether they died of peritonitis, secondary hemorrhage, operative shock or what, but I do know six children of my acquaintance failed to survive appendectomies in that period. Four of them were particularly rugged, red-cheeked country boys. No doubt there were others who lost their appendices and still lived. But I don't remember them.

Actually, I doubt if it is much of an exaggeration to say that surgery has advanced as far in the last forty years as aviation. Which indeed is quite an advance.

I have not mentioned the progress in treatment of mental ills because there seems to be confusion as to how far psychiatry may have wandered on unrewarding tangents. At the beginning of the century psychiatrists were called alienists and they devoted themselves largely to treatment of mental derangements.

In 1900 Baron Krafft-Ebing had published his classification of mental ills which was generally accepted, as well as his *Psychopathia Sexualis*. Sigmund Freud was working with Josef Breuer in Vienna and experimenting with hypnotism on hysterical subjects.

Then there was less tendency to confine the deranged or feeble-minded until they exhibited actual criminality. Then as now there was a great dearth of trained psychiatrists and competent asylum attendants. There was little opportunity for a psychiatrist to become wealthy by bringing comfort to rich neurotics and hypochondriacs; he was doomed to a life of unremitting toil at meager salary in the drab environment of a mental institution.

The "shock treatment," which seems to have effected some cures, especially among manic-depressives, had not been invented. Of much greater importance, virtually nothing was known of the ductless glands' effect on mental health—and vice versa.

There are many intelligent people, and even professionals, who believe greater progress has been made in psychiatry than in any other branch of medicine. I personally do not feel competent to take part in the argument.

In Chillicothe today there are ten practicing physicians and surgeons, including a clinic; four optometrists, three osteopaths and seven dentists. As I suppose is inevitable in a midwestern town, Chillicothe also has its share of chiropractors and a Christian Science practitioner.

Most of the doctors, I am told, are competent and alert to the advances constantly being made by medical science, through reading their professional magazines and by attending conventions.

But the greatest improvement in the field of medicine since my day is the Chillicothe Hospital.

When I was a boy the only hospital facilities in Livingston County were at St. Mary's Hospital, a small wooden building quite primitive in its equipment and operation. In those times no one went to the hospital unless his condition was desperate. Then he was carried there by friends on a cot or unhinged door. There was no ambulance in the county. I knew several who were carried to St. Mary's in that manner, and, while I have no thought that any would have lived otherwise, none of those I knew left the hospital alive.

Chillicothe now has a beautiful, modern three-story brick municipal hospital up on Eleventh Street efficiently operated with the finest of equipment.

I believe it interesting how the town got this hospital.

In 1911 bonds were voted and Chillicothe bought the privately owned electric light plant. In 1915 more bonds were voted for the purchase of the water company. Although antiquated equipment was replaced and rates lowered materially for both water and electricity, the public-owned utilities still made sufficient profit to retire the bonds, which included one million dollars for the improved power and light plant.

Electric rates ranged from one cent to 4 cents a kilowatt hour and water rates from fifteen cents to forty cents a thousand gallons under municipal management. These rates would have been lowered even more when the water and electric plants were paid for, but the City Council voted to continue the rates and build up a surplus for public works.

Despite opposition from certain factions which believed a hospital should be operated by charitable donations or by religious organizations, this gleaming new hospital was built and paid for by profits from the municipally operated water and electric plants.

No longer are patients carried on a shutter or cot. There are three ambulance services in town.

I don't see how even a moon-struck esthete could deny that this new hospital marks more than material progress. To my mind, also, the way Chillicothe got the hospital is an example of democracy working at its best.

Generally speaking, I suppose the most spectacular development in recent years lies in the field of so-called "magic medicines." Developments have been coming so very fast that even practicing physicians find it difficult to keep up with the march, and Dr. Perrin Hamilton Long of the United States Public Health Service predicts that the next five years may well see the whole spectrum of infection wiped from the slate. The sulfa drugs and the antibiotics such as penicillin and streptomycin and aureomycin already have saved countless lives and relieved untold suffering, slaughtering microbes, including the coccus family, in wholesale fashion and even discouraging a goodly array of ambitious viruses.

If human life is worth anything, if physical pain is something to be avoided, the development of these magic drugs alone proves that medical science has advanced the cause of worldly happiness and, yes, of culture, immeasurably in the last fifty years.

Also of some importance is the development by the United States Army Medical Department of the drug called Dramamine, which will enable all pallid-browed esthetes who deplore America to go to Europe with little danger of sea-sickness.

Perhaps some will be disposed to point to the large increase in fatalities from diseases of the heart and circulatory system as well as from cancer since 1900. But if we don't die young we must all eventually fall victim to degenerative processes. However, medical science not only has been learning so much about the nature of cancer that victory in this fight seems almost inevitable, but is making great progress in geriatrics, which can make growing old more comfortable.

In 1900 the life expectancy at birth of white males in America was 48.2 years, of white females 51.1 years.

Figures released by the United States Public Health Service in 1949 for the year 1947 showed that the life expectancy of white males in America had increased to 65.2 years, and for white females to 70.6 years.

Better than anything else, those figures tell the story.

XI

"SWEET AND HONEY'D SENTENCES"

THE MARKED DECLINE of oratory and particularly of elocution in the last fifty years is, to my mind, a signal advancement in American culture.

At the turn of the Century oratory was regarded as a high art over most of America. It actually was an interesting exercise in mob psychology.

The skilled orator with his flow of rhythmic sentences, augmented by "appropriate gestures," has a potency unrivaled even by jungle tom-toms in stirring the emotions of a primitive audience. Oratory, indeed, has much in common with the tom-tom inasmuch as even a reasonably civilized individual may find himself curiously stirred by its beat though he does not appreciate the significance of a single passage. White auditors of the Seneca chief, Red Jacket, reported themselves "swept away" by his eloquence although understanding no word of his tongue, and that, I believe, is the supreme test of the orator.

The prime purpose of oratory is to make gray appear to be deepest black or purest white, according to the purposes of the orator. The tricks of elocution—quavering voice, pauses, dramatic whisper, dreamy nuances, challenging bellow, plus the standard gestures signifying disdain, apprehension, reverence, righteous anger and a couple of dozen other shadings of emotion—are the tools of his trade with which he fashions the gaudiest hyperbole to dull the intellect and enflame the passions of his auditors.

While orators seem to grow in most primitive tribes, perhaps the earliest in written history was Gorgias, the Sicilian, who in the fifth century, B.C., appears to have been the father of Sophistry as well as the orginator of both the Sicilian and Greek schools of oratory. He talked the Athenians into coming to the defense of Leontini against the Syracusans and then talked the Greeks into relinquishing the property they had appropriated. He went to Athens and opened a school of rhetoric which inoculated Antiphon and Isocrates, Socrates and Plato, among others, with the elegant Sicilian roll which was reflected a century and a half later on Aristotle and consequently bounced down through such Romans as Cicero to dominate what used to be called the "classical education" in America, meaning that a college student was crammed to the gunnels with Greek and Latin language and lore, a little mathematics, perhaps a smattering of French or German, a sectarian adulation of the King James version of the Bible, then dubbed bachelor of arts and turned loose on the world as a man of superior education but in practical matters not knowing a gusset from a gasket and no better fitted for a happy, worth-while life than if he had spent his four academic years in a cataleptic trance.

Like the Russian thistle, English sparrow and Japanese beetle, oratory found the climate of America especially favorable for prosperous development, and by the middle of the Nineteenth Century nearly every crossroads hamlet had its local Demosthenes ready to spring to his feet with an impassioned oration when any occasion from a dog fight to a fete day attracted a dozen listeners.

The old lyceums nurtured the art and virtually every academy and secondary school in the land emphasized the importance of training, not in clear, logical speech, but in elocution. Colleges were not content to conduct classes but maintained *schools* of oratory, complete with deans.

As Robert Irving Fulton, dean of the school of oratory, Ohio Wesleyan University, wrote in 1900:

"The oration, as we conceive it, is the loftiest type of public speech and it marks the highest attainment of the public speaker. It is dignified and formal in style, clear in logic, forceful in thought, sound in philosophy, eloquent in language, emotive and persuasive in spirit, and, withal, it is constructed with the plot and motive of a great drama. It gathers up the salient facts of history and experience bearing upon the subject discussed, holds them up in the searchlight of the present day and generation, and weaves them into the fabric of the future. It moves the audience by persuasive, climactic impulses and stirs men to action. It must spring from the orator's own conviction and bring a message that is genuine, unmistakable and generally optimistic. Its object is to educate and inspire the masses, elevate the standards of morality and citizenship, or bring about great civic reforms and national movements. The stamp of its influence is clear in the national life and character of the past, it is a vital, living force in the civil policy of the present, and its promise of power and usefulness in the future is so great that it should be placed on the curriculum of every college and university that lays claims to a thorough preparation of youth for the duties and responsibilities of life."

Every college-trained orator acknowledged his debt to ancient Greece and Rome any time he got his feet on a platform, and he knew a great deal more about Pericles, Cicero, and the Delphian Oracle than he knew about Sir Thomas Gresham, Newton, William Pitt or John Marshall.

The orator was the American Great Man in frock coat and black slouch hat. He was pompous and peripatetic and he had a way of popping up in surprising places such as new mining camps and cattle towns in the West, delivering an oration and attaching to the squalid community of shacks and tents such classical appellations as Thermopolis, Syracuse, Athens, Ulysses, Apollo, Aurora, Attica, Urbana, Utica or Utopia.

From Patrick Henry through Daniel Webster, Edward Everett and James G. Blaine up to William Jennings Bryan the mark of an American statesman was his ability to sway a crowd, inflate its prejudices, arouse its anger, and by the shrewd employment of catchwords and rolling rhetoric, submerge rational thought until each auditor became merely one drop in a wave of mob emotion.

Bryan may have been the greatest American orator of all time. One can't tell by reading speeches because it's the delivery, not the content of the oration, which is important. Certainly at the top of his career Bryan possessed all possible attributes—the personal magnetism, a magnificent voice, an *incredible* voice, an unusual gift for the catch phrase and for rhetorical platitudes that seemed to be profundities as they sprang from his lips, an acute sense of the dramatic and an actor's memory, and an education which may have been pretty shaky on everything since the reign of Constantine but was well-grounded in Greek, Latin and the Holy Writ.

Bryan employed his talents to the fullest and, while they failed to take him quite to the White House, it is no exaggeration to say many of his followers suspected he was the reincarnation of Jesus Christ.

My father became acquainted with Bryan when they both were working in 1888 for the candidacy of J. Sterling Morton for Representative from the First Nebraska Congressional District. Morton (the originator of Arbor Day) was defeated in this Republican district, but twenty-eight-year-old Bryan, fresh from Illinois, sold himself to the Democrats of the region and particularly to my father.

I remember as a young boy hearing my father tell frequently of hearing for the first time the "Boy Orator of the Platte" speak in behalf of Morton. My father would say, "That young man hadn't spoken a dozen words before I knew he had been picked by God for a great work. I said to myself, 'There's no doubt about it. There stands the future President of the United States.' "

My father was a man of some standing in his own small community, and it is possible that the ambitious young lawyer took cognizance of that in making friends. At least they did become friends and hunting companions. I would have no idea what Bryan, who read both Greek and Latin fluently and who could quote Shakespeare and Milton by the rod, pole or perch, talked about to the horseman and hamlet merchant as they huddled behind a duck blind in a chill dawn. It may have been about bimetallism or the tariff or the rights of labor and the farmer or the teachings of Christ or prohibition or all these things, but whatever it was, Bryan was mighty convincing and my father became his devoted disciple.

Bryan cannot have been as sternly selective as was Jesus in Luke XIV, 26: "If any man come to me, and hate not his father, and mother, and wife, and children, and brethren, and sisters, yea, and his own life also, he cannot be my disciple."

Or even as in Luke XIV, 33: "So likewise, whosoever he be of you that forsaketh not all that he hath, he cannot be my disciple."

My father did not actually forsake anything. But in what he considered the interest of humanity at large he merely let his prosperous general store, furniture store, farm and tin shop run themselves while he devoted his energies to the promotion of this Man of Destiny, particularly in his little four-page weekly newspaper.

In 1890 thirty-year-old William J. Bryan was nominated for Congress by the First Nebraska District on a plank he wrote himself:

"We demand the free coinage of silver on equal terms with gold and denounce the effort of the Republican Party to serve the interests of Wall Street against the rights of the people."

The Republican incumbent, W. J. Connell, heard Bryan speak on free silver and publicly admitted he was convinced. He practically resigned under the fire of the "silver-tongued" orator and the Republican district sent a Democrat to Congress.

Such was the charm of this wavy-maned young man with the flashing black eyes, and so lulling, so soporific, so inspiring, so reasonable, so actually seismic was the power of that caressing, crooning, booming baritone voice in those days that his men followers were ready to die for him and women fainted in his presence.

Whether Senator William McKinley of Ohio ever heard Congressman Bryan speak in the Lower House is uncertain, but Senator McKinley somehow became converted to the free silver doctrine and was only weaned from his folly some years later when National Chairman Marcus Hanna bedazzled his soft brown eyes with a picture of undreamed-of splendor in the White House.

In any event Bryan was re-elected to Congress in 1892, but was defeated for the Senate in 1894 by John Mellen Thurston, chairman of the Republican national convention of 1892.

In 1895 my father's varied business interests had tangled themselves into such an unhappy snarl that he sold out and traded out of the mess to the best of his ability, acquired a grain elevator and weekly newspaper in the tiny town of Wheeling, Missouri, and moved from Nebraska.

I have suspected that my father may have been disappointed in Bryan's not calling him into the inner councils. But if this were true my father never spoke of it in my hearing, and certainly his loyalty to the silver-tongued orator was not diminished. The famous "Cross of Gold" speech came at the Chicago National Convention of 1896, followed by nomination of the thirty-six-year-old Bryan for the Presidency, but because I was only two years old at the time my knowledge of the campaign comes only from what I have heard and read.

Little local news was published in the Wheeling *Sun* that summer and fall, for this small weekly was devoted to the printing of speeches delivered over the country by the Honorable W. J. Bryan and to florid panegyrics of the Democratic candidate by C. N. Davis, editor and prop.

There seems little doubt now that Bryan's principal plank, the free silver issue, was economically and politically unsound. This, together with his unswerving devotion to old-time religion and literal belief of every word in the King James Bible are largely responsible for history's characterization of him as being "muddleheaded," "deficient in a sense of reality," and "profoundly ignorant of history, great literature and economics." It is largely forgotten that Bryan *did* sponsor some other things which were regarded at that time as socialistic or anarchistic, and among them were direct election of senators, a federal income tax, the eight-hour working day, and woman suffrage, and that he condemned the use of injunctions in labor disputes as well as the use of federal troops in breaking strikes.

Bryan sponsored these things and other revolutionary pieces of legislation which are taken for granted a half century later, but I believe there is ample evidence to show they were all abstractions to the "Great Commoner," minor abstractions which went to make up the Great Abstraction in which he lived. From what I know of Mr. Bryan, I suspect he lived mostly in a dream world, a dream which was broken pleasantly three times a day by the dinner bell.

But no matter how far-sighted and progressive were some of the measures advocated by the young Bryan, he will be remembered for his astonishingly reactionary, fundamentalist stand at the 1925 Scopes trial in Dayton, Tennessee, his final campaign on earth, when he snapped petulantly at opposing counsel, Clarence Darrow, that calling man a mammal was an insult to American womanhood. Darrow, the calm, devilishly shrewd jury lawyer, turned this trial against school teacher John T. Scopes into a circus by consistently maneuvering Bryan out of position and needling him into making ridiculous statements.

One evening some time later, Clarence Darrow, carefully nurturing the one highball he allowed himself, was discussing the "monkey trial" and I said it had been a great shock to me because I had been brought up to revere the Great Commoner.

Mr. Darrow looked at me with mild eyes and his lean, sallow face twisted into a smile. "It was a shock to me, too," he said. "Bryan had many admirable qualities. I'm sorry now that I poured it on the old man so hard, very sorry. But the truth never entered my mind really until he denied so emphatically that man is a mammal. Then I knew and it was a great shock, especially with him only sixty-five and three years younger than I. I should have realized earlier that this was not the 'Silver-Tongued Orator of the Platte,' or the man who put Woodrow Wilson in the White House. This was only a poor, harried, confused old man, quite senile and making a stubborn stand that he knew in his heart was very silly, sweating and fanning himself perpetually with a palmleaf fan and trying to comfort himself at mealtime with two big sirloin steaks. When I did realize that this was not actually W. J. Bryan I felt ashamed of myself and tried to be easier on the poor old fellow."

This, then, was the tragic end of one who was rated as a major prophet. In his day W. J. Bryan was an American yogi, living in a self-induced but highly contagious trance, worshipped by those who fell victim to his spell and hated venomously by those who feared him.

In 1896 Bryan put the fear of God into the hearts of Republican leaders all right, and they raised what then was a gigantic slush fund in a desperate fight to beat the menace by electing McKinley. It was a vicious campaign and hundreds of thousands of slips were put in pay envelopes on the Saturday before election reading, "If Bryan is elected, do not come back to work Wednesday morning. The plant will be closed."

It was no landslide victory for William McKinley—a switch of 19,446 votes in six states would have elected Bryan—and it is interesting to speculate on the course of subsequent history had Bryan been elected in 1896. What his economic program would have done to the nation's financial structure is problematical. No doubt the trusts of that time were powerful enough to have effected reprisals; and a chief magistrate who believed any compromise with evil to be a cardinal sin and anyone who disagreed materially with the views of W. J. Bryan to be in league with a literal devil, would have stood little chance in a poker game against some of the shrewdest operators in the world, each with a fistful of aces up his sleeve. His great talent of oratory would have done Bryan little good in the White House.

A strike of industrial and financial giants inevitably would have brought a showdown which might have resulted in Bryan's impeachment or in civil war. Despite Bryan's sympathy for the Cubans, however, there is little likelihood that the United States would have gone into the Spanish-American War and less that we would have taken over Hawaii, the Philippines and Puerto Rico.

Young Theodore Roosevelt certainly would not have been Assistant Secretary of the Navy, working out a crafty imperialistic scheme with Senator Henry Cabot Lodge, and consequently would not have had the opportunity to become the matinee idol at San Juan Hill and succeed to the presidency through the act of a madman named Leon Czolgosz—to the horror of Mark Hanna and other leaders of his own Republican Party.

The Union League Club members in New York and other complacent Republicans were inclined to take the nomination of the Boy Orator as a joke. But not Mark Hanna. The Republican national chairman, being an expert at mob psychology and therefore very much the realist, knew it was very unrealistic to be realistic with the American public.

Hanna had personally pulled the strings which nominated Senator William McKinley at the Republican National Convention in St. Louis, and the principal reason for his selecting McKinley was the fact that McKinley was tractable and morally immaculate, almost to the point of intellectual sterility. Had Hanna dreamed that the Democrats would do such a crazily unorthodox but devilishly clever thing as nominating Bryan, he probably would have picked a more colorful candidate himself. But being unalterably committed to McKinley, he knew he dared not pit him personally against the magnetism and reason-shaking oratory of the Democratic nominee. Hanna did not allow McKinley to go on campaign tours. McKinley stayed at home in Canton, Ohio, and spoke only from his front porch to those citizens who made a pilgrimage. Those would be unalterably Republican anyhow.

As Bryan got under way on his campaign tours which would carry him eighteen thousand miles over the country, his public reception spurred Mark Hanna to action. Hanna informed big business that the situation, far from being a joke, was critical and demanding of drastic action with important money. Big business was awakened to the peril and provided the important money which

Hanna, an old head in Ohio politics, knew how to use. Had Mark Hanna been no more alert and astute than many of the Republican national chairmen since his time, or had he been less convinced that the end justifies the means, or less talented in turning complacency into fear, silver-tongued Bryan probably would have talked his way into the White House. Likewise, if the Hatch Act of 1940 had been in effect in 1896, limiting campaign expenditures and prohibiting intimidation, threats or coercion, the election of McKinley might have proved impossible.

I couldn't guess what the United States would be like today had Bryan been elected in 1896. I only feel sure it would be quite different.

While I naturally have no recollection of the 1896 campaign, I do remember the Bryan-McKinley race of 1900 when I was six years old. I remember it particularly because Bryan came to our house that fall, but a month or so earlier I saw him and heard him speak in another town.

My father had taken me on a business trip and we were somewhere up in Iowa when he heard that Bryan was going to speak in a community fifteen miles or so away. There were no railroad connections, so my father hired a livery rig and we drove over, found the hall and were lucky enough to get seats on the aisle pretty well down toward the platform. I was very happy, with a feeling of preparedness for this event, because I had my blue soldier's cap with the black patent-leather visor and the gold letters *Bryan & Stevenson* on the front. Of course a Republican blackbird had spanged a white star on the top, but most of that had scrubbed off and wasn't very noticeable. I only regretted that I couldn't wear the cap there in the hall so everyone could see how I stood politically.

Presently there was a wave of excited cheering and applauding, and here came a group of frock-coated men down our aisle and they were headed by William Jennings Bryan, with his black mane brushed back over his ears and his wide, thin mouth set with grim determination. People were standing as they cheered and I climbed on top of my seat just as my father reached out and grabbed Bryan's arm. For an instant I was horrified at my father's effrontery, but only for an instant. Mr. Bryan turned quickly and his dark eyes glittered.

"Why, *Charley!"* he said. "What are you doing up here?"

"I came," my father said, oratorically, "to hear the next President of the United States."

Mr. Bryan was pumping his hand and grinning. "Come up on the platform with me," he said.

So my father, very excited and red-faced, took hold of my arm so firmly that it hurt and we piled out into the aisle and hustled forward with the other dignitaries. There were several rows of yellow folding chairs on the platform and we got a couple near the right end facing the audience, and there seemed to be thousands and thousands of men and women still standing down there on the floor, all cheering and smiling and waving handkerchiefs and small flags, and I saw several small boys staring at me enviously. I felt a little conspicuous, but proud and maybe a trifle haughty, and when we sat down I placed my soldier cap carefully on my knee with the gold lettering, *Bryan & Stevenson,* facing outward.

Then a tall, stern, very gaunt man was speaking, maybe a hungry Iowa Democrat, and he was making a "man who" speech, but no one was interested and the audience fidgeted and only cheered politely at the proper points while they stared at Mr. Bryan who was sitting there very grave of face, probably thinking of what he was going to say, and he wasn't wearing a stiff-bosomed shirt like my father's but only a plain white shirt with narrow black stripes like the ones the Dider Clothing Co. sold for seventy-five cents, and a low collar with a plain black string tie, but there was a godlike dignity about him and you could tell just by looking at him that he wasn't made of ordinary flesh and blood. Anyone could have told that if he only saw Mr. Bryan in a grocery store buying a pound of salt pork to cook with beans and didn't know who he was.

But at last the tall, gaunt man introduced the "next President of the United States," and Mr. Bryan was on his feet, tall and beautiful, smiling his broad infectious smile, and the crowd rose, cheering, applauding and whistling, so I put my *Bryan & Stevenson* soldier cap on my chair, stuck my forefingers in my mouth and really whistled. Presently, however, Mr. Bryan held up one hand and then both hands and the people quit yelling and clapping their hands and began clattering their chairs and sitting down and my father spread the tails of his coat and sat down and I picked up my soldier cap and sat down and fixed the cap carefully on my knees with the gold lettering toward the audience.

Then Mr. Bryan began to speak, and the crowd was a homeless cat purring with delight under the stroking of that magic voice. Never, I think, in American public life has there been such a voice. True, the voice of Daniel Webster has become part of our national folklore. But Daniel Webster was a man of enormous erudition, a man whose sharp brain cut straight through all stultifying distractions to the ultimate truth, a superb and fearless logician. Assuredly God has been very generous in bestowing gifts on certain great men of history. But it doesn't seem reasonable that God would have given Webster his most extraordinary brain *plus* a voice equal to Bryan's. That would have been prodigal. History does, I suppose, make its errors, and perhaps it is a mistake that history has recorded Daniel Webster as a demigod and William J. Bryan as a demagogue. And perhaps it is not.

At any rate Mr. Bryan's voice was a star-gauge pipe organ and Mr. Bryan was a virtuoso in its use. That day when my father and I sat on the platform Mr. Bryan was in magnificent form. His control of that crowd was equal to the control a master of legerdemain holds over his own fingers. At his will they sighed voluptuously, they moaned, they laughed uproariously, they cheered themselves hoarse and stamped their feet until dust rose in the back of the hall in a thin, gray fog. Had he called for it I have little doubt that this crowd would have risen almost to a man, seized scythes and the Iowa equivalent of halberds to march against any bastille he recommended. They might, however, have cooled down before they got there unless the particular bastille was in the immediate vicinity because one of the troubles with Mr. Bryan's oratory was its lack of staying power. It was very difficult for the most enthusiastic supporter to pass on Mr. Bryan's messages the day after a speech, and probably many of those who cheered loudest on this occasion voted Republican on election day. At least in the 1900 election Iowa gave McKinley 307,808 votes to 209,265 for Bryan.

For me, hearing Mr. Bryan speak for the first time was an astonishing emotional experience. Perhaps you could call it an esthetic experience and perhaps you could call it a religious experience, and maybe there isn't much difference between the two. In any event, sitting there on that folding yellow chair with my feet not quite touching the platform floor, I was swept clear away from myself, swept along on the waves of that caressing, crooning, booming, mellifluous voice. I had no idea at all what Mr. Bryan was talking about. I didn't understand a single sentence and I didn't try to understand. I simply rode along in the intoxicating flood, screeching cheers when the crowd cheered, laughing until the tears ran down my cheeks when the crowd laughed, muttering my own anger when the crowd growled its indignation at (no doubt) the wicked machinations of Mark Hanna (that bloated personification of evil with the dollar signs all over his checkered suit) and his puppet President, William McKinley. And I felt like crying and I felt like seizing the grand old American flag and carrying it triumphantly far ahead of the charging troops to plant it on the brow of the hill before I fell dead with my body literally riddled with enemy bullets, but not until Mr. Bryan himself informed me that both Mark Hanna and McKinley were definitely and finally taken care of, whereupon I could breathe, "Then I die happy."

When at last the speech was over and I came out of my trance, partially at least, my legs had gone to sleep from sitting so long with my feet off the floor and I could barely stand. The excited people on the platform, including my father, were wringing Mr. Bryan's hand and I wished more than anything that I also could touch the hand of this messiah and be glorified by contact with the supernatural, but I realized I was too small and unworthy for that privilege. However, when we were riding back to the other town in the livery rig, I took hold of my father's weather-beaten right hand—the hand which had shaken the hand of Mr. Bryan—and I looked closely at the palm. It *did* seem to glow a little in the twilight.

When it became definite that Mr. Bryan would visit Chillicothe and make a campaign speech, it was assumed he would come to our house for dinner and to spend the night, but I don't know whether my father had word to this effect or simply took it for granted.

At any rate there was furious activity in the household. Windows must be washed, carpets taken up and beaten and everything scrubbed that was scrubbable. A room must be prepared in case the Great Commoner could stay overnight, and, of course that meant my room. At first I supposed Mr. Bryan would sleep with me, but no, it seemed Mr. Bryan must have the room all by himself while I slept on a cot in my parents' room. All signs of my own occupancy must be eradicated and moved into the storeroom.

My mother and sister were dashing around at highest speed for at least two days, with towels wrapped around their hair, polishing silverware, cleaning places that ordinarily caught it only in the spring. I said, "My goodness, you don't think Mr. Bryan's going to crawl back of the bookcase, do you?" They ignored me and my mother, who had had experience years earlier that gave her great respect for Mr. Bryan's talents with a knife and fork and was really getting prepared, said, "Oh, I just wish you could get radishes in the fall. Mr. Bryan is so very fond of radishes and I remember him eating at least three dozen once."

She had baked pies—a lot of pies. Because she didn't know which sort he might prefer at the moment, she took no chances and baked apple, pumpkin, mince, cherry and custard.

Meanwhile Una had got the living room in shape—the chairs placed just so with the big easy chair on the left of the fireplace where a fire was laid all ready to touch off just as Mr. Bryan and my father came up the walk.

The clutter of current magazines was cleaned off the marble-topped center table, leaving only the huge gold-embossed family Bible and the red and silver *The First Battle,* Mr. Bryan's own account of the 1896 campaign with his portrait in silver on the cover.

Una stood puzzling over the arrangement and then she said, "Mama, I just don't think we ought to leave the Bible here on the table with *The First Battle.*"

My mother said, "What on earth? Mr. Bryan is a very religious man. He'd feel complimented to see his book right beside the Bible."

"No," Una said, "it isn't that. But the big Bible is all decorated with gold and it certainly won't look as if we're very good free silver people having such a big Bible with so much gold on it. It kind of overshadows the silver on Mr. Bryan's book."

My mother sniffed. "If Mr. Bryan were silly enough to think of a thing like that," she said, "he wouldn't be where he is now, running for President. Mr. Bryan knows they decorate big Bibles with gold and he'll respect us for having such a big nice Bible. The thing I'm worrying about is what to have for dinner. If I just knew what time he'd get here, we could plan, but I don't know. I know he likes beefsteak very much, but we don't know how long he can stay or anything and if he should have to rush away I certainly don't want to put in all the time he's here out in the kitchen. I think we'll have chicken."

On the afternoon when Mr. Bryan was to arrive, everything was still up in the air. They didn't know just when he would arrive or when he would depart. Other complications had developed also. My father may have had some faint political importance in eastern Nebraska, but this was Missouri. The Livingston County chairman of the Democratic Party had told my father there were many very important matters to be taken up with the standard-bearer and Mr. Bryan certainly would not have time to go out to our house. My father had said, "Sir, you don't seem to be very well acquainted with Mr. Bryan, so I can inform you, sir, that Mr. Bryan is not one to forsake old friends."

But my mother and sister didn't know for sure and they were worrying as evening came on and my father was downtown and, because we had no phone yet, there was no way of knowing what was going on. Would Mr. Bryan really come? And if he did, when?

Suppertime arrived and the dining table was set with the best china and the damask cloth and napkins and with autumn flowers for a centerpiece. My brother Glen arrived with Earl Ridenour and another friend who wanted to meet the Great Commoner and they hadn't seen my father. Mr. Bryan was in town all right and was going to speak in the park. That was all they knew.

I grew famished and was fed bread and milk and cookies on the kitchen table to "stay my stomach," and a couple of Una's girl friends came to see Mr. Bryan. They all sat around nervously talking and looking at watches while Una stationed herself at the front window watching.

Finally Glen and his friends said they would go downtown and see what they could find out. They went and didn't come back, and it was eight o'clock and then the curfew blew at half-past eight and I was getting very sleepy. At nine o'clock I went to sleep on the floor and they woke me up and persuaded me to go up and take a little nap on the couch before Mr. Bryan arrived.

It was broad daylight when I woke. "Didn't Mr. Bryan come at all?" I demanded.

"Oh, yes," my mother said, "he came all right. But it was pretty late. It must have been after ten."

"Oh, is he here now? Is he in my room?"

"No, he didn't stay all night. He didn't stay very long at all. Maybe an hour."

It finally developed that Mr. Bryan was accompanied by a number of unidentified men, some of them members of his own crew, some of them local politicians. Mr. Bryan already had eaten dinner, but he wouldn't mind having a little snack. When he went to the dining room he was followed by the strangers who made themselves at home at the table, polishing off the chicken and everything else in sight, including the pie—the apple, cherry, mince, pumpkin and custard pies. I don't believe our own family had any supper at all that night. But at least we were happy in the knowledge that William Jennings Bryan had shown Chillicothe we were pretty important people.

I for one was very proud and I didn't feel it was right to allow anyone else to occupy the chairs Mr. Bryan had used, especially the big chair by the living room fireplace. It seemed a sacrilege to allow just any visitor to plank his bottom in that hallowed chair.

On election night I was allowed to go down to the *Constitution* office with my father and brother to hear the returns, and the *Constitution* had its new astonishing typesetting machine in the window, which mitigated to some extent the awfulness of the reports from back East. Of course McKinley was elected—McKinley and Roosevelt—but at least Missouri went for Bryan.

I heard Bryan speak several times after that. The last was in 1908 when the portly Commoner was running against William Howard Taft, and although I was fourteen then, and able to understand most of what Bryan was talking about, I still was captivated by his eloquence. I also heard Mr. Taft speak, and it didn't seem reasonable to me that *anyone* could prefer Taft to our hero.

By 1908 my father would have been glad to accept a government appointment and I think Mr. Bryan had hinted he would be rewarded for his long service to the party. I remember letters coming from Mr. Bryan, short letters written in a bold, flowing hand with very black ink, but I have no idea what the letters said. They may have been only formal and conventional thanks for my father's good wishes and optimism, but my father was quite ready to accept a cabinet position.

In 1913 when Bryan became Woodrow Wilson's secretary of state, my father was sixty-four, in failing health and broke. But with unflagging optimism he wrote to Mr. Bryan, announcing his availability for service. As I recall, the reply came not from Mr.

Bryan but from a secretary, asking if my father would be interested in representing the United States government as consul in some town my father had never heard of in Central America—Guatemala or Honduras, I forget which.

My father got out the old atlas and looked up this place and didn't think much of it. He wrote Mr. Bryan he didn't believe that climate would be congenial to the chills and fever he had picked up in the swamps of Arkansas and that in any event he believed himself better fitted for postmaster of Kansas City, Missouri. The answer to that suggestion (also, I think, from a secretary) was that appointment of postmasters was outside the jurisdiction of the State Department and recommending that my father approach his representatives in Congress. So my father either wrote to or called on U. S. Senator James A. Reed, informing the Senator that Secretary of State Bryan recommended him for Kansas City postmaster. There was one thing, in particular, wrong with that. It wasn't so much that Senator Reed had never heard of my father or that my father's work for the Democratic Party had not been in Kansas City, but that Senator Reed simply hated William J. Bryan's guts and Senator Reed was one of the most talented haters in the country.

Next to Bryan himself, Reed was the best orator I ever heard. In his earlier days he was known as "Woody Dell" Reed because of his many poetically pastoral allusions, and he once won a night-long filibuster against a wagon-load of dynamite. That was when Reed was mayor of Kansas City, Missouri, and the flooded Kaw River had piled driftwood against the bridge which carried the water main from Kansas to Missouri, backing up the flood waters into the bottoms of Kansas City, Kansas. The Kansans wheeled a load of dynamite on the bridge and were going to blow it out to save Armourdale and Wyandotte, but the mayor of Kansas City, Missouri, mounted the dynamite and made a speech to the irate and apprehensive Kansans. He first told them if they blew the bridge out they'd have to blow him out too. Then he enthralled them with his best woody dell oratory all night long and when dawn came the flood was receding and the water supply of Kansas City, Missouri, was saved.

Senator Reed was a folksy fellow who affected rumpled tweeds and a red necktie and always began his orations with hands jammed into trousers pockets and speaking in a slow, hesitant, shy drawl until he warmed up. He appealed to the common people by saying "ain't" and "he don't." He was a consummate actor and a master of blistering sarcasm. He fascinated me.

When he came back to Kansas City in behalf of his own candidacy or to help other Tom Pendergast candidates, he was an indefatigable campaigner, making six or eight speeches a night in various parts of the city, and all of them different. I know because I used to follow him on my bicycle, hanging to the back of one of the cars in his caravan. It wasn't that I was vitally interested in politics at fifteen or sixteen or that I believed very much of what Jim Reed said. I just loved to hear him talk. He was as good as a show and didn't cost a cent.

Up until about twenty-five years ago it was virtually necessary for a successful politician to be a spellbinding orator and I think the decline in oratory may be credited to several things. One of these is the fact that audiences are generally better educated and more sophisticated and therefore less likely to be swept away by mere play-acting and chest-notes. They're more inclined to analyze just what the fellow is trying to say. Thanks to the movies, play-acting is no novelty to Americans now. The people are not at all susceptible to bathos, and a hammy performance by an office-seeker is more likely to win him laughs than votes.

Then there is the radio, which is no friend at all of the old-time orator. Fully fifty per cent of an orator's effectiveness is lost over the radio, not only because his "appropriate gestures" are not seen, but little of whatever personal magnetism he may possess manages to ride through the ether to the auditor. More important, the slow and impressive cadences of the practiced extemporaneous speaker become altogether too slow and are interspersed with appalling periods of dead silence which never would be noticed if the speaker were present.

In this connection I believe it may be permissible to relate something which was told me in strict confidence, inasmuch as it was a long time ago and both principals are now dead.

It was a very much off-the-record discussion of presidential possibilities with Alfred E. Smith, and I brought up the name of the then Governor of New York.

"Not a chance," said the Happy Warrior, "and I'll tell you why. He's a good guy and a good governor and I ought to know because I put him in there. New York voted for him because I endorsed him. They'd vote for him again because of his record. But that ain't the nation. To get anywhere outside his own home a politician has got to go out and campaign and make good speeches. He's got to be able to talk off the cuff, speak extemporaneously. He's got to be an orator. Well, Frank's got a good head for some things. Like I say, he's a good governor. But he can't make a speech. He can't talk off the cuff and he can't memorize. It takes a special kind of memory to be a politician or an actor and Frank just hasn't got it. When he has to make a speech he *reads* it. Well, what the hell! How far's a man going to get in national politics *reading* things to the public. They'd think if he didn't know what he was talking about well enough to *say* it, they'd vote for somebody that did."

Al Smith was only nine years older than Franklin Roosevelt but, politically at least, he was of an earlier generation. True, Smith did use the "raddio" to some extent, but his husky, raucous voice and individual mannerisms lost much of their effectiveness on the air. While Al Smith on the platform was a delight to any crowd, he seemed less logical on the radio, curiously ill at ease and even flamboyant.

Franklin Roosevelt, on the other hand, owed much of his success to the vacuum tube. He did not try to deliver orations. He went before the American people with what he called "fireside chats," and they were just that. Each auditor was given the impression that he was receiving a very intimate, frank report from the chief magistrate.

Roosevelt's voice was admirably suited for that sort of thing. It carried the impression of a warm, human personality, and it brought him the largest audience and most sympathetic audience that any American has ever enjoyed.

Franklin Roosevelt's radio technique set a pattern for smart politicians who wish to succeed, and it practically rang down the curtain on old-time oratory.

Recently I attended a sort of festival in the little town of Wheeling, across Medicine Creek to the east of Chillicothe. It was to raise money for the volunteer fire department, so they had concessions and bingo as well as entertainment from a portable stage. There were local talent vocalists and instrumentalists and comedians and, naturally, an address.

The speaker was Joseph D. Stewart, the popular postmaster of Chillicothe and civic leader, and it was an occasion which clearly called for a spread-eagle oration full of Hellenic allusions and quotations from Milton if any occasion ever did.

Well, my point is that Mr. Stewart didn't deliver any oration at all. He just talked to a few hundred of his friends, simply and informally.

The principal appeal of oratory is emotional, an attempt to sweep an audience away from calm, rational thought. When a people refuses to accept oratory as a substitute for reason and facts, it's a sad day for demagogues and phonies.

XII

"SPARE THE ROD—"

IT'S MY PERSONAL opinion that education in America, from kindergarten to bachelor of arts, has improved immeasurably in the last fifty years, and that the improvement indubitably is greater than recorded in any previous century. I say this in the face of further conviction that our schools, by and large, should be a great deal better than they are.

There seems to be much less agreement among educators as to the purposes of education and methods of inflicting it than in 1900, which indicates there is little danger of the subject becoming static. In fact, the business of teaching school, which once was relatively simple, seems to have grown so exceedingly complex that it's practically esoteric.

In my own opinion, the purpose of education is to train youngsters for a complete life in their own generation and environment. While it may never be possible to attain that abstract ideal, I feel positive we are coming much closer to it than we were fifty years ago.

I know that among the terrors confronting educators today the biggest and blackest bête noire is federal control and, knowing that it's a matter of history what federal control of schools can do, I'm certainly not advocating it. But I am not altogether convinced that any degree of subsidization carries the inevitable concomitant of direction. In a way, the GI Bill of Rights which sent so many hundreds of thousands of service men and women to college, was a form of subsidy.

In the 1949-1950 academic year, the federal government allocated one hundred million dollars among two hundred leading colleges and universities for research purposes, mostly into applied sciences, which no doubt kept the sheriff from several doors. This, of course, was a Godsend, but it also was a source of great anxiety in certain academic circles. While there apparently were no strings attached to these government gifts, most of the money was to be used on extremely practical projects. However, there would have been more than anxiety expressed in certain taxpaying circles if any great part of this appropriation had been used for strictly classical research. It's a problem, all right.

In this same academic year, private industry also has given about twenty-five million dollars to colleges and universities for applied science research. No one seems to be worried much about that, although there certainly are examples of a curriculum's being affected by large benefactions with private strings attached, as well as by powerful pressure groups of patriotic, religious or economic complexion. Sometimes party politics also has been known to show itself strongly in the affairs of tax-supported state institutions of higher learning.

In 1948 there were some nine hundred colleges and universities in the United States attended by about two and one-half million students. And, to the best of my information, many of those institutions were in financial trouble. Operation costs have increased greatly while endowments from wealthy alumni and other benefactors, upon which so many schools depended, have become practically obsolescent. Thanks to increases in the various forms of taxes and reduction in interest rates, people able to make huge endowments to colleges, even in exchange for honorary doctorates, are becoming increasingly rare. Consequently, tuition rates have been raised again and again; in some instances more than doubled in the last five years.

If this trend continues and unless there are more federal grants, it would seem that presently no one except a child of the rich will be financially able to extend his education past high school at independent colleges, and by independent I mean those not supported by taxes or by wealthy churches. If this trend continues, it would seem inevitable that many smaller colleges will be forced to close.

This prospect, I suspect, is not unpleasing to some intellectuals who have seen no reason to rejoice in the fact that the American college population has increased about seventeen times since 1900. These are the ones who superciliously declare that quantity is meaningless and who subscribe to the old English system of attempting to train an elite of gentlemen who will never, never forget the glories and obligations of their caste. These are the ones who call for a reversion to the "classical" curriculum, holding that education is useless unless it is useless. These are the ones who feel that the noblest work of God is the dilettante.

If the American attitude toward education now were the same as in 1900 and the financial affairs of independent colleges and universities were in their present condition, I suspect those who desire to maintain the institution of scholarship as a small and exclusive club would have their way. But the attitude has changed, and I think there's little reason to worry.

Fifty years ago the cult of lingual necrophilia was still in full flower. Its withering, especially in secondary schools, seems something less than a tragedy to me.

Realizing the debt our civilization owes to Athens and to Rome and the wealth of literature which has survived in Greek and Latin, accepting that there are many words and phrases which are impossible of exact translation into English, it still seems to me that the average citizen might gain a better approximation of what Homer or Cicero meant from a good translation by a professional Greek or Latin scholar than from his own labored reading of the originals. I don't happen to know any bachelor of arts who can *think* in Greek or Latin, even though he may have studied the subject eight years. Ten years after graduation, few of them retain enough Latin to translate that phrase from the Great Seal of the United States, "Annuit Coeptis—Novus Ordo Seclorum."

From my perspective—outside looking in—it seems the argument that studying Latin or Greek constitutes the finest mental training is most specious. I fail to see why learning the conjugations of a thousand Latin verbs is any better mental training than, for instance, learning the batting averages of a thousand baseball players.

Basically, I think, most Latin fans are medievalists, and they are inconsistent even in their medievalism because scholars of the Thirteenth and Fourteenth Centuries were not particularly prone to study subjects which seemed to them of dubious value. The study of Latin then was extremely practical because it was the universal European language. Of course it's too bad there isn't a universal European language now. I think the United Nations should do something about establishing one, but I also think they could pick a universal language of somewhat less complicated grammatical form than Latin. English, for instance. I'd leave the study of dead languages mostly to antiquaries, Jesuits, philologists and those scientists who employ Latin terminology for classification.

I might as a matter of course include serious writers among those who need a knowledge of Latin and Greek because it is a commonplace with scholars (and those who quote scholars) that no one can hope to write English well unless he has a sound knowledge of its immediate ancestors. There is, however, the fact that, according to Ben Jonson, Shakespeare knew "small Latin and less Greek"; that Abraham Lincoln, who wrote extremely well on occasion, knew no language except English; that Mark Twain studied no ancestor of his native tongue; that neither Herman Melville nor Rudyard Kipling could have learned very much Latin or Greek because neither went far enough in school, and the same can be said for one of the best contemporary literary technicians, Ernest Hemingway. If the scholars (and those who quote scholars) say all these would have written even better had they been well versed in Latin and Greek, it's something like the charge of statutory rape—easy to charge, difficult to prove, but equally difficult to disprove.

In 1900 very few high school students in communities such as Chillicothe, Missouri, had any idea of going to college. A high school graduate was considered well educated and actually was comparable on a population percentage basis to the owner of a bachelor degree now.

Most small towns in the Midwest, such as my birthplace, Unadilla, Nebraska, and Wheeling, Missouri, where my family moved when I was a year old, had no secondary school facilities at all. A youngster was graduated from the eighth grade in these villages and if he pursued education further he had to go away to do it. He was a privileged character.

Because my brother had been graduated from the public school of Unadilla, he had no opportunity for high school until we moved to Chillicothe. Then he and my sister, three years younger than he, enrolled together in the class of 1900. They took the recommended "liberal arts" course, although it was made plain they had no intention of going to college. I might even say this course was urged upon them *because* they had no intention of going to college, and this was to be their only opportunity for classical education.

So Glen and Una took four years of Latin and they took four years of Greek; four years of mathematics—including algebra, plane and solid geometry and trigonometry—English literature, which consisted of a study of such lights as John Ruskin, Ralph Waldo Emerson, Sir Walter Scott and Mrs. Humphrey Ward. Glen got a little of physics. Una, I think, had a year of ancient history.

Now this was strictly the classical course the girl of twelve and boy of fifteen were taking, the cultural course so admired by our scholarly retrogressionists. They were wasting none of their precious four years in the study of such practical, material things as typewriting and manual training and domestic science and dressmaking and human relations. They were studying no living languages such as French or Spanish or German. They had no general science or social science or biology or chemistry or world history or physical education or physiology or physical geography, or history and appreciation of art and music, or civics or mechanical drawing or automobile driving together with instruction in the life habits of the internal combustion engine; advertising, surveying, accounting and bookkeeping; merchandising, vocational agriculture, animal husbandry, or economics (home and otherwise) which the Chillicothe High School and a growing portion of the twenty-four thousand other high schools in America now feature in their curriculums.

No, this was the class of 1900 (cutely called the "Class of Naughty-naught") in the good old days when secondary schools still placed emphasis on the finer things of life. Instead of teaching boys and girls to be blacksmiths and milliners, the schools trained them spiritually and culturally. I myself can remember the zenith of that spiritual and cultural training when Glen and Una were laboring through Xenophon's *Anabasis* on the dining table after supper and my mother was very proud of her children, especially of Una with her dark hair in a braid down her back and barely sixteen, being able to make sense of those outlandish hieroglyphics.

One was really *educated* when one had read the *Anabasis* in the original Greek. Perhaps, had they gone on to college, they eventually would have struggled through the great Greek tragedies (completely bowdlerized, of course) but that might be carrying culture to extremes. When one had read the *Anabasis* one was really fitted adequately to meet the tribulations of life calmly and philosophically—provided, of course, it was read in Greek. The book obviously loses most of its potency in translation. Glen told me that himself when I at high school age failed to be utterly clabbered by a translation I had taken from the Kansas City Public Library. What impressed me most in this translation was that the *Anabasis* actually was concerned largely with a military retreat although "anabasis," according to the dictionary, was an advance. Glen, with his cultural background, however, was able to find a lesson in Xenophon's Greek: Americans are the greatest race of men ever to inhabit the earth, and this was proved by Stonewall Jackson's "foot Cavalry" frequently covering twice the distance in a day's march that Xenophon thought was remarkable for the Greeks under Cyrus the Younger.

Is it necessary for me to labor this point? Is it necessary for me to emphasize that I believe the Chillicothe High School "liberal arts" course of 1900 was neither liberal nor artistic?

Assuredly there is some advantage in knowing what effects the Persian wars had on subsequent civilizations, but I don't believe one learns that from studying Xenophon—even in the Greek. For all I know, it might be better for the high school student to have some notion of modern mortgage financing, methods of taxation and the basic psychological principles of human relations.

Today youngsters entering Chillicothe High School are given aptitude tests and they are encouraged to take courses in line with their abilities, ambitions and liking. Naturally, the curriculum is not entirely selective; there are still college entrance requirements, which are sensible. But even a candidate for college may be allowed a latitude which, to my mind, is nothing short of beautiful compared to the standards of fifty years ago.

In 1900 attendance was limited to those who lived in town or at least within walking distance. Now a large portion of the students come from farms and surrounding villages miles away, brought in by bus—boys and girls who could not have extended their education beyond the limits of a country school or village eighth grade half a century ago. Those who need money are assisted in getting part-time work according to their capabilities.

On the very material side I must mention the high school cafeteria, open for junior and senior high school students housed in the big building on West Calhoun Street. Even a generation ago, school cafeterias I have seen across this nation were execrable in the quality of food, high in cost (which frequently was higher than private lunch counters in the neighborhood) and lacking in cleanliness.

Recently I had lunch with some members of the Chillicothe

school faculty, including Superintendent Raymond Houston, in the big cheerful cafeteria, spotlessly clean and gleaming with stainless-steel equipment. The menu is varied day by day, but the cost is always the same—twenty cents for students and twenty-five for faculty.

The day I was there it was meat pie day, and it was a delicious beef pie with vegetables and biscuits. The servings were big enough to fill up a healthy, growing boy, with a generous helping of apple sauce, corn muffins and butter, a slab or two of cheese (government surplus), all the native fresh fruit you wanted and milk (or coffee for the faculty and visitors). Ice cream, if you wanted it, was a nickel extra. Naturally, it costs more than twenty cents to produce such a lunch, but the government's hot lunch program makes up the deficit. I asked Superintendent Houston if this donation opened the way to federal control and he said no. But they do pull up the American flag at nine o'clock in the morning and haul it down in the evening while a member of the school band plays "To the Colors" on his trumpet and faculty and students are supposed to stand at attention during the ceremony. Maybe that is a sign of encroaching native fascism, but I doubt it.

Now, as to education in general and especially in the elementary grades, I suspect the principal trouble in the schools fifty years ago was poorly trained teachers trying too hard to teach. I believe most intelligent educators realize better today that it is almost impossible to teach a youngster anything against his will, that the best a school can do is to provide girls and boys with opportunity to learn, and to inspire or encourage a desire to learn. The "You learn it because I tell you to. . . . You learn it or else" method belongs back in the good old days, the happily dead days of long ago when "No lickin', no l'arnin'" was the school room motto.

All school executives know now, or should know, that the ideal teacher is not a slave-driver but a guide, a superior person whose enthusiasm for learning is contagious. A good teacher points the way, reveals short cuts and waves a red flag before dead-end crossroads. This is part of the so-called progressive education.

However, there are grave dangers of progressive methods going too far, and these dangers are exemplified in the complaints about high school students who can barely read. I believe the attempt to teach speed reading is an example of progressivism going too far and that it can prove deleterious to a majority of students and disastrous to some. It seems quite evident from surveys of teen-age products of ultra-progressive schools that the child first should learn to walk before going out for the track team.

Of course this point can be, and has been, quite serious in individual cases, but condemning the whole progressive movement because of this patent fault is like condemning a fine automobile because of a faulty spark plug.

The other day at the Eugene Field School, where I used to suffer, I interviewed several rough-and-ready young customers, separately and out of hearing of anyone else. The principal question I asked was, "Lookit, do you really *like* to go to school?"

The first boy stared at me in astonishment. Then he grinned at anyone asking such a preposterous question. "You *bet!*" he said.

While I actually had expected the majority to reply, "Are you kidding?" or "Sure, and I love castor oil too," the boys, picked especially as looking like school-haters, all declared they had more fun at school than anywhere else and they had fun learning their lessons too.

From almost the very beginning I hated school, I loathed it not only because it encroached on my liberty but because it submerged my human individuality and forced me to submit to rank indignities. That is no minority report. I know that virtually all the boys and most of the girls shared my feelings.

The worst day of the year came in September when school opened; the gladdest day of the year came in May when school closed. The mournfullest sound in the world was the old bell in Central School ringing in the morning and afternoon. The most wonderful year of my life between six and fourteen was the year I was twelve when I didn't go to school at all but worked.

If intelligence is the faculty of comprehending and of adapting oneself to changing situations, I was about average among the boys and girls of my age. Certainly no more than average. But because of an excess of nervous energy the severe restraints were probably more odious to me than to those of more phlegmatic temperament. Even whispering was a whipping offense in those days, it must be remembered.

Though I did not realize it and my beloved sister certainly did not realize it, she innocently had started to weave a web of trouble about me long before I started to school. Being twelve years old when I was two, she found it as much fun to train me as teaching tricks to a puppy. That's what it amounted to, teaching me tricks.

My tin plate was circled by the alphabet, so it was natural for her to make me identify letters before I got my dinner. My learning the alphabet was great sport for us both. Then came the putting of letters into words with the assistance of blocks and picture books, and, partly because she made the thing a fascinating game and partly because of my own native curiosity, I soon was reading not only the picture books but *The Youth's Companion*'s Children's Page.

When I started to school at six I probably could read as well as the average child in the third or fourth grade, and Miss Lula Ellet, with beautiful blue eyes, pink cheeks, and taffy-colored pompadour, was astonished at my display of erudition and moved me up into the second grade after a week or so. The following spring half a dozen of us were given double-promotions, skipping the third grade, and then the fat really was in the fire as far as I was concerned.

Of course we were supposed to learn certain third grade subjects, such as the multiplication table, on the side. But I, at least, didn't. I just didn't learn it. I don't know the multiplication table very well today. The only way I can tell you nine times eight, for instance, is to say, "Ten times eight is eighty, subtract eight from eighty and that would be seventy-two, so nine times eight is seventy-two."

In the Eugene Field school the three rooms carried up through the sixth grade, and each teacher had an average of more than sixty children in charge. Proper ventilation was impossible, especially in winter with the coal stove roaring red-hot on one side, and the fetid mixture of sixty more or less unwashed children crammed two in a seat, plus the unsavory lunches brought by those who lived across the tracks too far to go home for dinner, plus soft coal gas from the stove, kept everyone including teacher in a state of semi-asphyxiation.

In cold weather one side of the room would be about fifty degrees fahrenheit, the other side near the stove about one hundred. So with the capricious Missouri winter climate, alternating day by day from sub-zero temperature with snow and ice storms to virtually balmy weather with slush and mud, almost everyone including the teacher was carrying his part of the communal cold at all times.

In these circumstances no teacher could give individual attention to any pupil, except with the rod for actual or assumed infraction of the prison rules. Teachers either did not know themselves the reason for a specified annual program for each class, or didn't believe it worth while to explain why we should know certain things. No effort was spent trying to rouse interest. It was quite sufficient that the Chillicothe Board of Education or the state board had laid down this course of study and we should learn it or else.

I didn't know how to study and was bored with trying to study things which did not interest me. Consequently, by the time I reached the fifth grade I was lost. If anyone ever took into account the fact I was ahead of my age group, at least no one bothered to drop me back where I belonged. No longer was I considered smart, but I suspect I may have been considered a smart aleck.

If something interested Chester Grace and me, we could learn it easily, without study. But if we weren't interested we didn't seem able to learn it no matter how much we tried to study.

For instance, in the fifth and sixth grades, our marks in geography were barely passing. Yet for our own amusement we used to draw maps of the United States, putting in all of the major railroads. We were fascinated by railroads and intensely partisan when it came to territorial competition. We considered the New York Central romantic, stupendous and enormously efficient, and the only route between Chicago and New York for any right-thinking passenger. No one except the ignorant and stupid rode any competing line. I remember discussing our teacher, Ralph Bond, in this regard: how Mr. Bond would go to New York if he went to New York. Mr. Bond, we were convinced, wouldn't even take the Pennsylvania. Mr. Bond probably would take the Erie. But, no, Mr. Bond wouldn't even go to Chicago. Mr. Bond would take the Wabash branch line from Chillicothe to St. Louis and continue on the Wabash all the way. Because we assumed the Wabash main line was as feeble as our little feeder branch, that was funny enough to convulse us and we began to refer to our teacher as Wabash Bond.

Of course neither Chester nor I had ever been to Chicago, let alone New York, and neither had ever seen a New York Central train. Our enthusiasm was based entirely on the fact that the Empire State Express, drawn by famous old 999 in a test run, had traveled 112 miles an hour between Batavia and Buffalo, New York.

If Mr. Bond had asked us to route a car of potatoes from Pocatello to Birmingham, we'd have started him out on the old Oregon Short Line with great excitement and switched him down with a minimum of mileage and a maximum of dispatch, combining geography with arithmetic and having tremendous fun out of both. But that would have been much too practical for Mr. Bond and the Board of Education. He couldn't have done a thing of that sort unless it was in his book. If it had been in the book we should have had to learn the answer by rote, and a misplaced preposition would have been more serious than an extra hundred miles.

Mr. Bond was a mousy and fearful little man and therefore something of a martinet. Probably because he felt very insecure himself, he was a tyrant over those under him.

Because Chester and I considered him stupid, we assumed that a couple of sparkling intellects such as ours would have no difficulty in outsmarting Mr. Bond.

The first exchange came when Mr. Bond ordered me to name the principal products of Sumatra and I hadn't the faintest idea where or what Sumatra might be. I did, however, have one special piece of information and this was printed in small type in the very front of the geography.

I stood up and announced confidently, "The principal products of Sumatra are iron and copper."

Mr. Bond smiled sarcastically. "How *very* interesting," he said. "But it says in the book that the principal products of Sumatra are coffee, pepper, rice, sago and gutta-percha."

"I'm sorry, Mr. Bond."

"Oh, you are, eh?"

"Yes, sir. You didn't ask me what this geography book says and this book was printed in 1892 and that was before they'd even discovered the iron and copper mines which of course changed things entirely, and when you asked me the *principal* products I thought you meant right now instead of when the geography book was printed, but of course if you mean what were the principal products way back in 1892 they were coffee and pepper and those other things."

Mr. Bond licked his upper lip and looked at the ceiling. "Hmm—I suppose you have been in Sumatra recently and learned all this first hand?"

"No, sir. I've never been in Sumatra in my life. But I read *The Scientific American* and things like that so I don't have to depend on an old-fashioned book that's out of date."

Mr. Bond probably was not convinced, but he made a strategic retreat. "I wish," he said, "that you'd bring that magazine to school with you tomorrow. I'd be very interested in seeing it."

I said I'd try to find it and when Mr. Bond turned his back someone, possibly Frank Scott or Chicken Page, let him have it in the neck with a bean shooter. With face flaming, Mr. Bond walked directly to me.

"Did you do that?"

"No, sir."

"Who did then?"

"I don't know."

"Stand up."

I stood up and he searched me and in my coat pocket he found one of those small metal tubes which used to comprise the barrel of a pen-and-pencil set, and a handful of beans. That was enough for Mr. Bond. He thrashed me soundly with a brass-bound ruler, and I knew one-third of the thrashing was for the bean and two-thirds for Sumatra.

Now the only sensible thing to do when receiving a flogging is to yell bloody murder, shed tears and beg for mercy. That gives the flogger the satisfaction he seeks and he lets up early. I certainly had no compunction against howling when my father beat me, but I resolved firmly not to degrade myself before Ralph Bond, moved partly at least by "stout fella" literature and partly by my contempt for the little teacher. So he jerked me around this way and that way, whaling my legs and rump with the ruler, each new blow arriving before the last had swelled to the zenith of pain, and finally, because I still refused to cry out, I was convulsed with the mounting agony and wet my pants. Not much, but enough to humiliate me, and I could feel that more than the welts when I regained my seat.

Mr. Bond went back to his desk, red-faced and panting. He slapped the ruler down with a bang. He stood looking over the two classes angrily until he got his breath back. Then he said, "Now let that be a lesson to you. Let that be a lesson to all of you. I'm going to have *respect* in this room if I have to thrash every mother's son and daughter of you every day."

Mr. Bond had taught me a lesson all right, but not the lesson he and other advocates of corporal punishment thought. He had whipped me severely because someone else stung the back of his neck with a bean. That did not teach me to respect him or even to fear him. As I sat there burning with a rage of humiliation and physical pain, I despised him and everything he represented, and I resolved that somehow, some way I'd get even. I wondered if I told my big brother if Glen would whip Mr. Bond for me, and I was afraid he wouldn't. I was afraid he'd tell my father who had promised me a *real* whipping if I ever got whipped in school. Mr. Bond failed to make me see I had been an odious brat. He only made me think of myself as a martyr.

So I plotted my own revenge, and in Chester Grace I had an able ally.

We used all the conventional means to bring discomfiture, embarrassment and actual physical pain into the narrow little life of Ralph Bond. And we devised numerous original projects also. It was Chester's idea, for instance, to rub concentrated oil of mustard into Mr. Bond's chair seat and we observed with scientific calm his growing uneasiness and the increasing glow of his face and his nervous abandoning of a sitting posture and finally we enjoyed his subsequent retirements when we could relax and chortle. No punishments resulted from the oil of mustard because Mr. Bond obviously was not sure what he had got into nor where. But he singled Chester and me out for rebels and whipped us for everything and nothing.

The little man did have a streak of shrewdness, despite his ineptness as a teacher. Time and again he beat Chester and me to the punch; time and again he sensed the development of an elaborate plot to show him up as a fool and whaled our backsides with his long heavy ruler before he could have possibly divined exactly what we were up to. Mr. Bond was temperamentally unfitted for teaching and was a bully and maybe a sadist. But he had an instinct for self-preservation which was too much for a couple of ten- or eleven-year-old boys.

Chester and I brooded over the injustice of it all. To be blistered for something which had not been accomplished yet and was, so to speak, still on the drafting board was bad enough. But when Mr. Bond took to whipping us for unidentified bits of deviltry without bothering to investigate, that was intolerable. He opened the door for crude tricks by other boys, including Highviewites, and even girls, who knew they were safe from detection because Mr. Bond would immediately advance upon Chester and me, ruler in hand.

Finally I got an idea and I informed Chester that I was going to run the little puke out of town.

"How you going to do it?" he demanded.

"You wait and see. You just wait until he licks me again for something I didn't do."

I had just managed to trade Max Blanchard out of a box of ancient thirty-eight caliber cartridges which would fit that old American Bulldog revolver my brother had given me on the assumption I couldn't get ammunition, and I had tried it out in the woods with Sliver Elvin. Of course we couldn't hit anything with the Bulldog, but it made a splendid bang.

The next day someone (not Chester or I) placed a tack on Mr. Bond's chair which he didn't even sit on. He picked it up and looked at it. "All right," he said, looking at Chester and me, "you think putting a tack in your teacher's chair is funny, but it's a pretty stale joke. I'll show you something a lot funnier." So he whaled our bottoms with his ruler.

On the following morning I went to school with the loaded thirty-eight in my hip pocket. And when I, with others, were called to the blackboard to do arithmetic problems, I ostentatiously pulled my coat up over the brown wooden butt of the revolver. There was a sudden chorus of gasps and then a curious silence fell over the room. I did my problem and went back to my seat, looking coldly at Mr. Bond on the way. He seemed slightly pale and was licking his upper lip nervously. He didn't have to be told what that revolver was for and neither did any of the staring boys and girls.

Mr. Bond marked my problem "A" without checking it. And for the rest of the day he couldn't have treated me with greater deference and politeness had I been chairman of the school board.

Chester scrawled a note, "What you going to do kill him?"

I wrote back, "Half kill him half scare him to death."

From school I went directly on my paper route and my father was home when I got there. I gave him our copy of the *Constitution,* but he didn't look at it. He looked at me and said, "Your teacher, Mr. Bond, came to call on me this evening at the office."

Why I hadn't expected that, I don't know. It was such an obvious thing for him to do.

Then my father, the old Plainsman, laughed. "Do you know what Mr. Bond said you were doing?"

"Why—no, sir."

"Well, he seemed pretty agitated and told me you were carrying a revolver to school."

"Gosh."

"I told him he must be pretty easily frightened, that all you had was a big, harmless cap pistol, but if it bothered him I'd make you leave it at home. Now I want to tell you something and you're big enough to know it. Carrying an imitation gun is the most foolish thing anybody can do. Never in the world carry a gun unless you're prepared to draw it, and never in the world draw a gun unless you expect to shoot. Nobody but a fool would carry an unloaded gun or an imitation gun. Now remember that, and give me that cap pistol. I'm going to put it away."

"Pop, that wasn't any cap pistol. I'm not fool enough to tote any imitation gun or unloaded gun. And I'd never draw my revolver unless I expected to shoot."

"W-h-a-t? Do you mean to say—"

"Sure," I said, and pulled the old Bulldog from my hip.

Pop dropped the *Constitution* and his eyes opened wide. "Where in tarnation did you get *that?* Of all the—well, what on earth were you carrying *such* a thing for?"

"Well, on my paper route I got to go through pretty tough districts. I got to go into three saloons and along the Levee and through nigger town and you can't ever tell when you might need protection."

"Stuff and nonsense. When your paper route gets so tough you've got to carry a six-shooter then it's time for you to quit your paper route."

"It's not a six-shooter, Pop. It's only a five-shooter."

He broke the revolver open and dumped the gangrened cartridges into his palm. "So I see. And about as pitiful a specimen as I ever laid eyes on. Probably blow up if you tried to shoot it—only these old ca'tridges would never go off. This thing goes down the old well where it'll never do anybody any harm."

And down the well the old revolver went, although I pleaded and promised I'd never shoot anything but Fourth of July blanks in it. "Hush," he said, "the less said about this affair the better. You could have been expelled for carrying a loaded revolver to school and maybe I ought to thrash you for it. I would too, except that Mr. Bond said you were a very nice gentlemanly boy who could do much better work if you studied more. So I'm going to see to it that you study your homework more."

But he didn't. My father didn't like to see me with nose buried in a book—even a schoolbook.

The following day Mr. Bond treated both Chester and me pleasantly and avoided asking us questions which might prove embarrassing if we didn't know the answers. The second day Mr. Bond ignored me but whipped Chester. The third day he slipped in from the rear when I was drawing pictures in the margin of my history instead of studying the book, jerked up my coat to make sure there was nothing on my hip, lifted me out of my seat by the collar and really gave it to me.

It was a rugged year with little Mr. Bond and he won many individual battles. It is not, however, he who wins the most battles but he who wins the last battle, so at the end Chester and I were victorious. Mr. Bond flunked a number of boys and girls whose position in the class was higher than ours. But he promoted us and we knew the reason he promoted us was that his arm was aweary from flailing our skinny bottoms and he couldn't bear the thought of spending another year with us. There definitely is more than one way of winning a war, as Hannibal learned from Fabius.

Corporal punishment of children is so barbaric that even the American Indians resorted to it seldom in correcting their offspring. It is degrading not only to the child but to the parent or teacher who inflicts it, and if there had been no other advance except the virtual abolition of corporal punishment in elementary grades I would say American schools have improved.

My old Eugene Field School is still being used in Chillicothe, although scheduled for replacement within a year. It has, however, been modernized. There is central heating now, and drinking fountains. Blackboards have been supplanted by the modern green boards, which are easier on children's eyes. They now have recesses and there are a few bits of playground equipment in the yard. More important, only the first three grades are conducted there now, instead of six, with one child to a seat instead of two in the second and third grades, and little chairs and tables in the first. There are about thirty children in a room now instead of sixty.

The old Garrison School also has been modernized, and now Negroes are encouraged to go through high school. I do not mean that Chillicothe has abolished segregation. A new Negro high school has been built, staffed by Negro teachers, and following the same general curriculum as the white high school.

I certainly do not defend Jim Crow. Jim Crow is fundamentally indefensible. But I will say that Chillicothe people, both white and black, do not seem to feel they have any race problem.

Recently I have had friendly conversations with several Chillicothe Negroes who showed no signs of race-consciousness—none of the old-time professional darkey obsequiousness. The objectionable term "nigger" is dying out.

Racial relations have improved greatly in the last fifty years. Eventually, I suspect, Chillicothe children, black and white, will go to school together. But serious trouble results from rushing that sort of thing.

Under construction is a magnificent new Central School on the site of the old monstrosity and it will be the last word in modern school buildings.

Now, because it has appeared necessary or desirable to move around the country more than is common, my family has had experience with schools in cities and small towns from coast to coast. Some of these public schools have been very good indeed. Some of them (notably New York City) have proved so bad that it seemed necessary to forget democratic principles and take up private schools. Consequently I realize that the public schools of Chillicothe are better than average and that Chillicothe is lucky to have an exceptionally capable superintendent. But the best superintendent in the world could do nothing without a far-sighted and intelligent board of education or, for that matter, without progressive civic leaders and taxpayers who have become interested in education.

Chillicothe schools are progressive, but never have carried so-called progressive methods to the ridiculous extreme I have seen elsewhere. There have been, and I fear there still are, schools where the grand motive seems to be avoidance of anything which could possibly frustrate the little chickadees or develop inhibitions, and where the children have a good time but learn nothing. Chillicothe is too practical to fall into any such psychoanalyst's dream as that. Any rational criticism of Chillicothe's educational system would be in the other direction.

In any event I take off my hat to Superintendent Houston, the Chillicothe boards of education for the last twenty-five years, and to everyone else, including the Parent-Teacher Association, whose vision, hard work and cash have contributed to the extraordinary advancement in their schools and methods. It is notably evident in all official announcements from superintendent or principals to faculty and pupils, in the relationship between teacher and pupil, in organization of the curriculum, that the prime purpose of the Chillicothe schools today is not to cram certain bits of approved routine knowledge into young heads but to develop civilized human beings. This, to my mind, is what schooling should be for. The finest lesson any boy or girl can learn is consideration for his fellows, which means sportsmanship, fairness and good manners. And that, in short, is civilization. And civilization, according to Webster's New International, is "advancement in social culture."

The Chillicothe High School now is conducting an admirable adult education program, directed particularly at present toward ex-service men and women.

Growth of the adult education idea has, of course, been phenomenal in the last fifty years and has been especially pronounced in the larger cities where there were colonies of foreign-born desirous of instruction in the English language. Now one can find night classes in virtually everything under the sun, from metalwork to Sanskrit, from oil painting to weight-lifting.

Fifty years ago American prisons dressed convicts in stripes and tried to rehabilitate them with the lash. Now most prisons have better success by giving inmates an opportunity to study courses tantamount to a high school education and to learn a trade. It's a fact that most convicts are unskilled laborers who never got past the eighth grade. I have heard more than one reformed criminal say the luckiest thing that ever happened to him was being confined in the right prison early enough.

Speaking of practical education, Chillicothe is the home of one of the outstanding business colleges in America, which draws students from every state in the Union. It is an outgrowth of the little Chillicothe Normal, which my sister attended for a year to study bookkeeping. Everyone who has motored in the Midwest is familiar with the orange arrows scattered along highways for hundreds of miles, announcing the distance to the Chillicothe Business College.

As to the general picture, and to higher education in particular, it seems to me that scientists now may be approaching the autocratic position held by the classicists in 1900. I think that change might be preferable, but not if the scientists are only semi-literate in all departments except their own particular trade. One of the silliest lectures I ever heard was pontificated by a Nobel Prize scientist on a subject about which he knew next to nothing.

Because the scientist is the modern popular hero and inevitably is regarded as an oracle, it is particularly important, in my opinion, that technical schools pay more attention to the *general* education of their graduates. By all means I think an engineer or physician or physicist or biologist should have a historical background—a background that integrates philosophy, the arts and the changing mores with political events.

I believe the bachelor of arts from a good liberal arts college today can be better educated, if he wishes, than his counterpart of 1900. He not only can tell you about Herodotus and explain the tactical innovation which won the battle of Austerlitz, but he may also have a pretty good idea of the inter-relation of political and artistic and economic and philosophical forces of a period and their manifestations in human activities. But I think he could use more general science in this day without hurting his classical education.

On the whole, it seems to me that education from top to bottom is progressing very well indeed in America. Progress may seem slow in some departments, but too great speed is dangerous and conducive to error.

We have a United States Commissioner of Education and a United States Office of Education and a lot of associations such as the National Education Association and the American Association of School Administrators and the Educational Policies Commission, and when they all agree on something it's likely to be pretty good. The fact that they *don't* all agree very often is perhaps wholesome. If there were complete harmony of opinion, it could mean lack of vitality among the rank and file and inevitable control by some strong clique. In that case it might be only a step for a quasi-official oligarchy of pedagogues to assume command of all the schools in America, a situation, it seems to me, just as full of danger in the long run as actual federal control.

I am sure I shouldn't hate school in Chillicothe today. I not only believe I should enjoy going to school under present conditions, but I believe I also might learn something.

Of course I do not know the answer to the problems of the hundreds of private colleges and universities over the country. But for the millions of boys and girls who are going to spend their lives as grocers and housewives and garage mechanics and postal clerks and stenographers and at the thousands of other occupations which make this nation roll, and who want more than a regular high school education, I think the answer lies in tax-supported universities and colleges and junior colleges and high school postgraduate courses where tuition is either nominal or free.

It seems to me that the junior college idea, which has grown, especially in the West, to wonderful proportions, is one of the finest developments of modern education. I have known young newspaper reporters who seemed to have acquired about as much general education in a two-year junior college course as does the average university graduate. But that, naturally, depends on the individuals.

In the last analysis, I suppose all improvement in education narrows down to improvement in the public's attitude toward education. When I was a boy I feel sure the average adult American considered knowledge of the three R's to be all the education a boy or girl needed. Each succeeding generation raises its sights a trifle higher. Gradually, the qualifications for teachers are being made stricter and eventually (we may hope) lagging salaries will be made commensurate so the status of teacher will carry the prestige it deserves and consequently attract more superior young people to the profession.

XIII

BOOKS ARE FATAL

One sure way for the man of letters to attract attention is to assail books. Thus, in a petulant mood, did Benjamin Disraeli declare: "Books are fatal—they are the curse of the human race. . . . The greatest misfortune that ever befell man was the invention of printing."

Any unqualified generality about anything in the world is apt to be nonsense. And any sort of general statement about books belongs in the same category with general statements about women, about any particular race or about mankind as a whole.

The only omnibus statement I'd care to make about books is that some are better than others but that I think even a moderately poor book is better than no book at all, if it is the product of some human brain doing its level best to cerebrate. I never yet met a person so stupid that I couldn't learn something from a half hour's serious conversation. An author may be ignorant, awkward and meretricious; he may be stultified by conceit, superstition or convention, and yet amongst the chaff some few grains of individuality will fall into his grist to reward the reader who is interested in the human phenomenon. The question is, of course, one of selection—whether there is a better book available to read or a more stimulating personality with whom to converse.

Although I am scarcely a bookish person, I have always been fascinated by books. There was a sense of solidity about printed matter between hard covers, lacking in magazine stories and articles, and from earliest childhood I experienced an almost sensual joy from handling a book, especially if it was my own property and I could read it again and again.

I still have the first real book I ever owned, though the cheap paper is yellow and brittle and the 7-point battered type has dimmed. It was *Robinson Crusoe*—496 pages of him—and in my sister's handwriting on the flyleaf is inscribed, "Christmas 1901. To Clyde, from Santa Claus." This is proof of my native naivete, that I still believed firmly in Santa Claus when seven years old, although I could and did read this long, stilted classic through immediately, and when I had come to the bottom of Page 496 I turned back to page one and started all over again and kept right on reading *Robinson Crusoe* over and over again until somebody got me another book. That was *Three Hundred and Fifty Aesop's Fables* "Literally translated from the Greek by the Rev. George Tyler Townsend, M. A." and I read this over and over until I knew three hundred and fifty Aesop's fables by heart.

The following Christmas Santa Claus brought me *The History of Julius Caesar* by Jacob Abbott with my brother's handwriting on the flyleaf, and I read this only two or three times. I don't know why. There must have been more things beyond my understanding in Defoe's ponderous prose than in the Caesar, which supposedly was written for "young people." It probably was easier for me to identify myself with Robinson and with the folk and animals of the fables than with Julius.

Those who hold that things were better fifty years ago than now may try to make a point by declaring it much worse for children to read a bulk of trashy modern juveniles than to absorb a few superior books.

To be consistent in that claim, I think they'd have to agree, in part at least, that books "are the curse of the human race" and that public libraries therefore should be closed. Had there been a public library in Chillicothe, Missouri, I assuredly would have read all the juveniles, good, bad and indifferent, on the shelves instead of reading *Robinson Crusoe* and *Aesop's Fables* over and over.

I did read all the juvenile books I could borrow from other children. I read *Black Beauty* and I read *Beautiful Joe* and unless my recollection, carried over nearly half a century, tricks me, they were sentimental trash. I read *Andersen's Fairy Tales* and *Grimm's Fairy Tales* and loved them. I read several of the *Five Little Pepper* series and, while I thought them sissy compared to *Robinson Crusoe,* they held my interest.

There was a problem connected with borrowing books, however, because, naturally enough, the lender expected reciprocation and I simply could not bring myself to lend my treasures to anyone. When I did weaken, I was in a fever of anxiety until I got the book back because of the danger of a page being torn or soiled or any of a hundred imaginable accidents happening.

Despite the fact that my father was so militantly opposed to storybooks, he was a tireless raconteur as was his father before him. Perhaps it was in the blood and perhaps it was only that he built up in me an appetite for stories at a very early age. To satisfy that appetite for *story* I was happy even to wade through miles of ponderous moralizing which was quite beyond my comprehension. It was something like eating a dish of bread pudding to get half a dozen raisins.

When I say there was *no* public library in Chillicothe it is not strictly correct, because there was a small semi-public library in the old high school. High school students and grade school pupils at least twelve years old were privileged to draw books.

My sister began to tell me about a wonderful book in the high school library when I was about ten and she could scarcely wait until I was twelve so she could thrill vicariously as I read it.

"Oh," she would say, "I just *envy* anyone who is reading *Little Women* for the first time."

The next year she would look at me with sparkling eyes and say, "Just think—only one more year."

So on my twelfth birthday I hurried to the library before going on my paper route, obtained an application blank and got my teacher to sign it. The following day I was duly registered and the lady librarian was pleased at my first choice—the battered and slightly tattered copy of Louisa May Alcott's famous confection. I could have it only one week because school and the library would close for the summer, but I assured the librarian I was a fast reader and would need only a few days.

I ran a good share of my paper route that evening with *Little Women* bumping comfortably along at the bottom of my sack, so anxious was I to get home and begin that long-advertised literary thrill.

Well, I couldn't read it; I just couldn't. I believe it was the first book I ever started to read and didn't finish. Una was disgusted with me. She thought I was merely being "contrary," but actually I should have got *Little Women* a year or two earlier. By my twelfth birthday so many nickel-dime novels—*Buffalo Bill, Nick Carter, The Liberty Boys of '76, Deadwood Dick, Frank Merriwell,* and other highly moral but intensely exciting pieces of literature had roared through my head that I scarcely could be interested in a story of gentle girlhood.

I was ill when school opened that fall. With what, I don't remember. Possibly it was chills-and-fever induced by going swimming in dog days and breathing the miasmic mists from swampy land, compounded by horror at the thought of going back to school. In any event, I was ill for several days but effected a speedy recovery when it was decided I might stay out of school for a year. My pal Chester had dropped back with his own age group and my having a year's vacation would put me with Chester again. So I went to work in the box factory, standing on a box before a workbench nailing egg cases and apple crates, until it was time to go on my paper route. That was wonderful and I resolved never to enter a schoolhouse again except, of course, on business.

It was naturally on business that I went to the high school with my library card only to encounter an unexpected difficulty. This was a new school year so I must have a new card approved by my new teacher. And inasmuch as I had no teacher I could not draw books. This was only slightly annoying because a survey of the shelves showed few books that looked exciting and I never bothered with the high school library during the following year when (under violent protest) I returned to the eighth grade. I didn't need the derned old high school library with its *Little Women* books. Mox Rupp had twenty or thirty volumes of Horatio Alger, Jr. Max Blanchard had ten or a dozen of the Rover Boy series. Francis Darr owned a shelfful of the Jack Harkaway books. They were all pretty generous about lending their books—much more generous, to tell the truth, than I would have been in their circumstances.

The principal trouble with a cloth-bound book, however, was the difficulty of hiding it. It made a bulge inside one's shirtwaist. My father caught me once with a borrowed book and it took some fervent pleading and promising to keep him from putting it in the fire.

The publishers of the nickel-dime novels were much smarter than the publishers of clothbound books. They knew what they were about. Because the nickel-dime novels had comparatively soft paper covers and because they were of approximately the proportions of *Time* or *Newsweek,* they could be carried inside a shirtwaist with little chance of detection.

I was quite well-to-do and I bought lots of the nickel-dime novels. I was quite well-to-do because I not only averaged two dollars a week from my paper route but could make a dollar or better any day I felt like extending myself nailing boxes, and I picked up extra change repairing bicycles in my spare time. While I had been buying my own clothes for a couple of years and contributing slightly to the family larder, I was able to keep myself supplied with such semi-necessities as a bowl of chili or a tenderloin sandwich at Peg's lunch wagon after getting my papers; ice cream sodas, candy and an occasional box of Sub-Rosa cigars (ten for a dime), a couple of nickel-dime novels a week, and I still had a glass jar practically filled with money. This jar reached its high point of

$28.10 in 1908 and I turned it over to my father, who had been wiped out in what he called "Teddy Roosevelt's panic."

The nickel-dime novels came from McIllwrath's book and stationery store and I kept them hidden in an innocent-looking wooden box in the barn, where I did most of my reading. Being rich and able to buy more of these thrillers than most of my friends, I, and our barn, became the central point of an informal circulating library. Sliver Elvin, Mox Rupp and other boys contributed to the stack, and any member of the gang was free to borrow simply by writing down in a notebook the title and date of the shocker he had drawn.

We were fascinated by these ridiculous tales, much as modern boys seem to be fascinated by the so-called comic books and cowboy movies, and some of us were influenced more than a little by the stilted nobility of our heroes.

I remember Mox Rupp's getting into a fight once and, as usual, coming out easy victor, and then, standing straight before his vanquished and blubbering foe, speaking a piece right out of Frank Merriwell—"I'm sorry indeed that you forced me to give you a whipping, but now that it's over I suggest that we forget it, let bygones be bygones. Now let us shake hands and be friends." But the other boy also was a reader of nickel-dime novels and did not relish being put in the role of the craven villain. He refused Mox's proffered hand and went away muttering and wiping his bleeding nose.

I believe, incidentally, that the comic books are legitimate descendants of the old dime novels, that they have no worse effect on morals or taste, and that they probably are easier on the addict's eyes.

Mr. McIllwrath, the purveyor of this literature, was a dour-looking little man with a big, straggling mustache and perpetually smudged glasses. I heard my mother refer to him once as a grumpy old bear, but he was a good friend of mine and he treated me as a valued customer.

One day when I went into the store to select a new Nick Carter or Liberty Boys, Mr. McIllwrath spoke to me in a lowered voice. "You like to read exciting stories, don't you?" he said, and his eyes narrowed behind their smeared spectacles.

"Why, yes, sir," I said.

"All right, I'm going to tell you something I wouldn't tell just anybody. Back in the store here, I've got the most exciting dime novel you ever read." He waved a hand at the display of lurid-covered nickel-dime novels. "All of those are just plain tame compared to this one, and I'm going to offer you a bargain because you're a good customer."

"Gosh," I said, "what is it?"

"Well, I'll tell you, son, it's going to cost you more than a nickel. It's going to cost you two-bits."

"Oh, gee, I don't know."

We were walking back toward the rear of the store, Mr. McIllwrath now inside the counter and I outside and there was an entrancing odor of books and paper and gum arabic and Lord knows what in the place. "Wait until I finish," Mr. McIllwrath said. "This book will cost you five times as much as a Buffalo Bill, all right, but there's five times as much reading in it and it's about five times as exciting. Pirates, murder, hidden treasure—everything."

He took from a shelf a cheap red, clothbound book and slapped it affectionately.

"Oh," I said, "that's a regular book."

"Yes, but *what* a regular book."

He handed it to me and I read the title—*Treasure Island.*

"Oh, I don't think so," I said. "It got love in it?"

He shook his head. "No love. One of the most exciting things I ever read myself. Now, son, I'll tell you frankly, as far as business is concerned, I'd make more profit selling you five Buffalo Bills for a quarter than this for a quarter, but I'd just kind of like to see what you think of this one. Tell you what I'll do. You buy this *Treasure Island* for two-bits and read it but keep it clean. Then if you don't tell me it's worth more than any five nickel-dime novels you ever read, you bring it back and I'll give you any five nickel-dime novels you want. Is that fair enough?"

That seemed eminently fair to me, so I bought the book and he wrapped it up and I put it inside my shirtwaist and went home by way of Polk and Woodward Streets so I could slip unnoticed into the barn to put this alleged super-dime novel into the box.

But first I unwrapped it and started to read a little just as a sample. Consequently I was late at the *Constitution* office and lost my turn at getting papers. The next day I nailed no boxes. Instead I huddled in the barn reading *Treasure Island.*

Never had I dreamed that such magic could be instilled on white paper by black type. This was no mere book. It was witchcraft. I was just the right age and had undergone just the proper conditioning to fall completely under Stevenson's romantic spell, losing my own identity in the character of Jim Hawkins, and I was practically oblivious to my own surroundings although forced by cramping muscles to shift positions occasionally. I read squatting on the three-legged milk stool, and I read standing before the barn window, and I read lying on the splintery workbench until, bleary-eyed, I came to the final words, "Pieces of eight! pieces of eight!"

Then I put *Treasure Island* into the box atop the stack of lurid-covered nickel-dime novels and stumbled out the barn door—and for goodness' sake—there was Chillicothe, Missouri. There were the several rows of old cabbage stalks in the garden plot. There was the sweet-smelling woodpile. There was the back of the house and up there my north window and the back porch roof—my nighttime exit and entrance.

I blinked my eyes and whispered dramatically, *"Pieces of eight!"* Then I went back into the barn and got *Treasure Island* and buttoned it inside my shirtwaist and reeled down Calhoun Street to Sliver's house.

Answering my shrill summons, Sliver came from the house grinning and eating a piece of bread and butter and applesauce and brown sugar and cinnamon.

"Hi," he called, then apparently seeing from my face that I had just gone through some profound emotional experience, he sobered and said, "Gosh—what happened?"

"Sliver," I said, "I can't tell you."

"Huh?"

"Well, I mean you got to go through it too, or you won't understand. It'd just sound silly. But look, Sliver, I just read the dernedest dime novel—"

"Dime novel? Are you bugs? You look funny. Your eyes are glassy."

"Sliver, you got to read it to see what I mean. It's not just the dernedest dime novel. It's the *damnedest* dime novel. Mr. McIllwrath sold it to me in secret and it's not supposed to get out. Maybe they'd arrest him if they knew he sold this to a kid. I don't know. Gosh."

Sliver stuck the rest of his bread and applesauce into his mouth, then wiped his mouth with the back of his hand, then wiped his fingers on his thighs. He mumbled something signifying intense interest as he chewed, and I pushed him into an alcove of the house where we were safely out of sight and unbuttoned my shirtwaist and took out *Treasure Island.*

Sliver swallowed and looked at me with puzzled eyes. "That it?" he asked incredulously. "Why that just looks like a *book."*

"Yeah," I said. "I reckon they put it up like that to fool people, same as they make pistols to look like a watch and you take out your pistol to shoot somebody and he thinks you're just seeing what time is it until he gets a bullet in the heart."

Sliver was impressed. He swallowed again and then took *Treasure Island* gingerly. "Gee," he said, "it'd sure enough fool anybody. Just a plain hard cover. Could be just a love book or anything."

"Yeah, but don't let your mother or big sisters catch you with it. They might look inside and then there'd be a big stink and get Mr. McIllwrath in trouble."

So Sliver read *Treasure Island* also under cover and was no less excited than I, and so did Mox Rupp with the same result.

The next Sunday was bright and warm and the three of us in our Sunday suits and hats walked out the railroad track and held a very serious literary discussion. Why was this long dime novel so much more fascinating and real than any other dime novel? The Alger books and the Rover Boys were interesting, in a way, but they simply didn't have this practically supernatural power to take you completely away from yourself.

"I don't know," Sliver said. "It's just like you were Jim Hawkins yourself every page of the way. Well, I wouldn't tell this to everybody, but I was reading this up in my room and Mama called me to go to the store and she had to call several times before I could get off the *Hispaniola* and back into my room, so I was all in a daze but I heard her coming upstairs and I quick shoved the dime novel under my mattress, but she could see there was something funny about me. Well, I went to the store and by the time I got back I was myself all right but I'll tell you kids I just didn't know whether I had ought to start reading again or not because maybe the devil was in it. There was sure enough *something* funny. But I crossed myself and then crossed the dime novel itself and went on reading."

Mox shook his head. "If the devil was in it," he said, "Long John Silver would have won. I'll tell you why *Treasure Island* is so real and seems like it's all happening when you read it, and that's because it all *did* happen just exactly the way it was written down. The other dime novels were just made up in somebody's head. Maybe a lie can seem true for a little while, but you put the honest truth alongside a lie and you can tell the difference every time."

So we walked back up the railroad track chanting:

"Fifteen men on the Dead Man's Chest—
  Yo-ho-ho, and a bottle of rum!
Drink and the devil had done for the rest—
  Yo-ho-ho, and a bottle of rum!"

It was with astonishment that I learned some years later that *Treasure Island* actually was a respectable book which could be read openly, and that some even regarded it as a classic. Sliver and Mox and I assumed that adults considered any exciting story bad—the more exciting, the worse.

It was a long time before I realized that Robert Louis Stevenson had employed his literary artistry to write what actually is a masterpiece among dime novels, with the selfsame morality standards and plot structure. *Treasure Island* could have been written in essence by any of the obscure hacks who poured out the nickel-dime novels and it would have attracted no more attention than any of the dog-eared books I had in the barn. It took the hand of a genius to endow *Treasure Island* with magic.

I don't know whether Mr. McIllwrath appreciated that reading *Treasure Island* would make run-of-the-mill nickel-dime novels seem stilted and unsatisfactory to us and consequently cut down on sales. If so, he may have got enough fun out of his little joke to compensate.

In any event, he did sell me several other regular books. The next was *Kidnapped,* which I enjoyed fully as much, and Sliver almost as much, as *Treasure Island,* and, intentionally or not, Mr. McIllwrath finally weaned us from nickel-dime novels altogether. I have often wondered whether the sour-faced old man was deliberately trying to develop a taste for literature in us. I suspect he was.

Perhaps his greatest triumph in this direction was selling me a copy of *Through the Looking Glass.* It was cheap binding but carried the old Tenniel illustrations.

I glanced at some of the pictures and shook my head. "Looks silly to me," I said.

"Well, it *is* silly," Mr. McIllwrath said, "but this is wonderful silliness."

"Oh, I don't think I want any book about some little girl named Alice."

Mr. McIllwrath looked hurt. "Now have I ever told you wrong

about any book? Didn't you like *Treasure Island* and *Kidnapped?*"

"Yes, but—"

"All right. Now I'm marking this book down from two-bits to twenty cents. You take it and if you don't like it bring it back in perfect condition and I'll give you two yellow lead pencils and some slingshot rubbers."

"Ten cent rubbers or five cent rubbers? Five cent rubbers and two lead pencils only makes fifteen cents."

Mr. McIllwrath scowled. "It'd seem you'd be willing to pay five cents for the privilege of reading the book."

"No, sir. If I don't like it, there's no privilege in reading a bum book about a little girl named Alice, and if I do like it there'd be no exchange and I don't need two yellow lead pencils at one time, especially when I already got one, but if you'll give me some ten cent slingshot rubbers and a ten cent bottle of mucilage, it's a deal."

Mr. McIllwrath agreed wryly, and I took Alice and found it delicious. Sliver also loved it, but Mox would have nothing to do with a book about a girl named Alice going through buggy adventures on the other side of a mirror.

Now, if I had stayed in Chillicothe would Mr. McIllwrath have jockeyed me along step by step and developed in me a taste for the best in literature? In certain circumstances, perhaps. But with the lessening of my family finances, I could not have spent money for books. As it was, I cannot remember buying a book from the time I was thirteen until I was at least twenty-one. Books were luxuries and the family needed whatever I could make for necessities.

There were two fortunate circumstances in my early life in Kansas City. One was the fact that the Public Library at Ninth and Locust Streets, lay between the old Central School and work. Then I was lucky enough to get Miss Sophia Rosenberger as English teacher, and Miss Rosenberger, an intense and warm-hearted little woman, was a genius at infecting her pupils with the excitement she felt over good writing. To her an apt figure of speech was a gift from God. She read us Shelley and Keats and Milton and made us see with her eyes and hear with her ears.

I attracted Miss Rosenberger's attention early. I seemed to fascinate her. She told me quite frankly that she simply couldn't understand how anyone could get through the fourth grade knowing nothing whatever of the principles of grammar. "It's simply incredible," she said to me privately, "that a boy your age wouldn't know an adverb from a preposition. I'd think you would have learned that much by osmosis."

"Miss Rosenberger," I said, "there is no osmosis in Livingston County."

But from Miss Rosenberger I learned some of the things which distinguish good writing from bad writing, and I learned the names of authors who wrote well, and I drew their books from the library on the way to work.

I had arranged my school schedule so the two study hours came at the end and arranged also to cut those study hours so I could get to work by one o'clock. The idea was that I should do my studying at home.

But by the time I got through work and ran the several miles home (to save carfare) and ate dinner and helped my mother with the dishes it would be nine o'clock, and it was easy to convince myself I was far too tired to study. So I'd go to bed and behind my closed door read until one or two o'clock in the morning. Miss Rosenberger liked Kipling. So I read every word of Kipling I could get hold of. She liked Mark Twain and O. Henry. So I read every word of them. When I found an author I admired, it was a matter of routine to go right down his shelf.

After my year of school, however, there was no Miss Rosenberger and I gave equal weight to suggestions from less competent persons. I read John Fox, Jr., and Thomas Dixon, Jr., and Harold Bell Wright and Winston Churchill and Rex Beach and Jack London and dozens of other lesser lights, and thought most of them wonderful—particularly Jack London.

In those days the Kansas City Library had open shelves, and I would wander through the fiction department, picking out volumes because the titles seemed inviting, knowing nothing of the book or of the author. Consequently, a sense of discrimination, which was budding under the tutelage of Miss Rosenberger, began to wither under the avalanche of trash.

There are intellectuals who are so pained at the quality of most best-selling novels today that they proclaim a galloping literary decadence. As I am a novelist who would enjoy a wider acquaintance with best-seller lists, it would be easy for me to chime in, but I have greater faith in the public's taste than in the judgment of intellectuals. Too often the intellectual is a wan midget on stilts speaking with the voice of a giant.

I believe American literary taste has improved in the last forty or fifty years because the American public is better educated. True, I have sampled the work of some popular contemporary authors which I wouldn't read unless I were paid reasonably well for the chore. But I also have had occasion to scan some best-sellers of the 1900-1910 period, and they were such incredibly bad sentimental flap-doodle that I, from some experience as an editor, don't believe any reputable publishing house would look at them today for the simple, sordid reason that publishing houses don't like to lose money.

Moreover, I believe the good writers of the 1900-1910 period would be better writers if they were producing today because a more sophisticated audience would make them more cautious in their flights of hyperbole.

Well, no matter, in those days the Kansas City Public Library was the greatest joy in my life.

I don't know whether it was occasioned by something I read or whether it was glandular or a combination, but by the time I was sixteen or so I became depressed by a sense of my own ignorance and decided that the library was the remedy. Among those thousands of books in the non-fiction department lay the secrets of the universe and here I was wasting my time with adventure and romance.

But I still knew no one to direct or advise my reading, and when I picked up a volume of history or biography it was just as likely as not to be the work of some romantic quack. I also drew now and then some book which was beyond my depth because I had not yet sufficient background to understand it. Such a one was Kant's *Critique of Pure Reason,* which I doggedly read from cover to cover with a dictionary beside me in bed, twenty years before I had acquired enough of the philosophical nomenclature to comprehend what in hell the man was driving at.

From all this haphazard reading and the dictionary habit I did garner that special mark of auto-education, a rather formidable vocabulary which I, as a private in the first World War, employed to put second lieutenants in their place and which, together with a slight facility for expression gained through Miss Rosenberger's osmosis, finally helped me get work as a newspaper reporter. And, in the newspaper business, which is much more interesting than repairing furnaces, I became acquainted with some educated people, several of whom took the trouble to lay out courses of reading for me and to advise me about simplification of a style inclined to be florid. It would be nice if I could say they led me so far on the path of scholarship that I now know the difference between a preposition and an adverb, but that would be a patent exaggeration.

Of course mine is a rather extreme case, but I must say that most of the pleasant things in a more than ordinarily happy adult life have come at least indirectly from the public libraries of Kansas City, Denver and San Francisco. That is why I feel so strongly about the importance of a good public library for any community. And that is why I am so happy now that Chillicothe does have a good public library.

I think it interesting how Chillicothe came to get the Livingston County Memorial Library.

Following the first World War, in which Chillicothe boys (many of them my friends) caught it rather bad, a committee of women was formed to plan a memorial for the men who didn't come back. Then someone got an idea it would be better to have a living memorial instead of a monument, and it was decided to establish a public library in memory of Livingston County's war dead.

It was easy getting this good idea, but it wasn't so easy getting the money to establish a library. The county had got along for going on a hundred years without a public library and donations were very slow. The women, however, were determined. They held rummage sales. They held watermelon and ice cream suppers. And finally they cracked the nut by putting on a carnival and rodeo, and the Livingston County Memorial Library was established. Even so, the going was rough for several years because it costs a good deal of money to keep a library in operation. But at last the library proved its worth to a point where the women were able to establish it as practically a public utility, equal in status even to the sewage system. In other words it now is supported by taxes.

All of Livingston County benefits from the library by means of a "bookmobile." This is a truck fitted with bookshelves, and the bookmobile, with driver and a girl librarian, makes the rounds of the county once a month, visiting especially the village and country schools—even such remote and once squalid rural schoolhouses as Jacksnipe and Hog Skin.

Each bookmobile "customer," school pupil or farm wife, is allowed to draw four books every visit and it is a big day in any district when the bookmobile arrives.

Except in the summer months, the bookmobile actually circulates more books in the rural districts than does the main library in Chillicothe. As an example, in March, 1949, the bookmobile circulated 7,851 books against 4,639 from the main library. But the situation was reversed in July when farm people, including children, have little time to read. Then the bookmobile circulated only 2,207 against 4,488 for Chillicothe.

Mrs. Kathryn A. Devereaux, the competent and gracious city librarian, is delighted at the reception the bookmobile gets in rural districts and particularly from the children. These farm girls and boys appreciate the privilege of drawing books and, according to

Mrs. Devereaux, are astonishingly careful with them. The library is especially well stocked with books of interest to children, modern juveniles as well as the classics.

Mrs. Devereaux and her assistants make it very much a point to recommend certain books to certain children. In this, of course, the rural schoolteachers co-operate.

One of the greatest problems of any public librarian, metropolitan as well as rural, is convincing holders of public purse-strings that more money should be appropriated for the purchase of new books. Politicians rarely read much except the newspapers, and I remember the bitter opposition that developed once in the Buffalo, New York, City Council when the city librarian wanted money for new books although records showed the library already owned "hundreds of thousands."

In this respect Chillicothe and Livingston County are fortunate in having as librarian an articulate and energetic young woman whose enthusiasm for her work overwhelms those who would be penurious. Of course Mrs. Devereaux actually needs more money than she gets. But she does pretty well. Few librarians in comparable communities are able to keep their shelves as well up to date. For example in August, 1949, her library purchased 271 new books and acquired twenty-five more by gift.

Public libraries in general are broadening and enriching their service to the community with lectures, children's story hours, musical recordings, picture departments, educational motion pictures including travelogues and science features, books in Braille for the blind, the circulation of books to patients in the hospitals and traveling exhibits to schools.

For example, the village in which I now live enjoys weekly lecture courses in the winter months on philosophy, music, literature, current events and world politics, sponsored by the local library association. The building also is utilized for art exhibitions, small concerts and meetings for the purpose of charity, cultural advancement or civic betterment.

In most states there is splendid co-operation between large and small libraries, aided by the union catalogue system. If a village library does not own a certain book, it can be borrowed from the nearest city at a mere cost of postage for the holder of the village library card.

But of course all this means less than nothing if one is not convinced that the reading of books is a good thing.

Martin Luther said, "The aggregation of large libraries tends to divert men's thoughts from the one great book, the Bible, which ought, day and night, to be in everyone's hand."

The only possible comment on that, as far as I am concerned, is to quote the first Caliph Omar at the capture of Alexandria. The father-in-law and successor of Mohammed said, "Burn the libraries, for all their value is in the Koran."

XIV

RELIGION

To state a belief that religion in America has improved in the last fifty years might seem a gratuitous assumption. How can one know? Assuredly there is no concrete evidence that the Almighty is flattered at the sight of red Neon halos flaming above the images of His saints or by floodlighting church steeples or by use of the radio by His spokesmen.

I don't know anything about the effects of the last half century on Buddhism, Mohammedanism, and Confucianism, but I suspect they have changed very little. I don't know very much about the Roman Catholic Church except that it has gained enormously in membership and political influence in the United States and lost a great deal in some other lands. Among the Jews, the Reformed congregations seem to have been gaining and the Orthodox to have been losing; and whether that is good or bad depends on your side of the fence.

Having been reared in the Protestant Church in that branch called simply the Christian Church (although sometimes incorrectly termed Disciples of Christ or "Campbellites"), I am in a better position to hold an opinion regarding this sect.

I think there has been some improvement. I think there has been some improvement, generally speaking, in the services of all Protestant churches because (again, generally speaking) Protestant ministers are inclined to be of higher intelligence and better educated than they were fifty years ago. The music also is better.

I have few tender thoughts for the church of my childhood. It was a place of boredom, cramped muscles and terror. There is, however, one very pleasant memory. In spring and summer and fall a stained glass window would be raised a few inches on the west side of the old church and through this slit on bright Sunday mornings I could see a small section of grape arbor and part of a green tree and the leaves would stir happily in the breeze and the sunlight would be golden and happy on the greenery, giving me assurance that all was right with the world outside despite the dolor in this House of Worship, and that eventually, if I only had the fortitude to live through the mournful present, I too would be happy outside in the sunshine of God's beautiful world. The slit in the window was my shield and my talisman. When, under the bludgeoning of the preacher's brimstone-laden voice, I found my throat constricting and my middle convulsing spastically, I would lift up mine eyes to the slit in the window from whence came my help.

Yes, I suppose I was a nervous small boy and I had a great many sins on my conscience. But because of that blessed small section of grape arbor and part of a green tree they never had to lead me screaming hysterically from the church as was the sorry fate of several other children.

Not long ago when I last attended services in the fine new First Christian Church of Chillicothe, Missouri, and sat in the same general sector where we used to sit in the old church, I was delighted to see that a new stained glass window was opened a slit on the west and through that slit I could see a small segment of green leaves in the sunshine. And, while I was not at all frightened by the sermon, the sight still gave me a comfortable assurance that beauty and rightness endure.

On this occasion, the music was good—for a Protestant church. The choir was garbed in wine-colored vestments, something which never would have been countenanced fifty years ago because a robed choir was the mark of Romanism. The choir also had good voices, well-trained by the capable Earle Dillinger, director of music for the public schools.

The sermon of the Reverend Robert E. Austin, pastor, was much less formal than the sermons of his predecessors forty to fifty years ago. I don't remember the Reverend Mr. Austin's actual text, but the theme, interestingly enough, was that we—and especially the young people—are going to the dogs unless we turn back to the good old days when people took their religion more seriously. According to the Reverend Mr. Austin, we have retrogressed shamefully. His remedy seemed to be a retrogression to the good old days which, as a matter of fact, he is not old enough to remember.

I didn't think he quite proved his point. To my mind, his sermon tended to prove the opposite, for the reason that he did not pound the pulpit, he did not bellow, he did not dwell with quavering voice on the horrors of eternal damnation. He actually never mentioned hell once in his entire sermon. He said nothing to give children the night terrors. There was nothing in his sermon to bring pitiful moans from the old people down front. Because of these things, I think sermons have improved, at least in the First Christian Church of Chillicothe, Missouri.

Of course the Reverend Mr. Austin lamented the passing of rugged individualism, which I do also in a way. But one might as well lament the passing of other picturesque institutions which changing conditions have rendered anachronistic—the narrow-gauge mountain railroads, for instance.

When I was a boy the word of a preacher was assumed to be the Gospel truth. If the preacher said something it was true and no argument, so I used to file away in my memory small bits of information gleaned from the pulpit such as: if you place a live fish weighing one pound in a vessel of water weighing twenty pounds the weight of the vessel of water will not be increased by one jot or tittle, but if the fish is dead the weight will be increased by the amount of the dead fish's weight; lightning never strikes twice in the same spot; there is dope in the paper of cigarettes which turns smokers into criminals; you shouldn't kill house flies because they eat the poison out of the air; blood will tell, in humans as well as in race horses.

The trouble was that in the good old days many preachers were careless with material facts, no doubt on the premise that material facts were unimportant in the face of the great spiritual truths they were purveying. In these days, however, congregations are better informed, so a preacher has to be more careful about everything he says. As far as I was able to see, the Reverend Mr. Austin was really mixed on only one material fact. He said 97 per cent of convicts in American prisons never had been inside a church as children, whereas practically the opposite is true. I was surprised myself several years ago when I looked into that particular matter in several of the larger prisons over the country, and found that approximately 92 per cent of the convicts had had more or less religious training as children.

But the Reverend Mr. Austin was making a point there and the nearest he came to mentioning hell right out was in warning parents that they will be taken to account unless they spare time to explain God and Jesus to their children. I wished he would go into particulars about how a parent explains God and Jesus to children, but I suppose regular members of the congregation already knew.

The thing that interested me was the Reverend Mr. Austin's taking cognizance of children at all. I think that is important, and I was told he takes an interest in youth activities outside the church. It's a fact that few criminals in adolescence were actively associated with such organizations as the 4-H Clubs and Boy Scouts, and a minister, if he has the personality, poise and common sense to be a capable minister, can do tremendous good in promoting youth activities. However, he must use good judgment.

In another town a girls' organization broke up recently because the directing minister was too fervent in intruding religion. The young lasses complained that the minister forced them to say the Lord's Prayer even before practicing basketball, let alone before playing it. No doubt the clergyman felt his charges needed prayer, but the girls said they attended Sunday School and church every

Sunday and said their prayers before going to bed. When they complained of an excess of prayer, the minister was vehemently indignant so the girls got mad and quit. That preacher gave it too much gas on an icy road and he skidded.

In my boyhood at the First Christian Church, the preachers didn't seem to have any interest in children at all. I would meet our pastor on the street and tip my cap and say, "How do you do, Brother Rankin," and he would blink, put on his automatic smile and say, "Uh, hallo, son," not knowing me from Marcum's dray horse although I'd been going to his church regularly ever since he had been in town.

There was a marked difference between the Protestant ministers and the pastor of St. Columban's Catholic Church. Father Kennedy was a round, jolly little man who liked children and who was at ease with children and knew how to make them feel at ease with him.

If I saw him on the street he would stop and talk with me. "How's that pitching arm?" he'd ask. Then, "Now, look, Clyde, you've got to get out and practice. That curve isn't going to do you a lick of good unless you learn to control it. Why don't you just bounce the ball off your barn when you haven't got anybody to catch you?"

Sometimes he'd show up when we had a game and if asked he'd umpire and enjoy it very much. But he never tried to boss the boys, Catholics or Protestants.

Father Kennedy was not proselytizing. I'm quite sure he knew my people were strong Protestants and that I'd never be allowed to enter his church. The only Catholic who ever attempted to proselytize me was my pal Sliver Elvin and I am sure he was not prompted by Father Kennedy or anything except a sincere desire to keep me from sizzling through eternity. Sliver didn't press the point. He just wanted me to go to church with him sometime when I was playing hookey from my own Sunday School, and I might have gone except that I was afraid I'd be thrown in contact with nuns. I had an unreasoning terror of nuns. I would as soon have met a couple of ghosts on the street as a couple of black-robed sisters.

But Father Kennedy was wonderful. A natural leader, intelligent and witty, he was loved by Protestant boys as well as Catholic. But perhaps he also preached hell-fire. At least the Catholic boys had a healthy respect for it.

Hell and the end of the world were tremendously important items in those days for practically everyone, adults as well as children. But I must say my father was an exception. He declared it was ridiculous to believe unbaptized babies were scheduled for eternal damnation or any other decent people, baptized or not. He wouldn't go so far as to deny the existence of hell, but he professed belief that it was reserved for burglars, saloon-keepers, certain Republican politicians and immoral women.

Nevertheless, I worried a lot, not only about hell but about the end of the world which, according to our regular preachers and visiting evangelists, was indeed imminent.

It was so with the boys and girls who attended the Methodist churches and the Presbyterian and Baptist also. That terror was not limited to the children of the First Christian Church.

According to the accepted belief, God tried to straighten out sinful mankind once with Noah's flood. Next time he had promised to do a thorough job with fire, and it was coming soon.

Once, seeing a grass fire from a distance, I was panicked for a moment. And I can remember, even when I was eleven years old or so, nailing up apple boxes under the open warehouse at the factory and looking across at the low hills and speculating how it would be when the angry, all-consuming flames burst from the ground.

Always there was the specter of the Day of Wrath close at hand, maybe tomorrow, maybe next week, but surely within a year or so. One ecclesiastical psychopath, maybe Presbyterian, maybe Methodist and I'm not sure which, went so far as to set a definite date which gave his congregation about ten days to prepare.

As the dread day approached children of his flock became more and more tight-lipped, pallid and hollow-eyed. Men swore off chewing tobacco. Women quit curling their hair and put aside their frivolous hats.

My father scoffed that if the end of the world were at hand it never would be the exclusive property of a sect that wasn't even Christian, that baptized by the wholly inadequate method of sprinkling a little water on the head instead of by total immersion as endorsed not only by John the Baptist but by Jesus Christ himself. But I had learned that my father *could* be wrong and I was far from convinced.

The Catholic boys pretended to take the whole thing as a joke. If Father Kennedy hadn't been given advance notice there was nothing to it. But as the day drew near even they were not too sure and their laughter became hollow and their eyes furtive.

Wednesday was to be the day of destruction and by Monday night I was in practically as bad shape as children of the elect congregation.

I can remember well how I lay in the dark—tense and quivering, my head in a confused whirl, my teeth clenched on the sheet, my hands gripping the coverlet in a desperate battle to keep from whirling off into nothingness. What was the world and what was I? What was the purpose of it all? Why the beauty and wonders of this fascinating life if only to feed the fires of God's wrath, day after tomorrow? It was terribly unreasonable, but I believed it; I was convinced it was coming. And the fires of the earthly holocaust were only the prelude to the fires of the eternal hell of which I had heard more from the lips of alleged divine authority than of any other subject in the universe.

In my near delirium I heard the clock strike eleven and twelve and one and two and finally I slipped from bed to my knees and prayed fervently not to the Great Jehovah but to gentle Jesus. I was not presumptuous enough to plead for complete repeal of what obviously was the climax of God's drama of the earth. But I did urge Jesus to take up with His Father the matter of a reprieve, a temporary suspension until I was a little older when I shouldn't be so much afraid. I fear I grew a little self-righteous and smug with

Our Savior, but I called his attention to the fact that I was not a "dirty kid," that I never had stolen anything except legitimate things, that I rarely told lies, that if I didn't love my teachers it was obviously the teachers' fault, that when I got into fights it was *always* the other kid's fault. I promised to quit playing hookey from both school and Sunday School, to quit smoking anything stronger than corn silk and to use no cuss-words more potent than "darn" and "gosh" even when I got mad.

The prayer comforted me a little. While I may not have had much faith, I still had hope.

Wednesday finally dawned with a cloudless sky, but it was a strange sky with a high mist that washed out the blue to the tint of an old work shirt that has been laundered a hundred times in naphtha soap, and the sun shone through with no warmth or happiness. The leaves on the trees hung motionless and resigned in the still air. Our old cat, La Barguelle, stretched and yawned on the back porch, her shrewd green eyes revealing knowledge that merry hell was to pay this day. But La Barguelle was a devil and her devious mind was calm with some esoteric but flawless scheme.

As the day wore on like the slow unrippled flow of the river, unshaven men scanned the pale heavens for approach of a destroying ball of fire. Tense women with uncombed hair pushed curtains aside to peer briefly now and then from windows or doors, and then returned to their prayers. Weary-eyed children came from their houses but didn't wander far. They sat on their front steps and bit their fingernails.

It was said that certain members of the elect congregation had made themselves ascension robes from the bed sheets they would need no more, but my father, pretending at least to hold the whole uproar in contempt, said they had better have made the robes of asbestos.

But the fire didn't come and the world didn't end and the prophet explained it all by saying the Lord had answered his entreaties to give the poor people a postponement so they might have opportunity to redeem their souls by aligning themselves with the only true faith—the Presbyterians or the Methodists, or whatever creed he represented.

I had my own private explanation. Jesus had paid heed to my own prayers. Inasmuch as the seat of all consciousness rested within my own small frame, I was obviously of much greater importance to the cosmic scheme than most people realized.

But the terror of hell and of the Day of Wrath still lived in me in spite of a growing sense of the reasonable. In that connection I remember a curious thing. I remember reading in about 1904 of the approach of Halley's comet and being very grateful that it wouldn't arrive until 1910. I calculated that I should be a big boy of fifteen or sixteen in 1910 and consequently not afraid, although I knew the sight of such a heavenly spectacle, at the time I was reading about it, would practically prostrate me with terror. Recollection of that ratiocination was amusing to me when I did become fifteen and viewed Halley's comet with wonder and interest but no trace of fear.

I am pretty sure Sunday Schools have improved since the first decade of the Century. When you reach bedrock there's nowhere much to go except up.

Our Sunday School teacher was a large odorous woman with decaying front teeth, a woman steeped in intolerance and superstition, profoundly ignorant, and bubbling with self-esteem. Mrs. Snilk was incredible, and I can't believe they make women like her any more—at least not around Chillicothe.

One morning Mrs. Snilk glared at me and demanded, "Didn't I see you with that South Methodist Grace boy the other day?"

"Maybe, ma'am," I admitted.

"Well, don't you never let me see you with him no more. Them what toucheth pitch is going to be defiled and never enter the gates of heaven. If you're defiled from Methodist pitch, you're pitchy yourself and I ain't going to have you in this here class defiling good Christian boys. Now you mind what I say."

"Mrs. Snilk," I said, "Methodists are Christians just the same as us. Chester Grace is my good friend."

"Don't you get sassy at me, young man. You get sassy at me and I'll tell preacher. I'll tell your pa and I reckon he'll show you who's a Christian or not. Next thing you'll be talking about Roman Catholics being Christians and you just dare and try coming to this class and defiling my nice boys with Catholic pitch. You just dare and try."

I don't doubt I was a disturbing influence. I knew our Christian Church was only about fifty years old and that bald old Uncle Jimmy Hutchinson who sat down on the mourner's bench was one of the founders. Consequently it didn't make sense that nobody could enter the gates of heaven except accredited members of our church. That would leave out a good many worthy people such as George Washington, Johnny Appleseed and Benjamin Franklin, not to mention Chester Grace, Sliver Elvin and Father Kennedy. But my mild inquiry convicted me of subversive utterances. And after I gave Mrs. Snilk's big, lubberly son a bloody nose and black eye the overalls were really in the chowder. I think Mrs. Snilk may have had wit enough to realize her son was acting as her proxy. But maybe not.

In any event I felt certain I could play hookey from Sunday School and Mrs. Snilk would not report me for fear of getting me back. I felt it was safe to play hookey as long as I met my mother and father outside to sit with them during church services. From then on my religious duties consisted of morning and evening services on Sunday. I was spared Wednesday night prayer meetings, although my parents attended.

At least once a year, and usually oftener, there would be an evangelical series, called a revival or "protracted meetings," held every night for ten days or a fortnight. Sometimes these would be conducted by the pastor, and sometimes there would be a visiting evangelist who got a share of the collections and perhaps a guarantee.

Such a one was the Reverend St. Charles Grewson, and his name was easy to remember because it was close to "gruesome." He was very tall and I imagine he thought of himself as Lincolnesque because he wore a Lincoln-like black beard and a long black coat. But he was thinner than Lincoln and deathly pale and his black-ringed eyes burned with the fire of fanaticism. His voice was sepulchral, his manner awesome.

The Reverend Mr. Grewson was inspired by the *Divine Comedy,* but, if he ever actually read it, Dante's poetry and mystic symbolism were lost upon him. I think it probable that the Reverend Mr. Grewson had read only snatches of the epic but had studied the Doré illustrations very carefully. At any rate the hell through which we were conducted nightly was the hell of Gustave Doré with embellishments from the Revelation of St. John the Divine as well as from the not untalented St. Charles Grewson.

One might have asked what manner of Christianity sought only to arouse terror? What of the ever-loving Father? What of the compassionate Christ? What of the First Epistle of John IV: 18: "There is no fear in love; but perfect love casteth out fear: because fear hath torment. He that feareth is not made perfect in love."

Night after night the Reverend Mr. Grewson took us, canto after canto, through all the horrors his unhealthy mind could dream up, contorting his gaunt, black-garbed body, employing all the tricks of the orator and ham actor, that hollow, doomful voice probing deeper and deeper into the souls of those who must suffer to hear him.

I can see him now, crouching forward with white talons clutching at the end of those long, long black arms: eyes blazing crazily in their black circles, and the slow, quavering voice intoning inexorably: "Oh, ye fornicators . . . Oh, ye blasphemers . . . there is no escape now. The sky is dark with the wrath of Jehovah, dark, dark, dark. By your own sins are ye bound, by your own transgressions are ye held helpless on the rock. Oh, yes, once ye were brave. Once ye were scornful of the warning. But you are not brave now. You are not scornful now. No, no. You struggle. You struggle against the bonds of your own sins, against the bonds of your own fornications and you who once were *so* strong and *so* scornful are as weak as a newborn babe. You cry out in desperation, yes in terror you cry out—" The Reverend Mr. Grewson's voice changed to a weak falsetto: *"Oh, Lord God, I repent now of my sins. Save me, save me!"*

He straightened to his great height and his cruel mouth tightened and he glared over the breathless congregation. "But, oh, ye sorry souls—the day of repentance is past. You gaze up into the murky sky for some sign of hope, but there is no hope. There is nothing but despair. But stop! The sky is not quite empty. There is something off yonder, a *tiny speck.*" He shielded his eyes like an Indian peering at the horizon. "It grows l-a-r-g-e-r. It is approaching, slowly, *slowly.* Can it be that deliverance comes at last? Can it be?

"NO! *NO!* Ye scornful sinners, your days of grace are past. That which approaches is not salvation, but the *vultures!* They are coming, coming, *coming*—"

The Reverend Mr. Grewson's long black arms began to beat up and down, up and down like the wings of a great black bird.

"They are coming, coming. . . . They are circling above you now. . . ." He circled behind the pulpit. He soared with outstretched wings and peered hungrily down at those in the front rows, turning his head this way and that on its long, obscene neck. "You know now. Ah, yes, you know now and you'd be willing to repent your fornications and rest in the gentle love of Jesus because you know that soon you will feel the weight of a vulture on your naked breast and his bright eyes will look into yours. But not for long will you see this because your eyes are a delicacy which he will enjoy nibbling first."

The Reverend Mr. Grewson crouched suddenly with wings extended and ugly head advanced and seemed actually to be swooping into the center of the congregation.

"He's COMING!" he bellowed.

A girl screamed piercingly again and again and there was a quick confusion while nearby men seized her and carried her up the aisle—a slim child of fifteen or sixteen—with her head drawn back tensely and eyes rolled to a ghastly white, a thin froth at her lips while her screams dwindled to a moaning gurgle.

Yes, a wonderful thing was old-time religion—so full of spirituality and the love of Jesus.

It really is a shame that we have grown so crass and material in our more enlightened areas that we now try to confine characters like the Reverend St. Charles Grewson in psychopathic hospitals where they can do no harm.

There are some grounds for worry, I think, on the effect of horror movies and some "comic" books on immature minds and nervous systems. But at least there are limits beyond which these producers dare not pass. Evangelists of the Reverend St. Charles Grewson breed knew no restraint. To my mind they were wholly vicious and inexcusable, and I can't imagine what quirk of spirituality induced parents to take sensitive young children to those meetings.

It seems to me that a purpose of religion is to dispel fear rather than to promote fear. It seems to me that a mark of the truly religious is ability to face the perils of life and uncertainties of death with uncringing calm.

In my boyhood, however, the good old-time religion saw to it that horror stalked, night and day, not only neurotic adults but most of the children.

The end of the world and yawning hell we had with us always.

It is true that in certain benighted regions evangelists of the Reverend Mr. Grewson stripe still spout with impunity. It is true that certain bucolic sects still expect the heavens to roll up like a scroll any time now. It is true that the fires of hell are far from extinguished in some ecclesiastical circles. But taking the nation as a whole, the situation is vastly improved since 1900. And the reason the situation has improved is that the public is better educated, more enlightened.

XV

"NEVER CALL RETREAT"

Now I AM not going to claim knowledge of an organized society of esthetes and intellectuals which considers democracy its mortal enemy and which is employing Machiavellian cunning to undermine democratic institutions. I do not know any such thing. Moreover, I do not believe such a society of medievalists, poetasters and votaries of the counter-clockwise clock could summon up sufficient political sagacity to be dangerous.

Attempting a concerted program of subtle reaction, that sort of organization would, I suspect, hurl itself into some such Agincourt or Lepanto as did that curious committee dominated by T. S. Eliot in presenting the Library of Congress prize to Ezra Pound, a deranged poet of the third magnitude whose trial for treason had just been averted by his official lunacy. Viewed from any perspective, from esthetics to politics, this action was neither brave nor bright. It didn't help Pound and it certainly didn't help poetry, but it made some of Eliot's most ardent admirers shake their heads in dismay.

There is little to fear, I think, from a reactionary revolt of the unworldly and unaware, organized or unorganized.

But there could be real peril in an unpremeditated by-product of that revolt.

When the tsetse fly attacks, he has one and only one objective in view. That objective is dinner. At most his bite is a minor annoyance and the host never will miss the small amount of blood extracted by the little fellow. There may be, however, an entirely unpremeditated and quite serious by-product to that small bite and that is encephalitis lethargica, or sleeping sickness.

Nostalgia is a habit-forming drug, a narcotic. It is a refuge of the aged, the rose-scented goose grease on the toboggan slide to senility.

When any large portion of a given people begins to moon over the glory that was Greece and the grandeur that was Rome, to sigh for the flowering of knighthood and the pageantry of feudalism as well as for the golden horse-and-buggy days, the drums already have begun to beat the long roll for retreat.

But why the retreat? It was valor in the face of adversity when Marshal Foch wired at the first battle of the Marne, "My center gives way; my right recedes; the situation is excellent; I shall attack." But our center hasn't given way. Our right hasn't receded. In the legendary words of the top sergeant, "We never had it so good."

Yes, I know about taxes. I know about the A-bomb and the H-bomb. I know about the possibility of war. I know about the conflict of ideologies, the decline in railroad earnings, about assembly lines and the shameless bathing suits. But we still never had it so good.

They say, "Ah, but we have lost our sense of spiritual values." Well, what sense of spiritual values? Do they mean we have lost or are losing our religion?

In 1900 the population of the United States was 75,994,575 and registered church members numbered 31,639,660.

Now, according to the *Christian Herald,* more than seventy-seven million Americans belong to churches. Church membership has *more* than kept pace with the increase in population.

Perhaps figures mean little in a case like this, perhaps there are more *nominal* church members in proportion now, perhaps the parishioners are less devout now than in 1900. I don't know how to measure intangibles. I don't know the spiritual market value of lip-service. I don't know any way to sift out the secrets in a man's soul.

I have heard ministers of the Gospel complain bitterly because there are so many Sunday diversions now, because highways are filled with cars and golf courses are busy on pleasant Sabbaths and people stand in line before movie houses. Of course the charge is true, and the degree of evil (or good) in this condition depends on one's point of view. I can only ask whether it's a very devout worshipper who attends church because there is no other place to go.

It's my observation that clergymen who are not complete bores draw pretty good congregations in spite of competition. And, again, the fact that the rate of increase in actual church membership is greater than the rate of population increase should mean something. People join churches of their own free will. I never have heard of actual coercion being used by proselytizers—at least not since Portuguese inquisitors forcibly baptized Jewish bankers. The prophets of doom can't mean that religion is losing ground in America.

I wonder if they mean we are losing our Christian sympathy for the unfortunate? That again is an intangible which can't be proved or disproved definitely, but available statistics tend to indicate just the opposite.

In 1900 American charities were comparatively unorganized and consequently campaigns to raise money were limited in scope.

The American Red Cross was not organized until 1905; the first Community Trust was organized in Cleveland in 1914; the Community Chests and Councils in 1918; the National Tuberculosis Association in 1904, to give a few examples. Since the turn of the century the methods of conducting charity drives have developed practically into a science, and I suppose there are grounds for argument that a substantial portion of the enormous sums collected are not contributed from actual charitable impulses. But, once more, who can know what was in the heart of John Jones when he contributed a thousand dollars to the Community Chest, whether he was actuated by vanity or by genuine sympathy for the unfortunate or by a curious mixture of the two?

If it can be claimed with some truth that the dollar increase in donations to charity since 1900 means little in terms of spirituality, there are several other points which must be taken into consideration.

For example, what percentage of 1900 donations was the result of the pure spirit of charity? Assuredly there were vain people in 1900 also. And, granting that the purchasing power of the dollar may have been quartered in the last fifty years; granting that the average working man today may have a larger surplus in terms of bread and shoes than his grandfather had; granting that his grandfather's donation of a dime may have entailed a greater sacrifice than our average working man's donation of a dollar; granting that charity solicitors sometimes use high-pressure methods; granting again that those with good incomes lose little because they can deduct charitable donations from income taxes, I still don't believe any sort of case can be made that our sense of being our brother's keeper is dwindling. In newspaper work I have seen too much evidence to the contrary.

Beyond the Community Chest drives for their multitude of related agencies, and the church drives and the sale of Christmas seals and the Red Cross and March of Dimes campaigns, there are hundreds of published appeals each year in any American city. I have never seen any such appeal go unanswered. It is my opinion that the American people by and large are astonishingly open-hearted and open-handed—even to the point of being suckers sometimes.

In some quarters of the globe it is the custom to call us dollar-grabbing materialists. But did anyone ever see an Englishman turn shudderingly away from a dollar? Or a Frenchman? Or a Russian or a German or Italian or an Oriental?

But the question does not concern whether we are more materialistic than other peoples; the question is whether we have lost much of our sense of spiritual values since 1900, whether we have traded our birthright for a mess of gadgets.

Well, how about Americans and the arts? No one could question the fact that more Americans are visiting art galleries with a better understanding of art than ever before, and no one could question the patent fact that more are listening to good music and, yes, *producing* good music than at any time in history. And I don't mean just *more* people; I mean a far larger proportion of the total population. Does that mean anything?

If I say that we proportionately are reading more good books today than in 1900—which I truly believe—then I suppose I am confronted with a matter of definition. Dr. Otis Paul Thudbury, for instance, may not agree with me at all as to the nature of a good book. Dr. Thudbury may not consider any book "good" which was written later than 1799. Or he may consider *The Crisis* and *Eben Holden* superior to *The Late George Apley* and *The Just and the Unjust,* a position he could defend only by sound and fury and quotations from Ralph Waldo Emerson.

What then *is* the cause of that strange discontent of the poetasters and intellectuals and the cream-faced loons who follow in their wake?

I actually don't know, but I could hazard a guess. I could guess they are disconcerted because the gap between their own eminent erudition and what they choose to call our "peasantry" is narrowing to the point where a farmer boy or coal miner can leap the strait and then leap back again if he doesn't like the climate. How can a scholar be a man of distinction when any considerable portion of the peasantry has learned that a man can read Euripides in the original and still be a complete ninny? In such circumstances how can a comfortably stratified society be maintained? Far better to return as nearly as possible to the dear days when only the nobility and the clergy had opportunity for education and the lower estate of the realm respectfully pulled its forelock in the presence of its betters. And if we can't go back to the glories of feudalism in one swoop, let us do the best we can. People were *so* much happier in the days of William McKinley, you know, when life was simpler and people were more humble and at least a *little* more stratified.

But I don't want to go back. I like it pretty well here now. And I think people, by and large, are kindlier, more considerate of their fellow man, better adjusted, less silly and more nearly civilized than they ever were before.

No, I haven't forgotten Dachau and Buchenwald. But the only thing new about the Nazi horror camps was the method. It must be recognized that man is the cruelest of animals especially when religious fervor raises to a frenzy his hatred of those who do not believe as he believes. There was Tamerlane's massacre of one hundred thousand at Delhi. There was Richard the Lion Heart's deliberate murder of his horde of prisoners at Acre. There was Charlemagne's liquidation of non-Christians, and the St. Bartholomew's Day massacre, and the massacre of thirty thousand Protestants in Ulster and Cromwell's reprisals, just for example. And it should be emphasized that the Dachau and Buchenwald horrors were instigated by the type of political regime which establishes elites, makes the will of the masses entirely subservient to authoritarian control, the self-same type of barbaric absolutism which has been responsible for practically all similar outrages in history, and which has either the outspoken or tacit endorsement of those esthetes and intellectuals who now moan that culture is declining horribly because of our democratic institutions and ideals.

It's the fashion these days to speak and write of the death of civilization if war comes. The prophets of doom, in giving these constant warnings, seem to carry the idea that the people want another war and that it's their duty as prophets to talk them out of it.

Well, the American people want no war. Of that I am sure. But, if through official bungling or necessity, war does come, I am also sure the American people will fight it out to the best of their considerable ability even though the nation's population might be more than decimated and a score of the larger cities flattened. Living conditions may become pretty stark. But civilization will not die.

I see little to worry about. None of us can live forever. And when the time comes it surely is no worse to go out in an atom bomb blast than in a plane crash or wasting disease.

The lack of historical sense among some of our supposedly erudite neurotics is surprising. War is one of the interesting but curiously contradictory idiosyncrasies of that astonishingly clever mammal, homo sapiens. Man is too smart, too adaptable, to go the way of the diplodocus and dodo. Unless science devises means actually to blow this planet to smithereens (which would relieve everyone of his worries), mankind will endure and will rebuild the wreckage of any possible catastrophic war within a decade.

Particularly ridiculous is the picture of survivors, skin-clad and living in caves. Not even an Eagle Scout could provide food and clothing for a family with a stone axe. The raw material is too shy and fleet of foot, and, in any event, why would a Missouri farmer, for instance, desert his fertile fields and herds and self-sufficient home to stalk through the elm woods armed with coup de poing or pogamoggan, hunting for an idiot woodchuck or turkey buzzard? In the words of the good old days of 1900: Man may be crazy but he ain't no fool.

Yes, there is unrest and in certain quarters near hysteria over the possibility of war. This is nurtured by certain articulate and fearful people who would know better than to yell "fire" in a crowded theater, but fail to see that their shrill warnings, far from serving any useful purpose, are planting the seeds of panic.

In spite of the fears of war, however, life as a whole is pleasanter now than it was fifty years ago because of greater creature comforts, because of inventions and discoveries from the realm of medicine to mere gadgets, and because we have a more humanitarian view of our neighbors. We really do.

In this long and perhaps prolix dissertation (if you can dignify it by such a fancy term) I have tried to show that culture in America has not declined in the last half century, but that in general it has advanced to a marked degree. I admit there may have been a leveling off of culture, but I'm not sure even of that. Conceding that there seems to be no logic to the sprouting and flowering of genius, it still doesn't make sense that the genius of one youngster will be stunted because another youngster also has opportunity to develop his lesser talents. Perhaps we now have no giants of the stature of Milton and Beethoven, but again, perhaps we have. Mozart,

Van Gogh and Melville were not regarded highly at the time they died.

If, through some chemical process quite beyond my understanding, genius flourishes only in the stratified society of an undemocratic political regime, then genius is a manifestation of unhealthy political economy, like the fungus obtruding from the bark of a diseased tree. In that case, I suppose, there is the question whether a land should be governed for the production of an occasional genius or for the prosperity and happiness of the people.

Now, by showing what life was like in a fairly typical small midwestern town in the early years of the Twentieth Century, I have tried to prove, largely by implication, how much better life is today than it was fifty years ago. I have tried to show how much less provincial and chauvinistic we are, how much better is our attitude toward ourselves and the world.

Consider the revolutionary change in public opinion toward social problems in general; consider the fact that in 1900 great corporations were operating virtually under laissez faire and to the detriment of the people at large; consider this when nostalgia-mongers yearn for a retreat into the Silurian ooze of the dear old days.

Those were the days when a progressive legislature in Illinois passed a ten-hour-day law for women factory workers and an outraged Manufacturers' Association took it to the United States Supreme Court and managed to get the law declared unconstitutional on grounds that the act was an infringement of liberty.

Those were the days when the Pennsylvania legislature passed a law forbidding a factory to work ten-year-old children more than twelve hours a day, and made the law stick. That was a piece of advanced legislation, all right, and it wasn't forced through by any labor unions either. But there wasn't too much opposition because it's a fact that the quality of work turned out by the average ten-year-old boy or girl begins to deterioriate after about twelve hours at the machine.

Those were the days before the Adamson Railroad Act when trainmen worked until they were relieved and when investigation of serious accidents frequently showed that an engineer or switchman had been without sleep from twenty-four to forty-eight hours; when in 1906 American railroad accidents took the lives of 9,703 persons and injured 86,008 seriously; when in 1905 there were 6,223 collisions and 5,371 derailments, and in 1906 there were 7,194 railroad collisions and 6,261 derailments, and spokesmen for the railroad companies actually attempted to put the blame on the Brotherhood of Railway Trainmen.

Those were the days before the principle of collective bargaining was accepted, when a strike was regarded as nothing short of insurrection against constituted authority and corporations were permitted to hire armies of mercenary thugs to protect strikebreakers, and (as I have seen personally not once but several times) to turn machine guns into a crowd of unarmed but jeering men, women and children.

Those were the good old days before labor-saving machinery and safety devices had changed the lot of a steel plant worker from living hell to just plain hard work, when the men habitually labored a twelve-hour-day for a usual eighty-four-hour-week and chairmen of boards solemnly declared they would be forced to close up shop if a ten-hour day were established.

Those were the days when coal miners, receiving an average of $10.09 a week for a seventy-hour week, were forced to live in company-owned shacks where sanitary conditions would have driven any self-respecting cat into the woods, when safety regulations were notable for their absence, and when George F. Baer, president of a great Pennsylvania mining company, could declare, "The rights and interests of the laboring man will be protected and cared for—not by the labor agitators, but by the Christian men to whom God in His infinite wisdom has given the control of the property interests of this country."

Those were the good days of contract labor when sovereign states leased bodies of convicts to private corporations and the private corporations were allowed to use the lash on the recalcitrant or ailing; when other corporations were permitted to maintain virtual slave camps in remote areas, recruiting men in the cities and holding them in peonage until the job was completed—and I also know about that personally.

Those were the days before the first pure food and drug act, when the manufacturers of patent medicines could and did load their products with habit-forming drugs not only for adult use but for "pacifying" babies, when no one was required to label a bottle with its contents; the days when diseased meat, decomposed or dangerously adulterated food were callously marketed under the dear old banner of "caveat emptor," and Senator Nelson W. Aldrich of Rhode Island, majority floor leader who unofficially was called "manager of the United States," fought the good fight for states' rights and against the curtailment of liberty attendant on enactment of such regulatory legislation.

Consider just a few of the pieces of social legislation which have been passed since 1900—most of them violently opposed by the proponents of rugged individualism—and see how many any rational citizen would wish to repeal today.

Take even the federal income tax amendment. Is there a more equitable means of collecting revenue?

Then there is the women's suffrage amendment, and popular election of United States Senators, the establishment of federal land banks, the parcels post, the Reconstruction Finance Corporation, the federal reserve bank system, the Norris-LaGuardia act outlawing yellow-dog labor contracts and limiting injunctions against labor, the Securities and Exchange Act, the Agricultural Adjustment Act, the Social Security Act, the federal guarantee of bank deposits and the various acts concerning collective bargaining of labor. Even the reactionary Taft-Hartley Act would have been considered arrant socialism in 1900.

Can anyone deny that the United States is better off today, materially, spiritually, morally, culturally, because of the bulk of this legislation? By "anyone," I mean any person whose cranial machinery is in working order.

Of course an intellectual might say that legislation has given the vulgar masses better working conditions and more leisure to the end that they have more time to be vulgarly idle and to attend vulgar spectator sports events.

For myself, I think there's a great deal to be said for the drama of spectator sports, and some of the most precious clutches of eggs in my memory have to do with moments when I had a hot dog in one hand and a bottle of soda pop in the other. Certainly the memory of mighty Babe Ruth slamming one clear over the scoreboard has precedence over the memory of Robert Mantell as Hamlet; the thirteenth round of the first Louis-Conn fight glitters brighter than E. H. Sothern as Shylock. While this indubitably brands me as a very common fellow, I still am honest about it and not at all ashamed. There's every reason to believe Julius Caesar and Pliny enjoyed the Roman Circus, and even austere Marcus Aurelius attended, although that may have been from a sense of political duty, like Calvin Coolidge going to the opening baseball game of a season.

If you go into a mill district public library you'll discover a lot of the workers are reading a good deal in their spare time—and proportionately less light fiction and murder mysteries than are consumed by some of the better uptown minds.

True, steel workers and other hardy men do like to foregather at a neighborhood oasis for an exchange of large talk when the day's work is over, but so did the glorious old Greeks and so did the grand old Romans and so did the Eighteenth Century Londoners and so do the uptown people now. And—I do not say this just to be patriotically common folksy—I actually have seen more evidence of cerebral activity in the saloon conversations of waterfront and steel plant workers than at some of the literary cocktail parties I have been obliged to attend. But of course the authors and editors and camp followers go to those cocktail parties to relax their weary brains.

If that should, by any chance, sound as if I believe a good many men who get quite dirty at their daily work are brighter and wiser and generally better informed than a lot of intellectuals, I'm quite willing to let the impression stand without correction. I'm willing to let it stand in the face of an erudite book reviewer who chided me for allowing a garage mechanic to refer to Chopin and George Bernard Shaw, when obviously no mere garage mechanic could have even heard of those two. You see I happen to know a journeyman plumber who has heard of Bach and Brahms and Mozart as well as Chopin and plays them quite well, and I happen to know a garage mechanic whose current idol is Reinhold Niebuhr, and I have had some correspondence with a burglar (who has only eighty-odd years to serve on a ninety-nine year jolt) whose Bible is the unabridged expanse of Frazer's *Golden Bough* and who professes to find great ragged holes in the logic of Arnold J. Toynbee's *A Study of History,* but the only observation I should care to make concerning the burglar versus Toynbee controversy is that Dr. Toynbee's diction is more grammatical than the burglar's but the burglar's prose is more lucid than Dr. Toynbee's.

A good deal has been written by various prophets of doom about the deadening effect of work on a modern assembly line. It seems, according to these students of human nature, that the brains of assembly line workers are bound to atrophy while their bodies degenerate into automatons. This, if true, is a doleful prospect. But I doubt if it is true—especially if the forty-hour week can be maintained in factories.

While it is certainly a fact that screwing nut N-345 J on to bolt B-345 J for forty hours a week gives no exercise to the brain, the worker still has some 128 hours a week for sleeping, eating and other pursuits including study, reading, talking, drinking, playing pin-ball machines, wenching, praying, bowling, attending extension classes, woodworking, going for long walks in the country, playing chess, attending the movies, inventing perpetual motion machines, painting pictures, plotting the overthrow of the government, engraving the Lord's Prayer on the head of a pin, writing books and thousands of other things I wouldn't know about.

Routine work is nothing new. It didn't come in with the assembly line. Long before anyone had thought of modern mass production methods, I was feeding a printing press ten hours a day and, while I certainly can't pretend I enjoyed the work, my mind was occupied with other things—usually mulling over what I had been reading, or merely daydreaming about the wonderful future.

Since Adam heard his sentence pronounced, "In the sweat of thy face shalt thou eat bread . . ." there has been deadly dull work to be done, and scrubbing floors or washing dishes or flailing grain or hoeing corn aren't exactly inspiring occupations. The old guild tailor, plying his needle by candlelight while he sat cross-legged in a damp and airless cellar, had small mental equipment if it was satisfied by the minor problems of the trade. So with the weavers and spinners and bearers of burdens and so with the toilers in the sweatshops before legislation robbed those employers of their liberty to exploit workers. Millet's "Man with a Hoe" was not the victim of an assembly line.

I'm not trying to glorify the assembly line. But mass production does make it possible for assembly-line workers to own motor cars, electric refrigerators, flush toilets and other creature comforts. And assembly line workers, actually spending less than one-fourth of their time on the assembly line, do in these days have the facilities and the opportunity to lead full and happy lives to an extent undreamed of for factory workers fifty years ago.

Frequently those who mourn the decline of culture in the last fifty years center their focus on the state of the legitimate theater today as compared to 1900. And as far as New York and other great cities are concerned, there isn't much to be said. The legitimate theater *has* declined.

Of course the principal reason is that the legitimate theater finds it difficult to compete with motion pictures, the radio and now television. Because of production costs, the price of tickets has soared and thousands who might otherwise be regular patrons cannot afford to spend eight to twelve dollars for a couple of seats, even if they could get the seats at market price instead of paying a three hundred per cent premium to a broker. And for the two or three plays a season which are really worth the market price of admission, one is obliged to make reservations so many weeks in advance that he well may be dead, ill or out of town on business by the time the great date rolls around.

Because of the large investment entailed, few producers and "angels" are willing to gamble on anything new. As the theater is basically a commercial enterprise and as a handful of New York critics are notoriously capable of killing a play at birth, it is simply bad business to touch anything unless it follows a tried and true formula. From what I hear, there's a pretty strict formula even for innovations.

It seems to me that the legitimate theater in New York may have run into a sort of natural law. When the saber-toothed tiger was unable or unwilling to adapt himself to changing conditions his importance in the faunal picture dwindled, although he must have been a quite interesting fellow in his day.

Grand as the legitimate theater was to city-dwellers in 1900, it was of small consequence to the two-thirds of America's population which lived in communities of 10,000 or under.

In Chillicothe we had a theater—Zibe Myers' Luella Opera House, and it was an exciting thing to go to a play there. I usually attended with several other boys and we would be in our seats nearly thirty minutes before curtain time, gazing tensely at the beautiful picture of the lake and hills and sailboat in the center of the curtain, and if you looked steadily enough you'd swear the sailboat was moving; then carefully reading all the advertisements around the picture—Sipple Clothing Co.; Dider Clothing Co.; Crelland's Jewelry Store, Spectacles Fitted and Watches Repaired; Star Brand Shoes Are Better; Crow Cigars for a Satisfying Smoke; The Farmers' Store, Where Your Dollar Goes Farther; Scruby Bros., Hay Feed & Grain —and there was always a strong smell of illuminating gas in the Luella Opera House from the footlights, a smell I always afterward associated with excitement.

Finally a young man would dart out from the left wings with an oil torch in his hand and, crouching almost double, he'd skip from one footlight to another, touching off the open burners with his torch while jokers in the audience applauded and boys yelled, "Howdy, Bob! Hurray for Bob! Hey, Bob, you missed one back there." But Bob never would look up or acknowledge that he appreciated the acclaim.

Then the curtain would rise and, because I always was in the front row, the players seemed grotesque instead of glamorous in their makeup and the beautiful young heroines frequently had wrinkled necks and gold teeth in front. To the best of my recollection none but shabby little repertoire companies came to the Luella. They would stay several days putting on the cheapest sort of melodrama, worse than the tawdriest back-alley producer of Hollywood C pictures would dream of filming in these days.

The best play I saw in the Luella was entitled *Over Niagara Falls in a Barrel,* and they had Niagara Falls painted on canvas and running like a roller towel in the hands of a pernickety dude hunting for a dry spot.

I remember one interesting sequence in another drama when the villain was wrestling with the gold-toothed but innocent little heroine and he threw her to the floor with a bang. Being in the front row I could see and hear very well, so there was no mistaking when the heroine sat up on the dusty stage and called the villain a compound name which couldn't be printed even in these days of tolerance toward such matters.

I was allowed to attend these cultural and educational entertainments when I could earn the dime, which was the admission for children under twelve, except on one occasion. Our minister had heard about this play and warned the congregation about its immoral and blasphemous character. It seemed the devil himself actually appeared on the stage in this play, so I was expressly forbidden to go, even though I had the dime.

About the only good thing one could say about the kerosene-circuit road companies which visited Chillicothe in those days is that only three or four of them came each season.

Whatever one may think about Hollywood, none of the major pictures produced by the major companies is as bad in story, direction or acting as the legitimate drama two-thirds of America was able to see fifty years ago.

Moreover, I, who have worked in Hollywood and do not love it, will say there are more first-class pictures produced in Hollywood each year than first-class plays produced on Broadway. Of course most motion pictures are poor things. So are most paintings and most books and most poems and most musical compositions and most sermons, and so they have always been and so they will always be unless human beings become a race of geniuses—a catastrophe which I see little reason to worry about at the moment.

Well, I have written a good deal about Chillicothe as I knew it in the first eight years of the Twentieth Century. How is it now? In particular, what physical changes have taken place?

At first glance the town seems much the same, although cleaner, brighter and busier. Visitors used to call it an attractive community, and it is more so now.

To some extent Chillicothe's society is still mildly stratified, but at least the geographical barriers are more tenuous. The place has grown and the tendency is for prosperous people to move to the West Side. There was more room to expand there and many beautiful new homes have been built. Our old district hasn't exactly run down, but has remained fairly static.

Speaking of building brings up the subject of architecture. And what glorifier of the good old days could argue that modern architecture, bizarre though some of it may be in striving for extreme simplicity and functional lines, is not superior to that of 1900?

In 1900 the height of elegance still was what has been called General Grant architecture in both homes and public buildings. Gaudiness was the keynote—grill-topped towers and mansard roofs and arched windows and decorative lightning rods, with a curlicue tacked every place they could tack a curlicue.

I think of these pretentious monstrosities as particularly indigenous to the Midwest, but you see them everywhere. They flowered lushly on the Pacific Coast, from central California northward. They can be found in Europe.

Highview is still largely a place of winding unpaved streets, but most of the old-time shanties have given way to neat new cottages—each with its garage. The garages tell the story. Movement back and forth across the Milwaukee tracks now is easy and without self-consciousness. I have been told by educators, police and social workers that Highview is no longer a problem center, that there is absolutely no stigma attached to residence there. The psychic barrier of steel railroad rails has been broken down by the motor car.

On the other hand, the Levee district has grown in size and squalor. Postmaster Joseph D. Stewart tells me there are approximately one thousand people living in that region now and, as a civic leader and social worker, he feels something has got to be done about it and soon. As a first move he favors the immediate establishment of a social center or neighborhood house there, because he realizes social problems of this sort are much more complex than a superficial observer might guess. After all, this is America and one can't be high-handed and arbitrary with American citizens even if one doesn't like the way they live. Nevertheless, sanitary conditions are bad in the Levee district and Mr. Stewart is quite conscious that an enterprising rat can travel from the Levee to West Calhoun Street in twenty-four hours and that flies can cover the course in a fraction of that time, especially with a southeast tail wind.

The Levee now is generally known as "Little Italy," which is a distinct libel inasmuch as Chief of Police Charles R. Barrett says he doesn't know of a single Italian family in this slum. The term apparently was borrowed from Kansas City where gang wars and crime have persisted in the Italian district for fifty years.

Chief Barrett is young, smart and efficient—a good representative of the clean-cut, modern scientific police officer. He has lifted the Chillicothe department out of politics, established a radio car system and developed close co-operation with the Missouri State Police. The department has nine patrolmen who keep the situation very well under control except, of course, in the Levee district.

In 1900 the police department consisted of an easygoing chief and one equally easygoing patrolman, although the 1900 conditions were such that the 1950 department would have been very busy attempting to keep law and order.

Patrolman Oliver Hicks is old enough to remember, and he says the improvement in Chillicothe's manners and behavior since the turn of the century is nothing short of remarkable.

I have touched on that particular advancement, and also on the improvement in the attitude of adults toward children (and vice versa); on public enlightenment regarding matters of sex; on the amazing advancement of medical science; on the improvement in educational methods; on progression of cultural subjects, under the narrow interpretation. In short I have tried to show that American people in general and midwestern people in particular have every reason to live fuller, more comfortable, soul-satisfying, happier lives today than ever before. And as far as Chillicothe is concerned I believe a great deal of credit is due a number of organizations, developed largely by public-spirited women, which have been working tirelessly for civic betterment and the advancement of culture. These include The Chillicothe Culture Club, the Junior Culture Club, the Sorosis Club, the Fact and Fiction Club, the Chillicothe Musicians' Club which brings in numerous notable musicians each season, the Wheeling Study Club and the Progressive Art and Study Club composed of Negro women.

Well, it seems to be human nature to think of the old days as golden days when, as the Kingsley character had it, "every goose was a swan." In 1900 they yearned for the days of romance before the Civil War. Before that scholars longed for the pure culture of medieval times. And in medieval times Dante Alighieri was aghast at the current materialism and spoke wistfully of the good old days before the spirit of avarice ruled the world.

In all the days of Christendom intellectuals have harked back to the glory that was Greece, but when Greece glittered at the height of that glory Aristophanes ridiculed contemporary culture; lampooned the popular hero, Socrates; sneered at Athenians as credulous fools and wished for a return to the good old days when there was some discipline in the land and culture was pure and unsullied.

Personally, I don't want to go back. I want to go forward and I believe we inevitably are going forward despite the prophets of doom, who, like the poor, "always ye have with you." I am not disappointed in Americans nor in the human race. Being a congenital pessimist, I do not expect men and women to be demigods. Considering their real nature and the chance they've had, I think human beings have done astonishingly well. And I just don't know how they did it.

Yes, I frankly am rather pleased to be a member of genus homo instead of, say, a horse or a wallaby. I really think people are pretty wonderful, particularly people who love life and do not fear death, particularly people for whom living is a bang and not a whimper.